KINGDOM OF NAUVOO

Gustavus Hills, draftsman, J. Childs, lithographer, Map of the City of Nauvoo, with insets of architectural rendering of the Nauvoo Temple and Joseph Smith, Lieutenant General of the Nauvoo Battalion, 1844, based on materials provided in 1842.

KINGDOM of NAUVOO

THE RISE AND FALL OF A RELIGIOUS EMPIRE ON THE AMERICAN FRONTIER

BENJAMIN E. PARK

LIVERIGHT PUBLISHING CORPORATION

A Division of W. W. Norton & Company

Independent Publishers Since 1923

For information about permission to reproduce selections from this book, write to
Permissions, Liveright Publishing Corporation, a division of W. W. Norton & Company, Inc.,
500 Fifth Avenue, New York, NY 10110

For information about special discounts for bulk purchases, please contact
W. W. Norton Special Sales at specialsales@wwnorton.com or 800-233-4830

Manufacturing by LSC Communications, Harrisonburg
Book design by Chris Welch Design
Production manager: Julia Druskin

ISBN 978-1-63149-486-4

Liveright Publishing Corporation, 500 Fifth Avenue, New York, N.Y. 10110
www.wwnorton.com

W. W. Norton & Company Ltd., 15 Carlisle Street, London W1D 3BS

1 2 3 4 5 6 7 8 9 0

For My Family

CONTENTS

KINGDOM OF NAUVOO

Prologue

There is a natural inclination in mankind for a kingly government.
—BENJAMIN FRANKLIN, 1787[1]

William Major, painting of Joseph Smith and the Quorum of the Twelve Apostles, Nauvoo, Illinois, 1845. From left to right, the painting depicts Hyrum Smith, Willard Richards, Joseph Smith, Orson Pratt, Parley P. Pratt, Orson Hyde, Heber C. Kimball, and Brigham Young. All of these men also participated in the Council of Fifty around this same time. LDS CHURCH HISTORY LIBRARY, SALT LAKE CITY.

A gloomy pall hung over the Mormon city of Nauvoo when Joseph Smith and his closest allies gathered to replace the American Constitution. The winter of 1843–44 had been exceptionally cold, and the spring that followed unusually wet. The downpour was so intense on April 14, a Sunday, that Smith, prophet and president of the Church of Jesus Christ of Latter-day Saints, canceled his public meetings. Despite the bad weather, Smith and his confidants were buoyed by the creation of a new, secretive political organization, one that they believed was destined to rule the world.[2]

The clandestine council gathered two days later, where its members breathlessly discussed a new founding document for their divine government, one that would replace the US Constitution. A committee composed of a handful of men had been toiling for weeks to draft the text, and the rest of the council was eager to see the finished product. They were not disappointed. "We, the people of the Kingdom of God," the document began, borrowing from the text they were seeking to supplant. What followed was a paradoxical mix of traditional republican language and revolutionary theocratic ideas. It was time, the document announced, for the kingdom of God to replace the governments of men. The men who crowded around to hear the constitution read out loud for the first time readily acknowledged the significance of the moment. They were at the cusp of a new form of divine governance.

Though the proposed Mormon constitution was incomplete and required further revision, the delegates could hardly contain their excitement. One remarked that it was "the greatest day of his life," and another noted that they were "treading on holy ground." After the festivities were over, William Clayton, who served as the council's secretary, went home, still elated, to reflect on the proceedings. "Much precious instructions were given," he noted in his diary. It seemed as if heaven had already "began on earth" and the millennium was rushing in. The entire world was about to be turned upside down.[3]

The men reviewing the document, informally known as the Council of Fifty, were part of one of the most radical religious and political endeavors of the American nineteenth century. They rejected America's democratic system as a failed experiment and sought to replace it with a theocratic kingdom. A new Mormon empire, they believed, was the only thing that could restore stability and justice to a fallen world. Democracy was a misguided effort that had run its course, and they were ready to offer a correction.

The detailed minutes from the council's meetings—meticulously recorded by a secretary, Clayton, who was convinced that their proceedings held the key to the world's future—were restricted from believers and historians alike for 172 years, even as rumors of their scandalous contents spread both within and beyond the faith's community. Finally, in 2016, the Latter-day Saint church allowed their release and publication, the culmination of several years of increasingly generous decisions by the church to grant access to its voluminous historical collections. The availability of these extraordinary sources, and the release of many other Mormon documents from the 1840s, has finally made it possible to offer a full-scale account of a significant and revealing—yet largely forgotten—moment in American history.[4]

THE CHURCH OF JESUS CHRIST OF LATTER-DAY SAINTS has often been seen as an anomaly in America. Joseph Smith's claims of deific visions, angelic visitations, and gold plates, not to mention the now-abandoned practice of polygamy, have made Mormonism an easy object of ridicule as much as a serious topic for study. The Broadway musical *The Book of Mormon* mixes mockery with sincere interest, yet still highlights the cultural chasm between the church and its surrounding culture. The Mormons, for their part, have often contributed to this view, through their insistence on exceptionalism and uniqueness.

To the extent that modern Mormonism is accepted in contemporary America, it is largely due to Mormons' ability to keep quiet about their distinctive beliefs and practices. Mitt Romney won the Republican Party nomination for president in 2012 by downplaying his faith and emphasizing Mormonism's common ground with evangelicals. Indeed, the Latter-day Saint church's conservative principles on gender and marriage have been a way to build solidarity with the religious right. In a pragmatic alliance that has allowed Mormons a space in the public sphere, both the church and the nation have agreed to overlook a long history of animosity and conflict. As evidence of this continued assimilation, church leaders in 2018 announced their intention to retire the term *Mormon* as a way to, among other things, close the gap between themselves and other Christians and distance the faith from its past identity.[5]

Yet while they have often been seen, and have frequently seen themselves, as outsiders, Joseph Smith, his followers, and their church were, in the first instance, products of their nation and times. Along with other marginalized groups that drew the ire of the white Protestant mainstream, like Catholics and Shakers—though not nearly as severe a backlash as African American congregations and numerous indigenous tribes—the Mormons constituted a minority group that fought, and often failed, to enjoy the protections and benefits supposedly guaranteed by the US Constitution. Far from a cult on the margins of American life, they challenged other Americans to live their ideals: whatever the Constitution might say, how, in practice, could a nation of diverse peoples and faiths hold together?

The Mormon challenge was rooted in the short-lived city of Nauvoo, founded by Joseph Smith in 1839 in Illinois, on the banks of the Mississippi River. Nauvoo was the crucible of the Mormon experience—the episode that saw their prophet murdered and their dreams of a religious empire dashed. If the Mormons are poorly understood by most Americans, Nauvoo is virtually unknown. To Mormons, it remains an important site. It shapes how they think about their tradition's past, and persists as a pilgrimage destination: hundreds of thousands stream into the small town every summer to watch plays, tour historic homes, play games, and take in speeches by experienced missionaries. The faithful see Nauvoo as a monument to their spiritual ancestors and beloved prophet, Joseph Smith. But to the rest of the country, the city is, at best, an exotic name, a historical oddity overshadowed by Illinois's veneration of its adopted son, Abraham Lincoln.

Historians know more about the Mormons and Nauvoo, but their view is a partial one. Very few histories of Nauvoo have been written for a general audience in the last fifty years, and the existing treatments have serious limits, especially when they argue, as they often do, that Mormonism diverged from American culture and society. Smith's theocratic bent seems incongruous in a period supposedly characterized by the expansion of democracy, and his emphasis on priesthood authority appears to clash with prevailing beliefs in individual freedom and social mobility. Yet while the Jacksonian era was one of democratic upheaval, it also provoked a cultural backlash. To many people, not just the Mormons, American society seemed to be spinning out of control. Early Mormonism's radical solutions were designed to solve problems many non-Mormons also perceived. Indeed, their success at winning converts stemmed from their ability to tap into widespread sentiments about social decay and failure.[6]

Of course, the case for Mormon exceptionalism rests mainly, both to critical outsiders and to many historical Mormon believers, on the practice of plural marriage, more commonly known as polygamy. Perhaps the first reason for Nauvoo's significance is that Mormon polygamy began there. Yet while polygamy is commonly seen as a decree imposed from on high—either from an omnipotent God or patriarchal leaders—in fact the practice developed, haphazardly, over several years, and was shaped by both local and national concerns. Joseph Smith, Brigham Young, and the many other men and women who were inducted into the controversial practice were, like many of their gentile contemporaries, struggling to find ways to bring order to their lives. Pointing this out does not excuse the leading Mormon men whose actions brought harm and pain to many people through polygamy, nor does it crowd out more cynical readings of their motivations. But even if the Mormon solution were unique, and even if Nauvoo dwarfed other radical utopias of the era, religious and sexual experimentation were common in antebellum America. Seeing the Mormons as outliers, and merely dismissing their polygamous practice as quixotic, can overshadow the overlap between their ambitions and those of other seekers on the American landscape.[7]

Another common misconception is that Mormonism is, has been, and always will be a fundamentally patriarchal religion in which women have almost no say over their fates. As we will see, despite the repressive practice of polygamy, women in Nauvoo were able to exert power and influence rarely seen anywhere in America at the time, and did far more to shape Mormonism, and to dissent from its emerging orthodoxy, than is commonly assumed. Their actions—including the creation of the Female Relief Society of Nauvoo, a women's organization that still exists to this day—both drew inspiration from and reacted to other women-led movements for change. The Nauvoo story, like the larger story of antebellum America, cannot be understood without accounting for the many ways in which women were not only victims or powerless participants, but also drove change and forced the hands of the men, institutions, and governments around them.[8]

Rather than an exceptional episode, then, Nauvoo embodied many of the contradictions and tensions of its time. Its story reveals not only the radicalism of the early Mormons, but also the tenuousness of the American experiment. Examining the rise and fall of this Mormon empire demonstrates how Americans still struggled with the concept and practice of democracy only a few generations after the nation's birth, and highlights the legacies and paradoxes of the country's commitment to one of its most cherished ideals, religious liberty.

YET THE MORMONS OF NAUVOO arguably went further than any other sect or group in addressing what they saw as the problems of American society. Their radicalism started with Joseph Smith, who continuously and tenaciously pushed his church in new and increasingly controversial (within the faith and beyond) directions. Smith frequently tested the boundaries of social acceptance and the patience of his neighbors, even if he only grew dearer to the hearts of his followers.

When the Council of Fifty gathered to discuss a new constitution on that muggy April morning in 1844, all eyes were intently focused on the Mormon prophet. At thirty-eight, Smith was a striking sight. He stood just under six feet and weighed a sturdy two hundred pounds. Observers often noticed his light hair, pale complexion, round face, retreating hairline, and large nose, set above broad shoulders and a fleshy physique. One journalist reported that "his figure would probably be called a fine one, although by no means distinguished for symmetry or grace." Nearly everyone commented on his gaze: his penetrating blue eyes were shaded by, according to one tourist, "the longest, thickest light lashes you ever saw belonging to a man." Though his outfits were, as one visiting dignitary put it, "neither very choice nor neat," he was a bold dresser, favoring elegant rings, a dashing blue militia cape, and a band of black crepe across his hat in honor of his younger brother, who had died in 1841. Smith walked with a limp due to a childhood surgery, yet exuded confidence and energy. One observer noted how the Mormon prophet possessed "a great deal of ambition and physical energy, qualities eminently useful for his calling." He knew how to command a room.[9]

The council meeting on April 18 saw Smith presiding in the second floor of a formidable two-story brick structure just a block north from his home. The building's downstairs was one of the city's first mercantile stores, and the upstairs hall had been the site of sacred— and secret—rituals for the past two years. (Smith presided over those ceremonies, too.) The structure was one of the few stately edifices in Nauvoo. Most residents lived in small cabins, fronted by even smaller gardens, though an increasing number of frame homes and brick houses were going up. Visitors to Nauvoo remarked on the dirty roads, empty lots, and poor living conditions.

The most noteworthy building, located on a hill at the city's eastern edge, was still incomplete. High on the bluff and overlooking the

river for miles was a magnificent stone temple—or at least the mak-
ings of one. The foundation for the building was 90 feet wide and 130
feet long, and when finished the spire would rise 150 feet above the
ground. The exterior had by then only reached a fraction of its eventual height, but even skeptics appreciated its appearance. One called
the imposing temple, with its 12-foot-thick walls, a "citadel" for the
Mormon kingdom. Travelers up and down the Mississippi River noted
its grandeur.[10]

Visitors, even as they witnessed the low living conditions of many
of the city's residents, nevertheless found a vibrant community. One
of the few urban centers west of Ohio, Nauvoo claimed at least 12,000
residents in 1844, nearly all of them members of the Mormon faith
and loyal to their prophet, and several thousand more in nearby settlements. At its peak, in 1845, Nauvoo was larger than Chicago. And
its inhabitants were ready to defend their city. Smith boasted to one
(aghast) tourist that he could raise a militia of three thousand men at
a moment's notice.[11]

Nor was that the only cause for concern for non-Mormons in the
region. Worried onlookers also heard gossip about polygamy, and about
dozens of women being married to a handful of leading men. Those
rumors, however, were mostly spread through hushed whispers—at
least for a time. Mormonism's leaders issued firm denials; there was
no public debate of the issue within Nauvoo. Yet the tensions between
Nauvoo and its gentile neighbors had been building for years, almost
since the arrival of the Mormons in Illinois. The Council of Fifty was
formed, in an indirect way, in reaction to these tensions, and to the
threat of violence by suspicious outsiders.

Many of Nauvoo's women held prominent positions in the city, and
they often dictated their own agenda. The Female Relief Society, which
boasted over a thousand members, was led by Emma Smith, wife of
the prophet, and was dedicated to rooting out sexual improprieties she
believed were pervasive in the city—including those committed by her
own husband. (Her concern was justified: Joseph Smith had secretly
accumulated over thirty plural wives by 1844, and brought a num-

ber of other people into the practice.) Like the Grimké sisters in their quest to abolish slavery, or the women leading temperance movements throughout the nation, Mormon women were not willing to stand idly by. Emma Smith had organized a series of meetings in March 1844, the same week as the Council of Fifty's founding, and during these meetings she denounced the illicit activities of her fellow Mormons.

Joseph Smith's actions over the previous year had already won him a host of enemies beyond his own wife. He had prompted complaints from gentiles across Illinois and found himself ensnared in legal thickets. People within and beyond Illinois claimed that he was in open rebellion against America's democratic system. Given that the Mormons were now secretly rewriting the Constitution, these critiques were not without merit.

Nauvoo sat near the American frontier, in more ways than one. It was close to the edge of American settlement, and also, perhaps, beyond the boundaries of the American political community. Contemporaries often remarked on this convergence. To many skeptical observers, the Mormons stood in the way of westward expansion and posed a threat to America's democratic experiment. Not only could Smith raise an army of Mormons, beyond state or federal command, but the Mormons rejected many laws that they saw as oppressive or unfair. Most fundamentally, they rejected the separation of church and state. State and federal governments had failed them, after all, in their flights from New York to Ohio, from Ohio to Missouri, and finally from Missouri to Illinois. This most recent uprooting came at the gunpoint of a state militia. If the government would not protect them, they would find ways to protect themselves, even if that meant challenging the foundations of American democracy.[12]

The beleaguered "saints," as they styled themselves, had concluded that democratic rule led to the oppression of marginalized people and voices. They could no longer believe that state authorities could fairly govern their constituents. "The States rights doctrine," Joseph Smith wrote John C. Calhoun, the senator from South Carolina and a powerful figure in national politics, is "what feeds mobs." Rejecting so-called democratic freedom, the Mormons felt the need to establish a new political order.[13]

The antebellum period is often viewed as an era of progress and reform. Industrialization streamlined domestic production, new communication technology linked disparate communities, and protest movements, at least in the North, fought to improve conditions for women, laborers, and various disenfranchised groups, including even, to a degree, free African Americans. But not everyone was thrilled with these developments. To many on the margins of society, democracy had only brought chaos and anarchy. Not only that, but the many routinely oppressed the few. Alexis de Tocqueville, the French aristocrat who had toured America the previous decade, coined the term the "tyranny of the majority" to describe this dynamic. How could a nation maintain order with such a diverse population?[14]

Joseph Smith and his radical faith offered one possible solution. Faced with the disarray brought by the voice of man, Mormons hearkened to the stability promised by the voice of God. This promise included priestly administration, coordinated voting, and patriarchal rule. In many ways, they were successful. The Mormons sent missionaries throughout the United States and abroad, and tens of thousands embraced their message. They established congregations in nearly every major American town and in countless rural communities. Several times a month, ships carrying new converts arrived in Nauvoo, many from across the Atlantic Ocean, docking at the makeshift port just blocks from the prophet's own home. They sought a Moses who could lead modern-day Israel out of its wilderness; the saints desired nothing less than to transform the world.

Most Americans were not as eager for such a profound transformation. Neighbors referred to Nauvoo as "the kingdom"—other Americans, both nearby and in the East, called the city a "Western Empire"—highlighting the Mormons' incompatibility with democratic society. Politicians simultaneously courted their votes while also seeking to curtail their power. Mormon dissidents within Nauvoo spread rumors of polygamous relationships, theocratic rule, and tyrannical oppression, some of them true. An eager American audience consumed the news of an unusual sect on the edge of their country. They were titillated, but also threatened. Could a government based on self-rule continue to function if self-rule led to rebellion? Did religious liberty lead to madness? Citizens worried that the Mormons could shatter their fragile nation, then less than seventy years old.[15]

From the start, America had been home to religious extremists and religious experimentation. When the first English colonists arrived in New England, many of them did so on a religious mission. The Puritans saw themselves as a people struggling within a fallen world, a godly union fleeing corruption. To erase sin, they established strict religious codes and empowered ecclesiastical leadership. The Puritans are central to the story of America, as is their idea of their society as a "city on a hill," a faithful example for unbelieving nations. Yet when Joseph Smith replicated many aspects of the Puritan experiment two centuries later, he was dismissed as quixotic at best, and dangerous at worst. Beyond diverging from the same evangelical tradition that Puritanism helped birth—and which had come to dominate American culture by the nineteenth century—Mormonism had the unfortunate fate of appearing at a time when opposition forces, drawing on political power and the power of the press, were capable of smothering marginal groups. The same land that had previously provided space for radical innovation was now prepared to manage any deviants. Just as the Mormons were forced outside America's political boundaries, so too has their narrative been sequestered from the larger tale of United States religion.

The story of Nauvoo is a story of America's religious frontier. It is also a story of democracy in crisis. Many historians have noted how slavery tested the boundaries of American politics during the 1840s, as the sectional divide seemed to trump national cohesion. But the Mormons, in their own way, presented a challenge to American unity as well. The saga of Nauvoo demonstrates how tenuous the democratic experiment still was. The rights reserved for American citizens, they came to believe, were only available to a different sort of people.

CHAPTER I

Soil

The public mind has been for a long time turning in our favor.

—JOSEPH SMITH, MARCH 20, 1839[1]

Ezra Strong, "The States of Ohio, Indiana & Illinois and Michigan Territory: From the Latest Authorities," 1836. LIBRARY OF CONGRESS, WASHINGTON D.C.

T here was little chance that Sarah Melissa Granger and Hiram Kimball would ever meet, let alone marry. Both were born in the East—Hiram in Vermont in 1806, and Sarah in upstate New York in 1818—but they took drastically divergent paths before making it to the same place at the edge of America's frontier.

Eager to take advantage of the economic possibilities that beckoned in the newly opened western settlements, Kimball—tall, fit, and with a full head of dark hair—left his parents in New England for a new life. Like many people from the American Northeast, Kimball followed the nation's economic boom, which enabled vast and swift expansion into new western territories. The Mississippi River valley was an especially popular location for people from the Northeast, as the river connected the region to the rest of a growing capitalistic empire. Kimball eventually became one of the few permanent merchants in a village known as Commerce, founded about a decade earlier on a particularly scenic bend of the river within the new state of Illinois. At least until that point, his life reflected the optimistic trajectory of the nation's new commercial society.[2]

Sarah Granger's move to the West, conversely, represented not so much America's possibilities as its limits. Her father, Oliver Granger, a former Methodist preacher, was one of the earliest converts to the radical Mormon sect. He moved his family, including teenager Sarah, who was of average height with brown hair, to the temporary Mormon hub in Kirtland, Ohio, in 1833. Sarah Granger quickly grew attached to the faith and was known for her deep engagement with its scripture. She even participated in an almost all-male adult school called the School of the Prophets. It was there, she later remembered, that she learned the intricacies of the Mormon faith. But due to growing conflict with individuals both within and without the faith, the Grangers and the rest of the church were eventually forced out of the city *and* the state. They arrived in Commerce in 1839, along with hundreds of other disenfranchised members of their church, as refugees. These newcomers outnumbered the earlier settlers, whose numbers included Hiram Kimball.[3]

Kimball, who held a vague affiliation with mainstream Protestantism, did not mind the new neighbors—at least not the Granger family. Despite their religious differences, he and Sarah immediately fell in love and were married the next year. Their union signified a merging between the Mormon church and the region of Commerce. Sarah and the thousands of other members of the Church of Jesus Christ of Latter-day Saints moving to the mostly undeveloped area drastically changed a river town known primarily as a trade hub into a City of God. Rather than serving as an outpost for America's expanding economic empire, one defined by individualism and capitalistic enterprise, the village came to represent an indictment of the nation's failings. Though he did not immediately join her religious sect at the time of his marriage to Sarah, Hiram was eventually baptized as a Mormon three years later. The transformation was impossible to resist. He would become a key figure in the city's commercial development, through his investment in a number of financial initiatives and service in civic positions, and Sarah similarly became a central part of the city's female community, which, she would muse, laid the foundation for her later suffragist activism. At the time, though, both Hiram and Sarah, individually and as a couple, were anxious mainly to establish a new Zion on the American frontier.[4]

It would have been impossible for an outside observer, or even Commerce's Mormons themselves, to anticipate the community's growth over the next half dozen years, not to mention the national attention it would command. They were seen by many Illinois residents in 1839 as downtrodden victims of religious intolerance and state-sponsored oppression. Their immediate agenda was basic survival. Illinois, a free state bordered on the west and south by slave states and known as a home to a quixotic collection of political groups with a wide range of dissenter commitments, appeared well equipped to welcome another marginalized community. But the Mormons, with Kimball and Granger at the forefront, would soon take advantage of the situation to build an empire of their own. Within only a few years, James Gordon Bennett, famed editor of the *New York Herald*, would write that the Mormons of Commerce—rechristened Nauvoo—appeared likely to swallow up the "lukewarm Protestant sects" and incite a "great religious revolution, as radical as Luther's to take place in the Christian world."[5]

MEMBERS OF THE MORMON FAITH HAD CROSSED the frozen Mississippi River in the winter of 1838–39 as pilgrims fleeing a hostile environment. A majority of the church had been forced out of Missouri after waging a quasi-war with its residents. Missouri's governor even decreed that all followers of Joseph Smith must be either expelled from the state or exterminated. One Missourian declared before Congress that it was necessary to remove the "great evil" that had corrupted their society. While Smith and a handful of other leaders were imprisoned, thousands of Mormons sought refuge wherever they could. Local accounts reported that hundreds were wandering the woods, searching for food and shelter. Many huddled in the abandoned town of Far West, located in the northwest county of Caldwell and previously the headquarters of the church, to plan their next move. They were surrounded by smoldering homes and anxious neighbors. It was understood that none of them could remain within the state when spring arrived.[6]

The Mormons, though in a pitiable state, were fervent in their belief that they had been deprived of their rights as American citizens, and they were anxious to seek redress. Among those leading the disenfranchised saints was Brigham Young. Born in Vermont in 1801, Young had red hair and a bad temper. His unrelenting drive and forthright proclamations later earned him the label "Lion of the Lord," but at this point he was still learning to be a leader. He and the other surviving members of the Quorum of the Twelve Apostles, one of the faith's governing bodies, organized an official exodus. Hundreds of men then entered into a mutual compact to provide the aid necessary to relocate the entire church, including those who were poor or otherwise help-less. The modern House of Israel was ready to escape its wilderness.[7]

Few Mormons were in a worse condition than Mary Fielding. Born in England in 1801, she had migrated to Toronto in 1834 and met Mor-mon missionaries in 1836. Shortly after her baptism she moved once again, this time to the church's hub in Kirtland, Ohio. There she met Hyrum Smith, the prophet's brother and a key leader in the faith. When Hyrum's wife, Jerusha, died in childbirth in 1837, he married Mary less than two months later. She immediately became the mother to his five young children, including a newborn baby. But she had little time to adapt to her new domestic life. In January the Mormons of Kirt-land were forced to flee Ohio, and Hyrum was imprisoned along with other Mormon leaders by Missouri officials the following November. "My husband was taken from me by an armed force," she wrote her brother, "at a time when I needed, in a particular manner, the kindest care and attention." It was indeed a difficult moment to be separated: she had just given birth to her first child. Without Hyrum's help, Mary was left to survive a frozen winter with a newborn, five other young children, and no shelter. She became so sick that she went months without being able to nurse her own child. Eventually she was able, with the help of others in a similarly desperate position, to shepherd her entire family out of the state. Others were not so fortunate. Dozens of Mormon women in Missouri lost children, husbands, and siblings during this long winter, and several claimed to have been raped at the hands of the Missouri mobs.[8]

People in Illinois, and especially the residents of the river town of Quincy, were quick to welcome the beleaguered group. A local newspaper proudly described their community as an asylum for the oppressed. Their generous welcome was partly rooted in state rivalry. Whereas Missouri seemed to not tolerate those that did not conform to their majoritarian culture, Illinois, which had been a state for only a little more than two decades, was eager to demonstrate civil reci-procity. A border state known for its politically diverse population,

ambitious leaders, and pluralist religious marketplace, Illinois desired
a reputation for civility on the frontier, especially in light of the violence that had shaped its short history, including the Black Hawk War
in 1832. Abraham Lincoln, who participated in that conflict with indigenous tribes, embodied the class of men then coming to power in the
state, and he was serving in Illinois's House of Representatives when
the Mormons arrived. Lincoln, like many of his colleagues, yearned to
be seen as an enlightened counterexample to Missouri, their backward
neighbor to the west.[9]

The Mormons were the happy recipients of Illinoisans' generosity. As the refugees arrived, Quincy's Democratic Association held a
series of meetings to organize relief efforts. They listened to the Mormons' traumatic stories and promised to find them shelter, food, and
employment. Recognizing them as a religious minority, they assured
the saints that they would be treated with "decorum and delicacy." The
association denounced the citizens and governor of Missouri for vio-
lating the rights that were promised by the Constitution. The *Quincy
Argus*, representing the state's Whig party, was similarly anxious to
reach out to the Mormons, and proclaimed Missouri's actions so repre-
hensible that "we could wish her star stricken out from the bright constellation of the Union." What had happened to the Mormons was an
affront to democratic society, both parties concluded. The Mormons,
though they were a fringe people—or perhaps because of that status—
deserved their help.[10]

But the Mormons' stay in Quincy could only be temporary. There
was a limit to the city's kindness, as the people were eager to move on
with their lives and cease diverting so many resources to one faith.
Once they had regrouped, then, the saints began to consider a more
permanent solution. To this point, they had been forced to relocate,
in succession, from communities in the eastern states (New York and
Pennsylvania), the Northwest Territory (Ohio), and the western frontier (Missouri). Though a central community had been crucial to the
Mormon faith, some wondered if it was time to take a different course.
Perhaps if they remained a minority spread across several towns and

cities, they surmised, they could avoid the problems that had arisen when they were a dominant body in one. Other marginalized religious faiths—like the Catholics, Jews, and Shakers—mostly drew ire only when they formed a large, centralized body. Lacking any specific direction from their imprisoned prophet, the saints were ready to disperse themselves, for their own safety.[11]

Yet the Mormons quickly stumbled upon a new opportunity. While Israel Barlow, a church elder, was wandering across the Des Moines River seeking shelter and provisions, he met a land speculator named Isaac Galland. Eager for new clients, Galland immediately made a business proposal, offering the Mormons property on either side of the Mississippi River in both Illinois and Iowa. The latter was a territory, which meant the saints there would be under the supervision of the federal government—an enticing offer, given that from the Mormon perspective, state governments were the primary threat. To further court the Mormons, Iowa's territorial governor, Robert Lucas, wrote a pledge that promised that their religious rights would be protected by the federal authorities. The saints were intrigued but hesitant, especially while Joseph Smith remained in a Missouri jail. They were still waiting for prophetic counsel, but now they at least had options.[12]

Smith, meanwhile, was busy planning his own relocation. He and his fellow prisoners had attempted several escapes that winter, without success. In April 1839, however, while on a routine move between prisons shortly after a grand jury hearing, the Mormons escaped their guards, who, according to Smith, were drunk. They later claimed that they had been allowed to escape, following an informal deal with the state that they would be freed once all of Smith's followers left Missouri. State authorities, in turn, could always raise Smith's status as a wanted fugitive in order to prevent any future Mormon settlement within their borders. Regardless, the runaways spent two weeks navigating back roads, in part by using code names, and Missouri officials later lamented that the Mormon prophet was no longer under their control. Joseph Smith, at least for the time being, was once again free.[13]

David Rogers, painting of Joseph Smith, 1842. This portrait hung in the Smiths' Nauvoo home. LIBRARY AND ARCHIVES, COMMUNITY OF CHRIST, INDEPENDENCE, MISSOURI.

The prophet arrived in Quincy on April 22, exulting in his liberty. He proclaimed that he had fled "that land of tyranny and oppression" so that he could "again take our stand among a people in whose bosoms dwell those feelings of republicanism and liberty which gave rise to our nation." The Mormons, he believed, were committed to the US Constitution as true patriots, in contrast to the Missouri authorities, and were willing to stand such an outrage against American principles. What had happened to Smith and his followers, he argued, was an affront to the nation's democratic system. It was therefore time to take a stand. He told his listeners that they were about to embark on a new project to redeem the nation and its democratic culture. The American experiment, in other words, could still be salvaged.[14]

Smith had, in fact, expressed interest in Galland's land even before his escape, and under his leadership the Mormons were now ready to stabilize the church and establish a new home. At a general conference held in early May in what appeared to onlookers as a Presbyterian campground just north of Quincy, the Mormon leaders looked both backward and forward. They agreed to purchase large properties on which they could rebuild their Mormon kingdom, and they decided to send delegates to the nation's capital to plead their case for federal redress. The saints were dedicated both to establishing a new city in Illinois and Iowa and to achieving justice for losing their previous one in Missouri. Sidney Rigdon, a fiery former Baptist preacher and second-in-command to Smith, was chosen to plead their cause to Congress. In the meantime, saints were to move to the settlements on either side of the Mississippi River. Rejecting the plan to scatter across the region and assimilate into surrounding communities, Smith and his followers retained their hope for an urban Zion. According to apostle Wilford Woodruff, the Mormons were "determined to build a city wherever [sic] their lot is cast" by being "industrious & determined to maintain the kingdom of God." The saints were ready for a fresh start.[15]

Though they originally set their sights on land in both Iowa and Illinois, they increasingly focused on the latter, with the warm reception from both Quincy and the Illinois government in mind. The saints soon narrowed their search to the land that included pieces of a small village named Commerce, located in Hancock County on a bend of the Mississippi River. A peninsula, the area featured flatlands measuring two miles north to south and a mile east to west, and seventy-foot-tall bluffs on its eastern edge. Streams carried water from the hills above to the river below, enabling the cultivation of a wide variety of small plants and groves of trees. Much of the land was made up of marshes. The shrubbery was dense enough to remind humanity of nature's indomitable grandeur. Yet the Mississippi River, which had long been the venous system of America's nascent capitalistic body, promised to connect the area to the broader commercial empire. The rapids transported goods and ideas across the entire North American continent, and from there to the wider world.

The region had already witnessed great transformations by the time the Mormons arrived. Previously the home to several Native American tribes, and known as Quashquema, much of the area's land was given as payment to veterans of the War of 1812, which largely disenfranchised indigenous communities in the region. As with veterans who were paid with land in other cases, however, few proved willing to settle in the unknown territory, and most sold their tracts to speculators. Eventually, enough white settlers moved to the westernmost region of Illinois following statehood in 1818 that a new county, Hancock, named after the famed revolutionary John Hancock, was incorporated in 1825. Starting in the 1820s, a group of traders, hoping to take advantage of the peninsula's proximity to the river, developed the land, calling it Venus. But their efforts came to an end as a result of the economic Panic of 1837. Another wave of speculators, like Galland, bought the property and renamed the town Commerce to reflect its potential as America's industrial age progressed. But their hopes diminished as they struggled to attract settlers.

The Mormons, therefore, provided an opportunity for the speculators to unload acres of unsold land. To the Mormons, the region's undeveloped status was a selling point, as it provided a chance to build a new city on their own. Through a series of transactions between April and August 1839, Mormons bought nearly seven hundred acres that included the heart of the peninsula for $136,500. In total, it was a large purchase and a considerable gamble. To confirm the new settlement's status as the headquarters for the church, Joseph Smith and his family moved into one of its few standing houses, a small two-story log home, on May 10.[16]

The constant turnover of landownership was common on the American frontier. Though the region was known for its beauty, its environment was difficult to tame. The saints later recalled it as a wilderness. The standing water in the flats required them to construct a drainage ditch to remove the springs' runoff water. The work became more urgent after an outbreak of malaria that first summer, due to the swampy conditions, that resulted in several deaths. But the water eventually receded and a new city began to grow.

The saints divided their new land into four-acre blocks, each comprised of four one-acre lots. Individual lots were sold to the incoming saints, who built small homes and developed meager gardens and orchards. The town's name did not survive the transition, either, as Smith rechristened it Nauvoo to signify a new and sacred cause: "The Name of our city (Nauvoo) is of Hebrew origin," he explained in a proclamation about eighteen months later, "and signifies a beautiful situation." Commerce, originally designed to be a small economic trading outpost of an expanding and integrated national economy, was replaced by Nauvoo, a godly city patterned on biblical precedent.[17]

Smith was eager to build his new kingdom on the banks of the Mississippi. He urged his followers who were spread across the nation to assemble in Nauvoo. This was not a new order in the short annals of Mormonism, but rather a revival of a prophetic tradition. The people of God were to be gathered just as they had been under the patriarchal leadership of old, in the days of Moses and Abraham. Smith prophesied that those who failed to heed his call would suffer the storms of an evil world. America, Smith declared, was headed for destruction due to its sinful nature. The world had rejected the laws of God in favor of the pleasures of man. The nation was awash with evil acts and religious confusion, which would usher in the end of the world. God could only suffer such wickedness so long. A storm was coming, and Nauvoo was the only safe refuge. Other radical prophets of the time agreed with this basic outlook, and the period witnessed an increase in millennial fervor. Just a few years later, William Miller, a Baptist preacher from New England, declared the world would end between 1843 and 1844.[18]

These eschatological calls came at a moment of patriotic pride, as most Americans possessed a buoyant faith in their nation's progress. The industrial revolution, coupled with westward expansion, seemed to open up possibilities for everyone—at least, for those who were able to take advantage. Mainstream religious groups like the Methodists, Baptists, and Presbyterians aimed to spread the message of salvation and the principles of democracy across the continent. America's future looked exceptionally bright. Against this view, Joseph Smith and other millenarian prophets prepared for a national collapse.

A staggering number of Mormons headed to Nauvoo as a result of

Smith's call. Disappointed with what they saw as the cultural degradation all around them, and anxious to live among God's elect, thousands flowed into the previously ignored parcel of land in Illinois. The Mormon message provided hope, redemption, and stability, and a stream of converts flooded the region to take part in Smith's experiment. At first, Nauvoo only contained around five hundred available lots; within a few years, population growth forced an expansion to 1,400. Though land speculation remained the dominant economic trade in the city, mercantile shops, bakeries, schools, tinsmiths, and a host of other businesses quickly appeared.[19]

The development of Nauvoo diverged from that of other outposts on the periphery of America's growing economic empire. While most Americans praised the economic transformation that brought more choice and opportunity, there were other groups, like the Mormons, who worried that America had lost its way. Like the Puritans before them, they believed the nation had forgotten its true purpose and was in need of a return to divine values. Too few people followed divine commandments, too many people were left behind while others thrived, and chaos seemed to reign. Nauvoo was to be an asylum for God's chosen people as they escaped a fallen world. Unlike other frontier cities that aimed to expand the nation's ambitions, the Mormon Kingdom was designed as its savior. The Massachusetts Bay Company, in the seventeenth century, represented a break from the corrupt Anglican empire; the city of Nauvoo, in the nineteenth century, reflected a similar divergence within the United States. Both challenged the conventional view of American settlement.

Early success in Nauvoo buoyed the saints' hopes. "The situation is very pleasant," wrote Mary Fielding Smith. By that summer she had recovered from her illness and was reunited with her husband. But she knew that cheerful circumstances were fragile. She admitted an ignorance as to how long they could enjoy peace. As a godly people, and especially after Missouri, Smith expected the same type of persecution that the early Christians had experienced. Indeed, to understand why Mormons hoped to reform American democracy, it is necessary to understand how they became its discontents in the first place.[20]

THE MORMON EXPERIENCE IN MISSOURI is one of the signal episodes of religious conflict in American history, and it prefigured Mormon settlement in Illinois. A state on the extreme frontier, Missouri was itself birthed in crisis. It was part of the territory acquired through the Louisiana Purchase in 1803, and early settlers flocked to the region seeking land and opportunity. The newcomers applied for statehood in 1819. But the state's admission became a national scandal when congressmen considered the legality of slavery within its borders. The question threatened the nation's stability. The original congressional bill of admission included an amendment that allowed slavery but implemented gradual emancipation, reflecting a broader concern over the growing power of the slave states, but the bill's rejection inaugurated a political firestorm. What was at stake was the meaning of American liberty.

The Missouri Compromise, passed in 1820, allowed Missouri to enter the union as a slave state, but decreed that future states incorporated above the parallel 36 degrees, 30 minutes north would be free, while those south of the line would permit slavery. Thomas Jefferson declared the compromise to be the union's death knell, as a geographic line now divided the nation into two competing societies. The episode seemed to amplify, rather than resolve, a national crisis. Even after the immediate controversy was settled, in Missouri, due to its contested makeup, conflict and violence still loomed.[21]

The bloody saga of the Mormons in Missouri was but one example— though perhaps the premier example. The first missionaries sent by Joseph Smith set foot in the state in late 1830, the same year the church was organized. But rather than focusing on converting American citizens, the saints had their eyes on the indigenous peoples just beyond the western boundaries of white settlement. This mission was prompted by a new scriptural text. Just a few months previous, in March, Joseph Smith had published the Book of Mormon, which claimed to be a sacred record of America's ancient inhabitants and their dealings with the Christian God. Smith was far from the only American to believe Native inhabitants were descendants of the House of Israel—nor was he even the only New Englander to produce a book that claimed as much—but his publication of a five-hundred-page book, supposedly a translation of golden tablets left by these ancient civilizations, was unique in both size and scope.

The text prophesied a day when the remnants of that population, who had migrated from Jerusalem to the New World six centuries before Christ, would rise up, with the help of righteous gentiles, and reassert their power over the American continent. The earliest Mormon converts understood themselves to be those righteous gentiles, and the Native inhabitants recently removed to the West as the descendants of those ancient pilgrims. The saints presented themselves as kinder alternatives to their white contemporaries in dealings with indigenous tribes, though they still subscribed to the racist beliefs and colonization policies of the era. Missouri, therefore, was once again to be a crossroads of competing civilizational visions.[22]

Though the missionaries never succeeded in achieving a mass Indian conversion, the region surrounding Independence, a city in Jackson County, Missouri, quickly gained significance in Smith's evolving theological vision. The county was named after the nation's president, Andrew Jackson, and it reflected his demotic and rough nature: local politics lacked civility, leadership positions were held by uneducated yet ambitious men, and disputes often resulted in extralegal violence. But Smith himself visited the settlement in the summer of 1831 and declared it Zion, the center place for God's earthly kingdom. Early Mormon converts in New York were encouraged to migrate to the area, and soon hundreds did.

Even as a competing Mormon gathering point in Kirtland, Ohio, became the de facto headquarters of the fledgling church over the next half decade, Independence retained its importance as the location for future millennial rule. The town already possessed a few hundred settlers, mostly from the South, who were anxious to take advantage of new western trade routes; their backgrounds and agendas were therefore different from those of their new neighbors. Soon the Mormon population in Jackson County grew to levels that frightened the original settlers, who saw them as religious zealots threatening their way of life—including, perhaps, the institution of slavery. To Jackson County's non-Mormon residents, the saints represented the dangers of democratization, as a few religious frauds could delude those from the bottom rungs of society, introduce communal unrest, and all the while claim protection under the banner of religious liberty. After a few years of escalating tensions, a mob expelled the Mormons from the county in the winter of 1833 and defended their actions as necessary to maintain societal peace. The safety of the many, they believed, justified the removal of the few. There was no room for the saints in this land of Independence.[23]

Missouri's solution to their Mormon problem reflected a broader American practice: removal and segregation. As the nation's politicians and intellectuals contemplated how to govern such a large and diverse population, especially nonwhite communities, geographic isolation was seen as a way to maintain distance while retaining some form of equality. President Jackson was implementing procedures to forcibly remove a number of Native tribes in the South to new western reservations through the Indian Removal Act, a callous policy rooted in white supremacy. Though Mormons shared the same skin color and European descent as their Missouri neighbors, their radical beliefs and countercultural message were seen as an impending threat and they were effectively denied some of the protections of American citizenship. Of course, Joseph Smith and his followers were never disenfranchised to the same extent as nonwhite peoples, retaining access to many rights that were denied to African and Native Americans.[24]

The Mormons were nevertheless cast as a body of citizens who could not remain among civilized communities. Repeated appeals by their wary neighbors to the governor of Missouri resulted in designated and explicit seclusion. In 1836, the state granted the Mormons their own county, Caldwell, in the northern part of Missouri to separate them from non-Mormon neighbors. The saints were once again forced to start over in a new location and deal with suspicious neighbors.

Once the Mormons arrived in Caldwell County and its county seat, Far West, they did not fare much better than they had in Independence. They were met with opposition from within and outside their faith, as Smith faced a leadership crisis that threatened his authority. The majority of the church, by then several thousand strong, relocated to the area in early 1838, after the Ohio settlement fell apart. The increasing Mormon population only heightened tensions. Several prominent leaders within the church clashed with Smith and were cut off from the community, and their dissenting voices further inflamed local animosity. Many wondered if the faith could even survive. Smith and other leaders felt that they, the true beholders of the American promise, were under attack. They declared their allegiance to the Constitution, as well as their frustration with the men who ran the state and the nation. "Exalt the standard of Democracy!" they cried. Few listened.[25]

In the summer of 1838, schisms within the church and pressure from without climaxed in a series of confrontations of threatening words and menacing deeds—and, ultimately, battle and bloodshed. When locals in a neighboring county refused saints the right to vote in an August election, Smith instructed his followers to stand their ground. Neither side backed down. Skirmishes broke out on the boundaries between Mormon and non-Mormon communities; both groups viewed their actions as means of defending rights and preserving safety. One member of the Missouri mob allegedly said "that a mormon had no more right to vote than a negro." Disenfranchisement, if not death, appeared to be real threats.[26]

The Mormons took a series of actions that embodied a political philosophy both radical and reactionary and that laid the groundwork for their later political practices in Nauvoo. They selected officers for militia leadership, organized civic meetings, and even drafted a secular constitution for a group called the Society of the Daughters of Zion, colloquially known as the Danites. The official name was a reference to a passage in the Book of Micah, and the common name came from the Israelite tribe of Dan; both titles were meant to invoke the armies of the Old Testament. The saints were a modern House of Israel, with the military strength to prove it.

The new constitution, drafted to justify extralegal activities, paradoxically reflected the Mormon desire to fit within America's democratic body. "Whereas in all bodies laws are necessary, for the permanent safety and well being of society," it began, "We the members of the society of the Daughter of Zion do agree to regulate ourselves under such laws as in rightiousness [sic] shall be deemed necessary for the preservation of our holy religion." They argued that they were devoted to defending the rights promised them by their American ancestors, those who fought for freedom and sacrificed "their lives, their fortunes, & their sacred honours." That last line, drawn from the Declaration of Independence, was intended to emphasize their patriotism. The cause of the current conflict, according to the Mormons, was that they had been stripped of the rights and liberties granted to them by the US Constitution, and it was within their right to follow the American example of resistance, even to the point of bloodshed. This right—the right to rebel—was not bestowed by the state, of course: it was directly granted by God, and those who opposed them were therefore "wicked and designing men." The Missouri mobs were both traitors and blasphemers.[27]

But the Danite constitution did not merely reaffirm American constitutional principles. The document also planted the seeds for political dissent, and even extralegal action. As ultimate power belonged to the people, the Mormons explained, they had the right to dispose of it when necessary. This idea, which drew from the British philosopher John Locke as filtered through the Declaration of Independence, was based on the notion of a social contract. But in the Danite context it was used to justify an opposition to legitimate American political bodies. "As it is inconvenient [sic] and impossible to convene the people in all cases"—that is, when democracy fails to bring about just conclusions—it was necessary to pass "the legislative powers . . . into the hands of a representation" authorized to take action. Power must be removed from the majority, in other words, and placed in the hands of the righteous few.[28] The Mormon Danite society, based on this radical idea of representative authority, was justified in its decision to form an extralegal body with the power to organize resistance.

Tensions only escalated from there. That same summer of 1838, Joseph Smith's counselor in the First Presidency (the three-man council that was the church's most authoritative ecclesiastical body), Sidney Rigdon, warned that any unjustified actions against the saints would court a "war of extermination." On October 27, after hearing exaggerated reports of Mormon insurrections, Missouri's governor, Lilburn Boggs, issued an executive order, later known as the Extermination Order, which declared that Mormons in the state "must be treated as enemies, and must be exterminated or driven from the State if necessary for the public peace." In the words of both leaders, extermination was the radical solution to democratic unrest. Only one side, however, had the resources to follow through on the threat.[29]

Three days later, though likely without knowledge of the governor's directive, a vigilante band of 250 Missourians marched on a small Mormon outpost called Hawn's Mill and massacred seventeen men, women, and children, many of them as they huddled helplessly in a central cabin. The massacre was a ruthless act meant to scare off other Mormon settlers, and rooted in the outright disgust many felt toward the faith. One of the perpetrators allegedly justified killing a young boy by explaining, "nits will make lice, and if [the boy] had lived he would have become Mormon." Once news of the order and massacre leaked out, a coerced, and possibly staged, meeting between Mormon and state officials took place. The state then imprisoned Smith and a number of leaders, who were to be tried for crimes including arson, burglary, treason, and murder. They were imprisoned for a long winter while thousands of Mormons were forced to leave the state, bereft and often shorn of their goods and property. Some of their wounds—both physical and psychological—would never heal.[30]

This was far from the only example of extralegal justice during the period. Especially on the frontier, where the hand of the government was mostly absent, justice was administered more swiftly by common citizens than by the inchoate and ponderous judicial system. Jacksonian democracy, which championed the common man and local community, seemed to sanction this form of deliberation. For example, in 1835, prompted by a group of white gamblers who fired into a crowd and killed an innocent bystander in Vicksburg, Mississippi, a mob captured and hung five men who were believed to have incited the riot, saving the state from a lengthy trial. They defended their actions through an appeal to the legal authorities' inadequacy, including the state's feeble investigative powers. The downfall of democracy, they believed, was that it made states so weak that justice was more swiftly achieved outside of the law. This was especially true, many felt, when dealing with minority populations on the frontier, who could act as they pleased.[31]

Smith and the Mormons never forgot Missouri. The violence of their enemies, and the negligence of the state, left lasting scars. Even after they fled to Illinois, the ordeal shaped the church's decisions and actions in Nauvoo. On the one hand, it reaffirmed that they could not rely upon state or local government for protection. This would lead Smith to formulate a political theory to secure rights for minority groups that simultaneously called for more local autonomy and protection from the federal government.

On the other hand, the Missouri experience also taught them that the democratic system could be manipulated in ways to protect their interests. Before, they had been willing to wait for Zion to be established following a period of millennial cleansing and apocalyptic justice. Yet their failure to maintain some form of peace, and the inability to merely wait for millennial reprieve, highlighted the necessity of implementing practices that assured long-term security. Learning from these lessons, they now sought ways to both work within America's constitutional order and explore methods that would allow them to control it for their own interests. The extralegal actions and political deliberations used against the saints demonstrated that America's chaotic democratic system was malleable enough for circumvention. Their ruin in Missouri forced the Mormons to consider new political solutions in Illinois.[32]

AFTER ARRIVING IN ILLINOIS, the Mormons petitioned for help from both political parties. When church members crossed the Mississippi River, their new state was anxious to boost its recently bankrupted economy and swell its stalled population. Both the Whigs and Democrats in Springfield, the state capital, were therefore quite receptive to the incoming Mormon body, so long as Smith and his followers were willing to follow traditional standards.

Illinois was known for its energetic practice of democracy. Most frontier states featured ambitious politicians who pushed the bounds of decorum, but Illinois, which produced both Abraham Lincoln and Stephen A. Douglas, was especially rife with men seeking broad acclaim and testing party allegiances. There were numerous scandals, as men were often accused of being overambitious or traitors to a particular cause. Personal rivalries dominated nearly every legislative action, and politicians recognized that they commanded a large stage. How they addressed a set of central issues—including the commerce provided by the Mississippi River—shaped national discussion and federal projects. Many viewed Illinois as the test case for whether western expansion would result in stable governance or anarchy. Local politicians were ready to prove the nation's hopes justified. Attracting immigrants and stimulating economic growth meant more seats, and more power, in Congress. Played right, Illinois's democratic system seemed ripe for manipulation.[33]

Some of the newly arrived Mormons were not willing to be cautious. Lyman Wight, who had been a member of the faith since its first year and had been imprisoned with Smith in Missouri, had earned, owing to his temper, the nickname "Wild Ram of the Mountains." When asked by Missouri officials if he was willing to stand by Smith and risk being killed, he allegedly responded, "Shoot and be damned." After escaping jail six months later, Wight, a tall, thin man with a beard, was anxious to lash out at those he felt were to blame for his misfortunes: the members of the Democratic Party. And the *Quincy Whig* was eager to provide a platform for Wight's accusations.[34]

The Wild Ram did not pull any punches. In a series of published letters, though he insisted that he did not mean to speak poorly about democracy, Wight warned that the Democratic Party failed to live up to its principles because it granted too much power to unruly mobs. Further, what had happened to the Mormons in Missouri, he explained, was a threat to the entire political system. For America's democracy to flourish, especially on the frontier, it was necessary to hold state institutions accountable, and Wight believed the Democratic Party had not done so. Minority groups like the Mormons, who were particularly vulnerable, had to band together in order to bring about broader change. Wight was ready to wage a holy war against the Democratic Party.[35]

Not all Mormons shared Wight's passion, nor his partisanship. Robert Thompson, who had also escaped the horrors of Missouri, worried that Wight's rhetoric could invite retaliation from Illinois politicians. Citizens in Quincy and surrounding areas had been welcoming, and legislators in Springfield accommodating, and he believed it would be foolish to risk those good feelings through political attacks. Thompson warned Joseph Smith that some might interpret Wight's condemnation of the Democrats in Missouri as an attack on *all* Democrats. The vulnerable Mormons could not afford to be cast as opponents to one of the nation's two dominant political parties. He further explained that there was a fine line that organized religions had to observe when it came to participating in America's body politic, and it was in their best interests not to cross it. Thompson encouraged Smith to remain neutral in partisan debates, and the Quorum of the Twelve were tasked with reining in Wight.[36]

In the end, church leaders took Thompson's advice. The First Presidency assured readers in a letter published in both Whig and Democrat newspapers that they did not hold a single party responsible for Missouri, and that the illegal actions were strictly confined to rogue mobs and conniving politicians. Missouri's malfeasance transcended party affiliation. Smith then privately, though gently, chastised Wight, telling him that despite good intentions, his actions could bring irreparable harm. The saints, he explained, were forced display "a little wisdom and Caution" and play the political game. Wight acquiesced and the *Whig* published his personal apology in its next issue.[37]

By refusing to align his religion with a political party, Joseph Smith attempted to follow American principles regarding the relation between church and state. The first decades of the nation's existence featured a formal, if uneven, process of disestablishment, or the separation between civic and clerical authorities. A majority of citizens understood America to be a Christian nation, but there were limits to any political and ecclesiastical alliance. Most Protestants, for example, drew the line where ecclesiastical actions infringed on personal liberty. Government bodies were not to favor one religious body over another—though the interpretation of the term "religious body" was often vague and flexible—and ecclesiastical leaders in turn were not to infringe upon individual conscience.

These ideas quickly became mainstream. As one New England preacher put it, for democracy to function, there needed to be two forms of religious liberty: "external liberty," or the civic rights granted by the state, and "internal liberty," or the freedom that each denomination granted individuals to act as moral agents without direct oversight. American democracy was to be a Christian coalition based on consent, not coercion. Ministers were forced to adapt to this new environment, which meant embracing the republican form of persuasion rather than ecclesiastical command. What resulted was, in effect, a quasi-religious establishment based on Protestant notions of liberty that dominated both political and cultural spheres.[38]

Minority religions that challenged this dispensation were met with swift justice. Though Native American tribes, African American sects, and minority religious groups like Shakers were continually attacked for their failure to follow these new political norms, Catholics were often the main target. Because they professed allegiance to a foreign pope and generally voted en bloc—an activity often described as "clannish" and "un-American"—American Catholics were identified as outsiders to the nation's political system. Anti-Catholic sentiment was present at the founding, and before, but the threat seemed to escalate as thousands of Catholic immigrants arrived in America during the 1830s and 1840s and settled both in urban seaport cities and on the western frontier. To Protestants, this seemed like a foreign invasion by individuals who did not share their democratic values. Catholics were forced to denounce their fidelity to the pope if they wished to gain full civil and political rights. Priests were also expected not to intervene in local politics, instead allowing congregants to follow their conscience. From the Protestant perspective, the Catholic faith demanded, according to one contemporary critic, a "substitution of authority for conscience," and they therefore did not fit within a political culture based on individual liberty.[39]

Debates over the place of Catholicism in American life provided a model for debates over the Mormons. The Mormon practice of communal solidarity, economic isolationism, and priestly leadership elicited the scorn of their neighbors. Within years of the faith's organization, Smith attempted to institute practices that would consecrate private property for public interests, an idea that countered the period's growing commitment to capitalism. J. B. Turner, a professor at the nearby Illinois College, therefore claimed that Mormons were "natural allies" with the Roman faith and its communitarian structure and theocratic standard. It was an unresolved question whether churches built upon hierarchical priesthood governance could coexist with Protestants in America.[40]

Other critics were anxious to extinguish the threat before it could take root. One local resident, Udney Hay Jacob, wrote to President Martin Van Buren, who succeeded Jackson in 1837, to warn him that the Mormons, then seen as a harmless group of refugees, would eventually threaten the entire nation. He urged Van Buren to eradicate the sect. The Mormons, similarly, claimed another observer in Quincy, held great political power all of a sudden. "Should they ever become disposed to exert their influence for evil, which may Heaven prevent," he warned, "they would surround our institutions with an element of

danger, more to be dreaded than an armed and hundred-eyed police."
There was potential for serious peril.[41]

But conflict seemed unlikely, given the warm reception the saints
received in 1839. As long as the Mormons followed the basic expectations for religion and politics, they could seemingly evade trouble. Smith
was, at first, willing to follow prevailing beliefs. He declared at the general meeting of the church in April 1840 that he had no wish to exert
political influence in Illinois. His imprisonment in Missouri seemed to
temper his audacity. Yet any perceived complacency did not last long.[42]

Thompson, when he warned Smith about the dangers of politicking, spoke of the possible repercussions. "If through the imprudence
and conduct of isolated individuals," he predicted, "3-4-or 5 years hence
our altars should be [once again] thrown down[,] our Homes destroyed,
our brethren slain, our wives widow[ed] and our Children orphan[ed]."
If that day were to come, Thompson would feel justified, knowing that
he had done all he could to warn them in advance. At the time, Smith
found Thompson's advice persuasive; later on, he found it too restric-
tive. In the end, though, Thompson turned out to be prophetic.[43]

WHILE EARLY REACTIONS FROM ILLINOIS POLITICIANS seemed promising, the Mormons maintained their belief that they could also receive
aid from the national government. Federal authorities, they hoped,
could correct state wrongs. Even while Joseph Smith was still imprisoned, he considered avenues through which to seek federal redress.
He encouraged his followers, who were only just beginning to gather
in Illinois, to start collecting accounts of the Mormon experience in
Missouri, noting the attacks, deaths, and rapes at the hands of vengeful mobs and a corrupt state. They could then compile these accounts
and submit them to federal authorities.[44]

His followers already had similar plans. Sidney Rigdon, his closest
counselor, proposed they assemble enough evidence to, as he put it,
"impeach" the State of Missouri due to its negligence at securing the
rights promised in the Constitution. The saints firmly believed they
could prove to the federal government—the final arbiter of constitu-

tional power in their eyes—that they had been wronged. National sentiment seemed in their favor, too, as newspapers in Washington had denounced the "band of robbers and murderers" who had persecuted the Mormons. Eventually, the Mormons gathered 481 petitions and Smith, Rigdon, and Elias Higbee set off for Washington to deliver their appeals to Congress.[45]

In a prefatory memorial meant to frame the petitions, Smith and his assistants provided a general narrative of events in Missouri—from their perspective as sufferers, of course. Everyone within the church, they argued, were "good citizens" who obeyed the laws of the land and were attacked merely for performing the duties and obligations of their faith. Missouri had stripped them of the rights and privileges promised to loyal patriots. Because of their private beliefs, they were beaten, robbed, and forcibly removed from their property and deprived of their belongings. The tale was a blemish on America's record of freedom. The women and children who were forced to flee the state "marked their footsteps on the frozen ground with blood." Yet the Mormons believed that the government could still address these wrongs.[46]

The vast majority of the petitions provided explicit details and demanded substantial monetary reward. Many had good cause. Isaac Leany requested $10,000 for each of the two bullets lodged in his chest, $5,000 for each of the two bullets to his hip, and $500 for each of the two bullets that had pierced his arm. Nathan K. Knight asked for $5,000 for being shot through his lungs. A number of the complaints were remarkably meticulous. Benjamin Crandell listed stolen acres of property, corn, hogs, calves, cows, wheat, equipment, guns, and twelve months of missed labor, which in total was worth, he claimed, $2,307. Others were vague. Some, even if they escaped physical wounds, sought redress for political slights: James Bingham demanded $10,000 for "being deprived of citizenship in the State of Missouri." The price of disenfranchisement was steep.

But the largest appeal came from Joseph Smith himself, who, due to property losses, damages, pending lawsuits, and false imprisonment, boldly demanded $100,000. Combined, the petitions totaled over $2 million. Many of these estimates were clearly exaggerated, and some of the details were likely stretched. But they demonstrated the saints' level of disgust with the state of Missouri, as well as their firm belief that the federal government could reverse the damage. These were the poignant voices of citizens who believed their rights had been trammeled and hoped their allegiance to a democratic system was not in vain.[47]

Mormons were not the only Illinois residents appealing to federal power after being wronged by a state. In 1839, the same year mobs forced the LDS Church out of Missouri, a young Abraham Lincoln delivered his first major public address. Speaking to the Young Men's Lyceum in Springfield, Illinois, the ambitious lawyer declared that national stability depended on forging an "attachment" between the government and the people. Mobs, or any extralegal body that aimed to circumvent law in order to bring about vigilante justice, threatened the democratic order. Lincoln was specifically referring to another Missouri incident, this one racial in nature: a free black man in St. Louis had been recently chained to a tree and burned. This "mobocratic spirit," Lincoln said, may be packaged in a patriotic hue by its proponents, but it eroded the law's efficacy and was an imminent danger to the "undecided experiment" of American self-rule.[48]

Especially in the West, many were calling for more law and more order. Tocqueville made the same observation as Lincoln in the second volume of his *Democracy in America*: the reciprocity required to maintain democratic balance between citizenry and government seemed to erode on the American frontier, where tyrannical majorities stamped out dissent. In an era where federal oversight was mostly invisible, some argued for strengthening it in order to protect equal justice and minority rights. The Mormon appeals were just further evidence against democratic excess.[49]

The Mormon quest for justice enabled a wide range of voices to enter the public sphere. The individual petitions sent to Washington, including those carried by Smith in 1839, allowed ordinary members of the church, including women, to express their grievances. Lemira Calkins, identified as a widow, demanded redress for being driven from her home, an event that had inflicted pain on her and her family. Lydia English claimed the experience was so extreme that her husband died as a result of his inflictions. She asked for $5,000. Another woman, Nancy Cary, wrote that her husband was captured after Boggs's extermination order, and then a Missourian struck him with a gun, fracturing his skull. He died two days later. She requested a mere $275. Catherine McBride recalled helplessly watching her husband cut "to peases with a sythe blaide."

These women generally asked for less money than their male counterparts, but they spared few grisly details. The seventy-three-year-old Sophia Higbee, who also lost a husband in Missouri, confessed that no earthly sum could compensate her. These were passionate appeals from women who feared that mob violence had forever destroyed the supposed American promise of domestic bliss. For some, even narrating their grief was too painful. "We have been requested in several letters to give a history of the proceedings of the mob in Missouri," wrote Almira Covey, "but this is more than I can do." The pain was still too fresh.[50]

The antebellum period featured a growing number of female voices in the public sphere. Cast as the guardians of domestic virtue, women often led various movements for cultural reform. Especially once Jacksonian Democrats scaled back the federal government's role in improving everyday life, individuals and organized groups sought to transform the world around them by mobilizing relief and reform efforts. This was particularly true of evangelical women dedicated to refining society. One woman swept up in the reformist spirit of the age was Emma Hale Smith, wife of the Mormon prophet. Born and raised in rural Pennsylvania, she was the niece of a Methodist minister and an active participant in local revival efforts. Her decision to elope with a transient laborer and religious seeker like Joseph led to her being disavowed by her well-established family. From that moment, her life was intertwined with her husband's attempt to reform the world.

David Rogers, painting of Emma Smith, 1842. This portrait hung alongside her husband's in the Smiths' Nauvoo home. LIBRARY AND ARCHIVES, COMMUNITY OF CHRIST, INDEPENDENCE, MISSOURI.

Emma Smith never gave up her emphasis on dignity and respectability, nor her independence. A tall woman with chestnut hair who dressed conservatively and possessed a strong will, she never hesitated to correct her husband and other church leaders. In Kirtland, voicing a Methodist belief in temperance, she chastised the Mormon brethren for their use of tobacco. Her arguments led to a new dietary code that was closely aligned with Methodist beliefs.

The other Mormons recognized Emma's power. Though she did not add her own petition to the cache that was sent to Washington in 1839, she had certainly experienced her share of suffering. Her first three children died in childbirth, and another adopted son lived only ten months. By the time of the saints' bloody conflict with Missouri, she had four young children to care for. It took all her courage and determination to make it through the crisis. As her husband spent the cold winter in a dreary prison, she guided her family, as well as several other families that looked to her for leadership, out of the state, all while keeping one eye over her shoulder for another mob. As she crossed the frozen Mississippi, she carried not only her youngest children, but also her husband's sacred manuscripts, which were sewn to the interior of her skirt. Emma Smith sacrificed a great deal for her husband's kingdom.[51]

Sacrifice was a common theme for Mormon women. The men of the church were frequently called on missions that took them away from home for weeks, months, and even years, leaving their wives to fend for themselves and their families. This put additional strain on women in the home. Just as the saints were settling in Nauvoo and dealing with the malaria outbreak, Joseph Smith appointed the Quorum of the Twelve Apostles to go to Britain and teach the gospel. They were to travel alone. This mission was a long time coming, but it now arrived at an inopportune moment. Their wives, still recovering from Missouri, were left to build a new home on their own. "I never needed more grace, patience or your prayers than I do at present," Leonora Taylor admitted to her apostolic husband, John. At the time, Mormon families including Taylor's were scattered among deserted army barracks across the river in Iowa as well as the few makeshift adobe homes available in Nauvoo. "Sister Tailor's [sic] going in with me," wrote another apostle's wife, Phebe Woodruff, "as she had to move out of brother Youngs house." Leonora and Phebe were now sharing a room with yet another woman, Sarah Pratt, whose spouse was on the other side of the Atlantic Ocean. Their husbands—John Taylor, Wilford Woodruff, and Orson Pratt—won many much-needed converts in Britain, and on their return helped build up the city of Nauvoo, but it was often their wives who were left to build the new settlement. Their lives would not get easier in the coming years.[52]

The delegation carrying the Mormons' petitions to Washington, as Emma Smith and other women built up Nauvoo, was led by Joseph Smith, but also included Sidney Rigdon—or at least it was initially supposed to. Few men had played as large a role in early LDS history as Rigdon. Nearing age fifty, he had served as an elder statesman since the church's first year. He was previously a minister for several schismatic Baptist traditions and brought his oratorical skills to his new faith, which needed them. Rigdon was ordained to the First Presidency in 1832, and was seen as Smith's right-hand man ever since. At times, his eloquence helped bring legitimacy and respect to the fledging movement; at other moments, as in Missouri, his rhetoric could get them in trouble. He had been imprisoned with Smith and other leaders the previous autumn, but had been released two months earlier than the rest and helped organize the scattered Mormons in Illinois before Smith's arrival. His experience and statesmanship were crucial as the church navigated new political contexts, which is why he was chosen to accompany Smith to Washington. However, after he became violently ill during the trek, the group decided to leave Rigdon behind in Cincinnati—a development that portended Rigdon's Nauvoo experience, as he would continually be found on the outside looking in at Smith's newest activities. Indeed, Rigdon likely had no idea how much the following years would test his—and his family's—allegiance to the man he and the rest of the Mormons believed was a prophet.[53]

Those who remained with Smith arrived in the nation's capital in late November. Though no longer the swampland of the eighteenth century, Washington remained a small, underdeveloped city, reflecting the nation's youth. But that did not diminish the awe visitors who hailed from rural parts of the country felt, and the Mormons had reason to believe it would be a fruitful trip. Every delegate from Illinois, both Democrat and Whig, made a point to meet with Smith and his associates. One of the state's representatives in the House, John Reynolds, offered to introduce them to President Van Buren. (Reynolds later reminisced that Smith appeared "fair and honorable" to him, save for "his fanaticism on religion.") For the first time, the Mormons felt they were backed by their elected authorities. Though it is unlikely Smith and his associates expected Van Buren, who was nearing the end of his first term as president, would take direct action—executive orders were nonexistent in the era—they likely hoped he would support their petitions to Congress.[54]

But the meetings tempered their expectations. Led by Reynolds, Smith was brought to the White House, then known as the President's

House, on November 29. While the prophet marveled at the stately structure—it was "a very large and splendid palace, surrounded with a splendid enclosure decorated with all the fineries and elegance of the world," he reported—he was less impressed with its current occupant. Van Buren was as slick a political fixer and operator as existed at the time, and the Democratic Party, then only a little more than a decade old, revolved around his agenda. The prophet described the president as "a small man, sandy complexion, and ordinary features," and possessing a "considerable body" that was "not well proportioned." Even Van Buren, Smith quipped, admitted that he was "quite fat." Drawing on the language of a famous Christian creed concerning the trinity—with which the Mormons, who believed in an embodied God, disagreed—Smith concluded that Van Buren "is without boddy or parts." They judged Van Buren as hardly a man.[55]

More disappointing than the president's physical features was his political outlook. Ever since the first Democratic president, Andrew Jackson, was elected in 1828, the power of the federal government had been, with the exception of punishing Native and African Americans, in abeyance. The Democrats believed that authority lay with individual state bodies. Jackson left office in 1836 after two terms, but Van Buren, his handpicked successor, continued the Democratic agenda. Unlike Jackson, however, Van Buren lacked the personal charisma to win the party's loyalty, which forced him to carefully tread the political scene. This balancing act led him, according to Smith, to determine the Mormon cause even before he had ever heard it. After Smith presented his case, the president merely replied, "What can I do?" Van Buren's understanding of the balance of power limited his options. "I can do nothing for you," he reportedly explained, because "if I do anything, I shall come in contact with the whole state of Missouri." The president was worried he would lose the necessary votes from a state he needed in his reelection bid.[56]

The Mormons reached a similar dead end in Congress. Their memorial was only briefly debated before being dismissed by the senators. At issue was jurisdiction—did the federal government have the right to interfere in state conflicts? Elias Higbee, whom Smith left behind to handle the petition when he returned to Nauvoo, argued before the Senate Committee on the Judiciary in late February 1840 that this was a much broader problem than mere anti-Mormon animus. While there were "15 thousand souls" who were kicked out of Missouri, he estimated there were thousands more also deprived of their rights throughout the nation. Only federal intervention could solve a problem of this magnitude.

But several days of testimony failed to convince senators that they should get involved. Garret D. Wall, senator from New Jersey and chairman of the committee, informed Higbee that redress could only be granted by Missouri. The committee's official report concluded that the Mormon cause did not authorize the involvement of the federal government, because no crimes were committed by federal officers. Only the state could redress wrongs committed by state actors. The verdict was the same when the committee's report reached the Senate floor a few weeks later. At least for the time being, the saints had to look elsewhere for redress. For the disappointed Smith, the dilemma seemed clear: how could they gain redress from the state for actions committed by a state-sanctioned mob? Local democracy, it seemed, could only result in majoritarian rule.[57]

The Mormon delegation concluded that the national legislature had devolved into insignificance. They described Congress as full of men who were so devoted to displaying their oratory skills, exhibiting their elite etiquette through "bowing and scraping, twisting and turning," and gaining acclaim from party officials, that the end result was more "folly" than "substance." Hyrum Smith, Joseph's brother, agreed that congressmen were prejudiced against particular constituents, and that their only allegiances were to factions and bodies numerous enough to keep them in office. In many ways, the Smith brothers were not wrong.[58]

Joseph Smith's firsthand exposure to national politics was a formative experience. He was forever haunted by Van Buren's statement that the president could "do nothing" for the beleaguered saints. But rather than losing faith in the power of the federal government, he instead concluded that the wrong people were in charge. Smith believed that American federalism, if wielded properly, had the power to protect the rights of minority groups. The saints had to claim their inherent political power. Because Van Buren proved unwilling to help, "he shall not have our votes," Smith privately mused. When the prophet decided to leave DC and return west, he was turning his back on America's traditional democratic system. Nauvoo would be built on a different foundation.

Crucial to Smith's new political project was a simple electoral calculation. According to one observer, Smith was devoted to turning the entire church against Van Buren, whom he described as "a huckstering politician," as well as any other figure who refused Nauvoo support. If politicians were driven by electoral politics, then the Mormons needed to learn a new way to exert power. Smith recognized that there was a political game in American democracy. They would continue to appeal to the government for redress—several more batches of formal petitions were gathered throughout the next five years—but the saints also explored other mechanisms for influence. There were multiple avenues for reparation.[59]

The prophet had reason to be optimistic. When he returned to Nauvoo after his journey to Washington, Smith found a city that was both growing and thriving. "It is almost incredible to see what amount of labor has been performed here during the winter," he wrote. One resident estimated there were already nearly three thousand people living in Nauvoo itself, with a few thousand more residing nearby. Phebe Woodruff wrote her husband, apostle Wilford Woodruff, who was still in Britain, that the city was growing exceptionally fast, and that nearly all the best lots were already taken. Within a year of first settlement, they already raised at least three hundred homes. Among those new families making Nauvoo their home was that of Hiram and Sarah Kimball, who married that September 1840. They, like their neighbors, expected to remain for a long time. Even as politicians—at both the state and federal level—had failed to grasp the potential power of this new kingdom, the saints were eagerly planting roots in the Mississippi Valley's fertile soil.[60]

CHAPTER 2

Seeds

When we arrived [in Nauvoo] we found the people like the net cast into
the sea & gathered of all kinds good & bad.

—ELISHA ATWOOD, JULY 19, 1841[1]

GEN.^L JOSEPH SMITH ADDRESSING THE NAUVOO LEGION.

Robert Campbell, "General Joseph Smith Addressing the Nauvoo Legion," water-
color and ink on paper, 1845. This depiction was created shortly after Smith was
killed in 1844, and in the midst of growing tensions with neighbors. The legion
always represented, to the saints, their last line of defense. LDS CHURCH HISTORY LIBRARY,
SALT LAKE CITY.

Nauvoo was a town on the rise in the fevered spring of 1841. "The sound of the ax, the hammer, and the saw," the local newspaper remarked, "greet your ear in every direction." Around three hundred homes had been built the previous summer, and about the same number were planned for the coming summer, as the city swelled to several thousand inhabitants. Besides the continuous stream of followers who gathered in Nauvoo from nearby states, every few months brought new groups of eager converts from Great Britain. Between 1841 and 1842, over two thousand Mormon immigrants crossed the Atlantic Ocean and settled in Nauvoo. It was impossible not to feel optimistic about the town's future. The setting was better than one could hope, penned a Mormon in a letter urging his brother, still in Pennsylvania, to join the City of God, as Nauvoo was already one of the prettiest towns along the river.[2]

The nation itself witnessed a significant change with the election of William Henry Harrison as president in 1840. Harrison represented an ascendant new political party, the Whigs, who were devoted to reforming the country. The Whigs claimed that America could once again return to its glory days after years of neglect under the Democratic Party. Reformers of all stripes tried to capitalize on the momentum. Even after Harrison died in April 1841, a month after taking office, many assumed the nation to be in the middle of a major transition.

Amid such local and national excitement, the Mormons decided to hail their progress with a celebration. April 6 marked eleven years since Joseph Smith had founded the Church of Jesus Christ of Latter-day Saints, and though the saints commemorated the date every year, this anniversary seemed especially notable: they were laying the cornerstones for their new, grandiose temple.

Situated on a majestic bluff that towered over the city below, and visible for miles down the busy river, the structure, once completed, would be the architectural capstone for the community. The festivities—including parades, bands, and sermons—certainly signaled its importance. One of the central components of the celebration was the Nauvoo Legion, a city militia organized just two months before, but that had already enrolled over six hundred men. They paraded past seven thousand saints who flocked to Nauvoo from the surrounding region. Cannon fire starting at 7 a.m. announced the arrival of Mormon generals. Two hours later, Joseph Smith, whom the saints had granted the title of Lieutenant General of the Legion—an honor not bestowed on any American since George Washington—appeared on a central stage to accept a handcrafted silk flag from "the Ladies of Nauvoo." The prophet knew how to orchestrate a show.

The militia, led by Smith, then marched to the site of the future temple, where they lowered, in order, the southeast, southwest, northwest, and northeast cornerstones. Each stone was presided over by a different ecclesiastical office, and the thousands of attendees scrambled for a good position to see every moment. Once finished, the militia, band, and choir performed once more before retiring. The city's newspaper concluded that few had ever witnessed "a more imposing spectacle than was presented on this occasion," as there was a "multitude of people, moving in harmony, in friendship, in dignity." They doubted a similar display could be found anywhere else in the American West. They were likely right. Especially after the tragedy of Missouri, the Mormons were exuberant to find themselves in such a situation.[3]

Present at the festivities was a newcomer to the Mormon scene, John C. Bennett. Though short in stature, he commanded attention. He was one of the prominent new converts, all of them men, whose arrival was heralded by Smith. It was, in part, due to Bennett's efforts that Nauvoo had recently received a generous charter from the state legislature, and Smith believed that he had found a colleague who could bring respect and prestige to the fledging faith. The prophet described Bennett as "a man of enterprise, extensive acquirements, and of independent mind, and is calculated to be a great blessing to our community." But the Mormons didn't know that Bennett also possessed a checkered history. Though only a resident of Nauvoo and convert to the faith since the previous autumn, Bennett had already been elected mayor of the city and major general of the militia. Two days after the cornerstone ceremony, at a general conference for the church, Bennett was appointed "assistant president." His meteoric rise only made sense within a community yearning for credibility. At least in early April 1841, it seemed a successful gamble.[4]

Not all who attended the festivities on April 6 were impressed. Thomas Sharp, a newspaper editor in the nearby town of Warsaw, was alarmed by what he saw. He was not the first to worry—there were distressed editorials as early as 1840—but he soon became the most vociferous in sounding the alarm about the Mormons. An armed militia led by an ecclesiastical figure seemed to obliterate the boundaries of church and state. "We believe [the Mormons] have the same rights as other religious bodies possess," he wrote, "but whenever they as a people, step beyond the proper sphere of a religious denomination, and become a political body," Americans must "take a stand against them." Mormons rebuffed the charge. After reading Sharp's remarks, Joseph Smith publicly cancelled his subscription to the Warsaw paper, denouncing it as a "tissue of lies." For the time being, the Mormons would shrug off the accusations, as a majority of outside responses seemed positive.[5]

But neither Sharp nor his criticisms went away. Just as the saints placed the stones for their impressive temple, they were also planting seeds for conflict. While only a few onlookers noticed at first, the Mormons in 1840 and 1841 were laying the foundations for a new community that would attempt to both correct and redeem American society.

JOSEPH SMITH WAS NOT THE FIRST PROPHET to envision a sacred city on North American land, of course. John Winthrop's famous "City on a Hill" sermon embodied the early Puritan quest to establish religious communities during the colonial era, and was followed by the Moravians, William Penn, and others. There was something about the American soil that seemed to invite spiritual settlements to take root. Even after the founding of the United States, citizens throughout the young nation retreated to religious outposts to take shelter from what they believed was a fallen world. Communitarian groups like the Shakers, followers of a British protest sect and led by a female prophet, organized closed societies designed to separate themselves from the ills of modernity. They were followed by other radical movements—both religious and secular—that hoped to establish utopias within the new nation. Nearly every "reading man," complained Ralph Waldo Emerson in 1840, had "a draft of a new community in his waistcoat pocket."[6]

Perhaps the contemporary community most like Smith's Zion was the Shawnee Prophet Tenskwatawa's holy city, Tippecanoe. A leader of the Native resistance movement in the first decade of the nineteenth century, Tenskwatawa established the community along Indiana's Wabash River. Known as Prophetstown to its white neighbors, the city was a refuge for thousands of indigenous people from many different tribes who together opposed further American colonization in the Northwest Territory. They were directed by the Great Spirit to settle there, explained the prophet's brother and famed fighter Tecumseh. Tenskwatawa dictated the religious and moral values for the pan-Indian city-state. The leadership also oversaw the building of the city's streets, buildings, commercial areas, and residential neighborhoods. Tenskwatawa preached a radical theological and political doctrine and denounced white American culture. And like Joseph Smith's Nauvoo, Prophetstown proved a nuisance and threat to neighboring governments, culminating in violent conflict. Tenskwatawa and Tecumseh lost their war with America, but their attempt left a legacy—both inspiration and cautionary tale—for other religious communities on the nation's cultural and geographic fringe.[7]

Smith first conceived of an urban Zion shortly after the church's founding. The idea appeared in his earliest scriptural texts. The Book of Mormon focused on establishing a righteous civilization, with pronouncements focused on a "people" rather than individuals. The virtuous would found cities, control government, and set the parameters for who belonged to the communities; the downfall of nations would follow from a society's inability to follow God's commandments. When Smith offered his revision of the Book of Genesis, he added entire chapters that detailed righteous Zions of old—civilizations that hewed to the dictates of a prophet and were collectively taken up to heaven.

These visions became tangible when Smith visited Independence, in Missouri's Jackson County, in 1831. Upon his arrival in the undeveloped region, Smith dictated a revelation declaring the location as the central point of the eventual City of Zion. Far from leaving this an abstract idea, Smith and his counselors drew up detailed plans for the city. These included lots for temples, a grid system for streets, and even the orientation of individual houses. Crude instructions surrounding the sketch took up nearly every inch of the paper, as if Smith and his scribe had tried to cram in as much information as possible. Very little escaped their attention. "When this square is thus laid off," Smith explained regarding one plat, "lay off another in the same way, and so fill up the world in these last days." While some of America's most animated preachers urged believers to flee the corruption of the city, the Mormons envisioned a righteous metropolis. Their city on a hill doubled as a city-state.[8]

The saints had reason for optimism during their first few years in Illinois, as they received quick and overwhelming support during that season's legislative session from influential state figures who were anxious to court Nauvoo's votes. Powerful politicians and lobbyists promised to pass legislation that explicitly benefited Nauvoo, and one of them, James Adams, even converted to the faith. Meanwhile, the Mormon community was growing rapidly. Three thousand converts had already immigrated to the city, and the Quorum of the Twelve Apostles were currently in Britain, seeking even more. They were not disappointed. "We have witnessed the flowing of the saints towards Zion," the apostles wrote in May, as "the stream has begun and we expect to see it continue running, till it shall have drained the salt or the light from Babylon." The United Kingdom was currently facing the backlash of an industrial revolution that left thousands in poverty, and many were willing to trust a new, foreign faith that promised salvation and a new start on the American frontier. Church leaders planned the first mass migrations to Nauvoo for that fall, with many expected to follow.

Smith, vindicated by this success, continued to urge that the world was ripe for destruction, and that the faithful must relocate to Nauvoo as soon as possible. Those who waited too long "shall scarce escape with their lives." As with Noah before, the earth was on the verge of an apocalyptic cleansing. This time, however, rather than huddling on a boat while the earth around them flooded, God's elect were to gather in a city as the world burned.[9]

Smith understood that he needed able men—he would never, at least at this point, have considered women for the role—to help him administer and defend his new Zion. Perhaps the most consequential convert to arrive in Nauvoo that summer came not from Britain, but from within Illinois. In late July 1840, Smith received a letter from John C. Bennett, who had just been appointed the quartermaster general for the Illinois state militia. Bennett—short, slender, with dark hair and intense eyes—boasted impeccable credentials: he had served as the brigadier general of the Invincible Dragoons, a respected division within the state militia, and he claimed to be an insider at the state capitol. He also expressed fondness for Smith's project. Bennett surprised Smith by announcing his intention to move to the town as soon as the following year. Yet if his first letter exhibited reserved admiration, he quickly revealed an odd obsession: he wrote three more letters over the next three weeks, each increasingly anxious. Eventually, in August, Bennett concluded he would travel immediately to Nauvoo and make a new home there. Smith welcomed the prospect and promised to embrace the apparently earnest seeker. Bennett reached Nauvoo in early September and was quickly baptized.[10]

Bennett, it would later be revealed, had spent most of the previous decade on the run. By his mid-thirties, he had already worked as a physician, minister, and university administrator, moving nearly a dozen

Engraving of John C. Bennett in uniform. Bennett experienced a meteoric rise within the Mormon community, particularly due to his military experience, as represented in this portrait. FOUND IN *THE HISTORY OF THE SAINTS: OR, AN EXPOSÉ OF JOE SMITH AND MORMONISM* (BOSTON: LELAND & WHITING, 1842), III.

times in about as many years. His fierce demeanor, sharp wit, oratorical skill, and immense charm won him confidence and support initially, but his schemes always fell apart within a couple years. He had been thrown out of a Masonic lodge in Ohio in 1834, around the same time he left his wife and children behind, as he hoped to start over again in Indiana. He then repeated the process once more, though this time without a family, in Illinois. The Mormons provided a new opportunity in his perpetual climb.

Unaware of this background, Smith anxiously welcomed Bennett into the flock. The prophet was often quick to trust people with education, training, and status, and so he put the fledgling statesman to work. Bennett spoke at the general conference that October on the political oppression the church had already faced, and pledged to help them avoid future problems. He certainly impressed his audience. Both Phebe Woodruff and Vilate Kimball praised his eloquence in letters to their apostle husbands, still away in England. The assembly collectively put their faith in the new convert by sustaining Smith's motion for Bennett to help draft Nauvoo's city charter.[11]

Smith and Bennett set to out to secure legal protection for the city. They used five other city charters passed in recent years as models, and much of Nauvoo's language was borrowed from these examples. (Indeed, the entire section on legislative powers was taken directly from Springfield's charter.) The combination and expansion of particular provisions found throughout the different cities proved to be a potent mix of ideas providing Nauvoo with substantial power, including its own militia. It was not so much Smith and Bennett's document itself, however, but rather the way the Mormons interpreted it, that would cause conflict. To casual readers, the charter mostly reflected boilerplate city governance; to Mormons, it granted them the political sovereignty they had long coveted. For once, it seemed they were allowed to govern themselves. As a demonstration of the immense significance they assigned to the charter, the saints referred to it as their "Magna Charta."[12]

Bennett received surprisingly little resistance when he brought the charter to the state capital in late November, as the Mormons were still riding the initial wave of generosity. The bill was presented in Springfield on November 27, passed by both the House and Senate on December 9, and was signed by the governor, Thomas Carlin, as well as the Supreme Court justices, on December 16. Spearheaded by Whig senator Sidney Little and the young Democratic senator Stephen A. Douglas, both parties granted substantial support to the charter. Bennett noted that Abraham Lincoln congratulated him once it was signed into law. Thomas Ford, who would become governor in two years, later recalled that Bennett had succeeded in flattering both sides. Each political party, in return, was eager to win the Mormon vote. Most of the state's politicians, including Ford, later came to regret these hasty actions. But in the meantime, the Mormons had benefited by correctly playing the state's political game. The charter went into effect in February.[13]

Nauvoo's residents held their first elections on Monday, February 3, 1841. As a sign of his growing status, Bennett ran unopposed for mayor. Those elected to citywide positions were mostly ecclesiastical leaders,

including all three members of the First Presidency. Of the four alder-
men and nine councilors, only two, Daniel H. Wells and John T. Bar-
nett, were not of the Mormon faith. (The two men represented the small
population of non-Mormon settlers in the area.) The City Council then
moved the next day to establish a city militia, which they christened
the Nauvoo Legion. The militia's officers included Joseph Smith as lieutenant general and Bennett as major general, and the council passed a
resolution that no adult male within the city was exempt from service.
The two institutions—the City Council and the militia—were intertwined. Nothing was more crucial to the regulation of laws and liberty,
Bennett declared in his inaugural address as mayor, than their battalion.
Nauvoo was now organized—and recognized—as a formidable force.[14]

Few aspects of Nauvoo's settlement were as divisive as the legion. To
Mormons, given their prior experiences, an armed force was necessary
for the protection of their lives and liberty. They were determined not to
face so helplessly the same attacks they had in Missouri, wrote one resident, John S. Fullmer. Eliza R. Snow, known as the faith's poet, called
the legion "a strong bulwark of Freedom." But to outside observers, the
militia was an ominous sign. Few cities possessed their own militias,
as most residents served in state or county legions. Though technically
part of the state militia—service in the Nauvoo Legion exempted men
from other armed-service duties in the state—the nearly all-Mormon
force appeared to be a private army in the hands of a religious leader.[15]

And an imposing army, at that, as it was estimated to number
around 1,500 men by the end of 1841. Bennett, as the state's quartermaster general, was able to amply supply the legion. One nearby journalist estimated that they possessed 5 six-pound cannons, 500 muskets,
460 pistols, 85 rifles, and 123 swords. Though perhaps overstated, this
rumor reflected a growing anxiety concerning Nauvoo's power, and
raised significant questions: To whom did Nauvoo's citizens cast their
primary allegiance—to their prophet, or the state? Would Mormonism's control be isolated to Nauvoo, or could it spread further? Illinois
residents held their breath as they waited for answers.[16]

WHILE NAUVOO'S ELITE WERE ATTEMPTING to create a new city during the transitional year of 1840, most of the residents were trying to avoid death. The malaria that afflicted the saints during the summer of 1839 had returned with a vengeance. Nearly every family was touched by what they called "swamp fever." Funerals were a weekly occurrence. Joseph Smith had previously reassured the saints that the sickness was not a sign of God's disapproval, but the toll grew to the point that the prophet wondered whether the saints had brought the misfortune on themselves. If the faithful could only cease expressing their discontent, he proclaimed at a meeting in July, good health would return. What was the use of building Zion if the faithful could not live to see it? In the end, even the Smith family could not escape the plague's wrath, as the prophet's beloved father, Joseph Smith Sr., succumbed a couple months later, a catastrophic blow to a family that had already lost so many. The malaria eventually abated as the saints drained the swampland, which decreased the number of disease-carrying mosquitos, but in the meantime they continued searching for meaning behind the tragedy.[17]

One of the most significant answers emerged during one of the many funerals that summer. The saints gathered on August 15 to mourn the loss of Seymour Brunson, but when Smith rose to speak he was prompted to address another Nauvoo resident. In the audience was Jane Neyman, who had recently lost her husband, William; her son, Cyrus, had already died several years earlier. Salvation for someone like Brunson, an adult convert who had been baptized in the faith, seemed assured—but what about those who did not have a chance to receive the prescribed ordinance of baptism, like Cyrus Neyman, who died before hearing the gospel? What was the fate of those who perished outside the faith? This was a poignant question that had plagued Christian theologians for centuries. It was also a pressing issue for younger denominations across America, as the sheer diversity of the religious scene seemed to bring much confusion but little assurance. Many worried that there might never be a satisfying answer.

But on that languid summer day, surrounded by hundreds of

mournful saints, the Mormon prophet offered a radical solution. Smith drew from a puzzling passage found in the Apostle Paul's letter to the Corinthians—"else what shall they do who are baptized for the dead? If the dead are not raised at all"—and proclaimed that believers could act as proxies for those who had come before. That is, saints could stand in for deceased loved ones by performing their ordinance vicariously. Surrounded by a community humbled by death, Smith proposed the idea that baptisms could transcend the grave. Those in attendance were ecstatic. "The day was joyful because of the light and glory that Joseph set forth," wrote Vilate Kimball. "I can truly say my soul was lifted up." Out of a city of sickness came an antidote for religious trauma.[18]

At first, there was limited counsel on how to perform the ordinance. The first recorded vicarious ritual, which saw Neyman baptized on behalf of her son in the Mississippi River on September 13, was haphazardly done. The man performing the ritual, Harvey Olmstead, made up the rite's wording on the spot; the woman serving as witness, Vienna Jaques, rode into the water on the back of a horse so that she could hear what Olmstead said. Many others followed suit. From that point on, according to Vilate Kimball, the waters were "continually troubled," as the saints were anxious to liberate their ancestors from spiritual bondage. But questions remained regarding proper procedure.

Speaking at that October's general conference, in front of the largest gathering of Mormons yet assembled, Smith added further guidelines, including that only those whom saints had personally known could be baptized. He also told them that those performing the baptism must first be visited by the deceased in angelic form. The ritual would change over the years, but it stood as a testament to the Mormons of God's grace and the significance of their living, modern prophet.[19]

Smith's teachings concerning vicarious baptisms quickly merged with another central topic of the October 1840 conference: the construction of a new temple. The saints had previously built a temple in Kirtland, Ohio, and planned two more in Missouri that were never completed. Constructing a temple in Nauvoo would signify that the city was a permanent settlement for the church. For its site, they chose a prominent spot located on a lofty bluff, which would give the temple a commanding view of the valley and river below. Smith announced his desire for the temple in spring or summer 1840, purchased the designated four acres of land that fall, and announced plans for its construction in October.[20]

Every Mormon in the city was expected to contribute. Leaders asked residents to offer a "tytheing" to God by donating one day in ten to the massive construction project. If the faithful supported him, Smith promised, they could build a temple grander than Solomon's. Like their previous temple in Kirtland, the building would serve as a meeting space for the saints to learn the gospel, prepare for missions, and be "endowed" with power through ritual washings and anointings. Smith further predicted that it would attract a stream of visitors who would be an economic boon for the community. Nauvoo would be a gathering place for both committed saints and curious tourists. The Mormons started quarrying rock and digging a foundation, with plans to lay the cornerstone the following spring.[21]

The plan for the temple soon changed, however. Smith announced in December that it was to be much larger and more intricate than the one in Ohio. Whereas the Kirtland Temple mostly reflected the style of New England meetinghouses, the exterior of the Nauvoo edifice would resemble gothic cathedrals in Europe more than evangelical chapels in America. And it would be much grander in size—when finished, it measured over 120 feet in length and 90 feet in width, featured three floors, and boasted a weathervane 165 feet tall.

The prophet further hinted that the building would be a site for new rituals. A proclamation in January 1841 explained that the temple would be home to new, and still developing, priesthood ceremonies. The ordinance of vicarious baptisms, for example, should only be performed in the temple. The saints were instructed to build a font within the structure's basement. But that was not the end of the temple's purposes. In a new and sweeping revelation, Joseph Smith dictated that God wished to reveal things in the new temple that had been kept hidden throughout the history of mankind, including further rituals, beyond vicarious baptisms, referred to as "the fulness [sic] of the Priesthood."[22]

The wording was significant. As Smith's plans for the temple crystalized, so too did his fascination with priesthood governance. Over the winter of 1840–41, as the saints worked fervently to secure their city charter, the prophet, through a series of increasingly radical sermons, retold the story of humanity's—and even the earth's—origins, centering the cosmos around a divine yet materialist structure. Prior to the creation of the earth, humans were floating "inferier intelligences" that required a path to corporeality and further development. God—himself a being with flesh and bones—created a new planet out of existing cosmic materials in order to provide spirits with a chance to receive bodies and lived experience. Human existence was predicated on priesthood authority, the commanding principle of God's kingdom. Every eternal thing came from God, while any principle not of divine origin—including other forms of authority—was of the devil. Priestly keys, Smith explained, had been passed through every generation of humanity, and had served as the channel through which every truth and practice is revealed.[23]

Priesthood governance, in short, was God's method of bringing order to civilization. Any and all authority, Smith declared, was based on this sacred genealogy. This was a sharp rebuke to America's secular system, which diffused power and embraced chaos. It also enhanced the authority of priesthood leaders like Smith. The only way to reassert control was to become heir to this priesthood lineage by following the prophet's direction. The world had lost its way and required a course correction. Joseph Smith was willing to provide one.[24]

When the saints gathered to lay the cornerstones of the temple on April 6, 1841, their actions reflected the divine order through which society should operate. Everything revolved around priesthood authority. Smith, representing the church's First Presidency, lowered the southeastern stone; the other stones were overseen by the High Priesthood (southwest), High Council (northwest), and bishops (northeast). The Mormons exulted in this restoration of celes-

"Elevation of the Temple: Now in Erection at Nauvoo." The Nauvoo Temple, originally imagined to replicate the smaller structure in Kirtland, Ohio, soon became much more grandiose in design and purpose. LDS CHURCH HISTORY LIBRARY, SALT LAKE CITY.

tial procedure. "Jesus is a God of order, regularity, and uniformity," Sidney Rigdon pronounced, and the cornerstone ceremony was an example of that design. Nothing escaped God's eye, for every action was directed by priests.[25]

More than just a major architectural achievement meant to draw outsiders to the city, the Nauvoo temple served as the central axis around which God's kingdom rotated. It overlooked the city below and provided purpose for all activities, both spiritual and earthly. Not only would the temple dominate the gaze of local citizens, but principles behind its creation prompted the city's actions.

WHEREAS THE TEMPLE'S CORNERSTONE CEREMONY was witnessed by thousands, an equally important ceremony took place that same week, only this one was under a strict order of secrecy. On April 5, the night before the laying of the cornerstones, Joseph Smith met with Louisa Beman and Joseph Noble in a small grove, shielded from prying eyes.

Noble was a longtime member of the church and close confidant of the prophet, and Beman, who had disguised herself as a man by wearing a coat and hat, was his sister-in-law. Emma Smith, unaware of the meeting, was not present. All three knew that what they were about to do was neither legally nor socially acceptable, yet each believed their actions were both justified and necessary.

Acting as officiator, Noble married Beman to Smith as a plural wife. In the evolving Mormon terminology, this was referred to as a "sealing," and Smith and Beman were now understood to be wed for all eternity. While the cornerstone dedication, taking place the next day, received extensive newspaper coverage, none of the three individuals involved in the polygamous ritual left a contemporary record of the occasion. Only Noble ever discussed it, and he did so nearly thirty years after the event. For a faith that placed such immense significance on written records, the lack of textual evidence underscored the ceremony's strangeness. Yet the ideas behind the temple's construction also justified the private union: God's plan was to restructure society around a new order, and priesthood authority would create new relationships according to eternal principles. Humanity's arrangements were giving way to those of God, as mediated through a prophet. The priestly "keys" that were a staple to Smith's temple teachings also unlocked a new heavenly system of domestic ties.[26]

Whether Smith's marriage to Beman originated the Mormon practice of polygamy, we cannot know. Rumors had followed the church ever since it was founded in 1830. But many new religious and social movements during the period experimented with radical sexual practices, so outsiders may have simply assumed the same about the Mormons. Some later claimed that Smith took a plural wife in Kirtland, Ohio, during the 1830s, though the reliable evidence is very thin. It seems more likely that the doctrine originated in Nauvoo in 1840, when Smith began envisioning a new society and revealed the centrality of priesthood keys, familial networks, and eternal unions. Joseph Noble and others recalled that it was during the fall of that year that Smith first taught them the practice.[27]

While the precise origins of the practice remain murky, what is clear is that the theology that Smith used to justify it evolved substantially in the years following 1840. Critics, both during Smith's life and afterward, argued that he merely invented religious justification for his personal proclivities, and his dedication to his polygamous project did indeed, at times, suggest that it was an obsession. Yet Smith was never intent on merely vindicating promiscuity. There would have been much easier ways to justify extramarital affairs, after all. His understanding of, and reasons for, such a radical marital experiment, however, was slowly pieced together as new individuals were added and new ideas were considered. The eventual product of Smith's theorizing on polygamy was not a superficial endorsement for extramarital sex, but a vision of a multilayered patriarchal hierarchy that governed the cosmos. As he did throughout his prophetic career, he constructed a new religious world that gave radical meaning to human activities. The number of participants in the practice grew substantially, even as it remained largely a secret: by 1844, Smith had wed over thirty women, and almost one hundred other men and women had entered the controversial order.

The reasons for a certain type of man to embrace the practice are clear, but why would a woman enter into a polygamous relationship? The nineteenth century witnessed expanding, though still limited, opportunities for women in America, and even if the fight for suffrage was still in its infancy, the widespread acceptance of companionate marriage models, in juxtaposition to explicitly patriarchal structures, promised to improve the lives of both wives and mothers. The separation of public and private duties may have kept women's voices—not to mention votes—out of the political realm, but according to the men who pushed for modest reforms like anti-temperance, it also theoretically increased their authority within the domestic sphere. Many religions empowered their women congregants, as seen in the female divinity found among the Moravians and Shakers, or even in the activism of Methodist women (of which Emma Smith remained an example even after her conversion to Mormonism). Further, communitarian experiments like the Shakers, with their emphasis on abstinence, and the Oneida community, with its introduction of shared marriages, recast the family in ways that struck at the heart of a traditional domestic home.[28]

Amid so much change, however, some desired a return to more traditional and patriarchal practices. In New York, the controversial prophet Robert Matthews, who christened himself as Matthias, established a religious commune based on female subjugation and male empowerment. Other, more mainstream advocates sought to curtail women's activism. While Americans had always worried over the sanctity of the home, the tumultuous nature of the new marketplace, which plunged many into poverty, and the separations caused by constant personal movement during westward expansion caused many to grow increasingly concerned with what they viewed as the degradation of the home. This was especially the case on the frontier, where traditional boundaries were continually challenged by new and rough realities. Joseph Smith's proposed system of sealing allegedly offered, through the authority of priestly networks, a safety net in a world of tumult. The most common refrain found in the writings of women who entered plural marriage in Nauvoo was the appeal of the security and permanence the ritual offered. They looked not so much for an intimate relationship as for the assurance of familial networks that transcended life and death.[29]

Smith was sealed to two more women before the end of 1841: Zina and Presendia Huntington, tall sisters with brown hair and soft features. The women had a lot in common with Louisa Beman: all three hailed from families with deep roots in the Mormon faith and close friendships with the prophet. Presendia even visited Smith when he was imprisoned in Missouri. They had each individually earned the prophet's trust. Further, all three women were known for profound spirituality, and Zina Huntington even claimed to sing in tongues and speak with angels. A spiritual union with the prophet—the physical nature of the relationship with Smith was never made clear—was therefore not a great leap for women deeply committed to the Mormon gospel and the revelations of their prophet.

Daguerreotype of Zina Huntington Young and Presendia Huntington Kimball, circa 1858. The Huntington sisters were two of the first women sealed to Joseph Smith as plural wives. PIONEER MEMORIAL MUSEUM, INTERNATIONAL SOCIETY OF DAUGHTERS OF UTAH PIONEERS, SALT LAKE CITY.

Some still recognized the costs, however. Zina later recounted that when she first heard about the "law of celestial marriag[e]," she immediately understood that it would be a great sacrifice because she knew that outsiders would never again view her as an "honerable woman." Polygamy would bring her closer to God, at least as defined by Smith, but also push her further from respectable society. Along with Beman, the Huntington sisters were venturing into uncharted territory with their beloved prophet.[30]

But they differed from Beman in that they already had husbands. In 1827 Presendia had married Norman Buell, with whom she had two surviving children, aged twelve and two. More recently, in March 1841,

Zina married Henry Jacobs, months after she was initially approached by Smith. Rather than embracing the polygamous proposal when first offered, Zina chose a union that was much more aligned with conventional expectations. Yet, upon further reflection, and perhaps further prodding, she changed her mind. She concluded that her faith in the prophet required following through on his proposal. After additional consideration that fall, Zina was sealed to Smith on October 27. She was already six months pregnant with her first child with Jacobs.[31]

Six weeks later, on December 11, Smith was then sealed to Presendia. Their brother, Dimick, performed both ceremonies. It was a family affair. Both women continued to act in public as wives to their first husbands, but their eternal lives were now secretly conjoined with the prophet's. The situation demanded confidentiality. "It was something too sacred to be talked about," Zina later confessed, and though the ceremony meant the world to her, she dared not breathe a word of it for years. Instead, she and her sister lived the new principle in sacred silence. The very secrecy of the rite suggested its transgressiveness.[32]

Their marriages, and Beman's, were only the beginning of Smith's new polygamous experiment, which would soon grow to such an extent that it cast a shadow over Nauvoo's daily life. For the time being, though, the circle of participants remained small, as Smith was the only man to take on plural wives. A few months later, in January 1842, he was sealed to his deceased brother's spouse, Agnes Moulton Coolbrith. This union, perhaps even more than the other plural marriages, followed a practice found in the Bible, or at least the Old Testament: the Law of Moses, as outlined in the Book of Deuteronomy, stated that on the occasion of a husband's death, it was acceptable for the brother to take the widow as his own wife. Smith may have felt that he was simultaneously expanding his priestly network while also performing his familial duty. Over the next two months, he was sealed to three more women, each of whom had husbands who were active members of the church: Mary Elizabeth Rollins, Patty Bartlett Sessions, and Marinda Nancy Johnson, the latter of whom was married to apostle Orson Hyde, then on a mission in Europe. That a majority of Smith's earliest plural wives were already married underscores the complexity of familial merging taking place in his new priesthood project.[33]

It is impossible to know how many of these marriages were consummated. Joseph Bates later claimed that Louisa Beman, who was not already married at the time of her sealing, spent the night of the ceremony with Smith in his own home, which was located across the Mississippi River and therefore away from prying eyes. The Huntington sisters, however, along with the other women who had husbands other than Smith, either denied or refused to confirm that they had been physically intimate with him. They understood the union to be spiritual in nature, a convergence of families throughout eternity, with limited direct implications for their current life. For the time being, how participants in Smith's polygamous system were supposed to think about their new relationships, and to conduct themselves, was far from clear.[34]

Though Smith never publicly confessed that the practice existed, polygamy became a constant feature of his life. Few major endeavors he undertook over the following years were unrelated to his clandestine domestic arrangements. As committed as he was to the ritual's significance, arguing that it was necessary to individual exaltation, he was similarly committed to its secrecy, knowing that its exposure would lead to Nauvoo's downfall. For some in the community, and perhaps especially the women who accepted and participated in it, polygamy became a way to grow closer with the prophet and their God. It also became a bond between Smith and the men he eventually introduced into the order.

But for others, polygamy would become a wedge creating distance between the ideal and reality of Mormonism's Nauvoo experiment. Over the next few years, a number of men and women would reject the doctrine and oppose Smith's new marital project. These conflicts rippled throughout the communities and extended beyond it, and eventually became serious enough that even Smith could not contain the fallout.

———

DELINEATING AUTHORITY—both spiritual and secular—in a religious city-state like Nauvoo was a complicated task. Who possessed the final say in a community that blended religious and civic leadership, and who defined the boundaries for community acceptance?

For Nauvoo's first eighteen months, until the City Council was officially formed in February 1841, an ecclesiastical body, the High Council, served as its government. Since its members did not have civic authority, however, their only mode of punishment was excommunication, and they used that threat for actions ranging from the operation of unauthorized ferries to the selling of unlicensed land. Even after the establishment of a civic government, the boundaries between church and state remained blurred. Ecclesiastical leaders filled a vast majority of the city's secular offices, and major decisions for the community were made and announced at church conferences. One resident detailed a plan for raising money for the temple's construction that demonstrated the overlap: all residents were expected to go before a city justice to swear that they had given an honest tithe, and then the justice produced a certificate confirming their offering to the "trustee in trust" of the church, Joseph Smith. This method ensured that every citizen contributed to the sacred cause, and it relied on the civic authorities to do so.[35]

Once the official city government was duly organized, Nauvoo's newly elected leaders went to work passing and implementing new laws. The new ordinances included regulations on the sale of whiskey as well as provisions for forcing stray dogs from the city. The City Council was mainly concerned, however, with establishing true freedom of conscience and religion. On the one hand, they believed Nauvoo could be an example for the rest of America of how liberal society could function—and an indictment of those who had previously failed to protect the Mormons. "Be it ordained," the council declared, "that the Catholics, Presbyterians, Methodists, Baptists, Latter-day Saints, Quakers, Episcopalians Universalists, Unitarians, Mohammedans, and all other religious sects and denominations whatever, shall have free toleration and equal Privileges in this City." All denominations were granted the privilege to hold public meetings, which the council, and many others within Nauvoo, believed were the key to preserving free speech. Yet there were limits imposed on these public meetings, as anybody found guilty of inciting a riot or mob would be swiftly punished. The city of saints was to be a paragon of both liberty and order—especially now that they, the constituted majority, wielded civic control. Even if the ordinances were primarily for show—there were no large groups within the city who were not Mormon—they represented the community's ideals.[36]

The Mormons of Nauvoo were also, at least to a degree, somewhat liberal on the question of racial integration. An editorial published by the church newspaper in October 1840 declared their desire to create a city that would welcome people from every nation, including the "degraded Hottentot." "Hottentots" was a reference to southwestern African tribes, and was invoked pejoratively to suggest the "uncivilized" nature of black people. Yet the Mormons, in the laws they passed in Nauvoo, welcomed such newcomers, at least rhetorically. The City Council's bill guaranteeing religious liberty explicitly included "Mohammedans," a nineteenth-century shorthand for African American Muslims. Perhaps this sympathy was based in a sense of perceived kinship. When describing their expulsion from Missouri, the apostle Parley Pratt wrote that Mormons had been deprived of the rights typically assured to white citizens, as if they were "some savage tribe, or some colored race of foreigners." The saints of Nauvoo were quick to present themselves as open to all of America's outcasts, as long as they were willing to participate in their city's redemptive project.[37]

At least one African American convert took advantage of this hospitality. Elijah Able, who had been with the church for a half dozen years, participated in both the civic and ecclesiastical life of the city. He was even allowed to purchase a plot of land in Nauvoo, a rare occurrence for free blacks in the state. Illinois was in the middle of enacting a gradual emancipation plan, and as a result of post-emancipation migration, there were few free blacks outside of urban centers like Chicago, Springfield, or across the river in St. Louis. Able was a rare sight, especially in his role as a member of the House Carpenters of the Town of Nauvoo. However, his other job, as the city's undertaker, a position that admittedly few others desired, reflected his minority status. Within the church, he was ordained a seventy (an office that was focused on missionary work), participated in baptisms for the dead, and served as a missionary in nearby states. Nor was he alone. The saints also received in 1840 a man from the nearby Oneida Nation, Lewis Dana, a skilled interpreter who converted to the Mormon faith and promised to spread it to surrounding tribes. Encouraged by this news, one apostle predicted that the day had come for mass indigenous conversions. The gospel net was to gather all kinds to Zion.[38]

Joseph Smith's views concerning race, especially in the institutional and legal realms, had been changing since the faith's founding. Mormonism's earliest scripture, including both the Book of Mormon and Smith's revelations, implied a remarkably universalistic approach to race, similar to the projects of earlier evangelical movements that pushed for abolition. "All are alike unto God," the Book of Mormon declared, "black and white, bond and free, male and female." But whereas most white evangelical denominations slowly moved away from their antislavery positions and embraced a more segregationist outlook, Mormonism seemed, at least for a time, to stick to its stated principles. The church's radical theology taught that racial distinctions could be erased and redeemed, and the Mormons did not establish distinct congregations for different races, as other religions did.[39]

Yet there were practical concerns, as well as ingrained cultural beliefs, that tempered the Mormons' theological openness. One of the church's earliest congregations in Ohio featured a charismatic black convert whose enthusiastic religiosity discomforted leaders to the extent that he was pushed away from the faith. In Missouri, the saints' slaveholding neighbors grew anxious of the church's perceived antislavery positions, which in turn caused Smith and other leaders to affirm their opposition to radical abolitionism. And while the first Mormon missionaries were dedicated to bringing the gospel to Native Americans—who they believed were heirs to God's continental kingdom—the failures of early missions and the outside suspicions of a Mormon-Indian alliance led them to pull back on these efforts. Despite their professed good intentions, Mormon views of blacks and Natives in reality remained close to those of other whites in the period.[40]

Further, the same scriptural texts that proclaimed the possibilities of racial inclusion also contained the seeds of a segregated society. When Smith prepared his own translation of Genesis in the early 1830s, he appropriated contemporary ideas concerning race into the text. Zion, Smith's revision insisted, would be filled with a combination of all of Adam's descendants, except the descendants of Cain. Cain's offspring, according to the text, were black, and therefore had no place among God's people. White Christians had long used the spiritual genealogy of Cain and, more commonly, Ham, as an excuse for slavery and racial exclusion, and now those concepts were written, by Smith, into Mormonism's scriptural canon. And while the saints in the 1830s and 1840s did not interpret these passages to mean a strict restriction on those of African descent, the groundwork was laid for such a practice. At the very least, Mormons were anxious to prove their status as white Christians and American citizens through their commitment to expected racial boundaries. By the time Nauvoo was founded, church leaders recognized these proper barriers: the city charter specifically limited citizenship to white men and outlawed interracial marriage. Mormon racial universalism could only go so far.[41]

The central question the new city government would face, though, concerned neither race nor religious freedom, but sexual scandal. Developments in the summer of 1841 had lasting significance for Nauvoo's future. Above all, John C. Bennett's meteoric rise to the top of the Mormon faith came to a halt. Smith learned earlier in the year that his new right-hand man might not be the boon for the church he had originally imagined. Early in 1841, Vilate Kimball claimed that some prominent individual in the city, likely Bennett, had tried to seduce a young woman. While Smith admitted that the accusation was troubling, he chose not to take action. He may have been worried that digging into it would expose his own polygamous activities. Further, Bennett had become too valuable to the city to justify disciplinary action. Smith still had grand designs for him, and in April, prompted by Sidney Rigdon's prolonged illness, he promoted Bennett to the position of assistant president of the church. But Smith's concern was such that he sent a trustworthy friend, George Miller, on a fact-finding mission to see if there was anything in Bennett's past that could cause problems for the church. Miller's early reports, as it turned out, were not promising.[42]

Though Smith was not willing, at first, to press matters with Bennett, the situation became increasingly fraught later that summer. Hyrum Smith, Joseph's brother, and William Law, a counselor in the First Presidency, were visiting Pittsburgh when they wrote a letter to the prophet concluding that the rumors—that Bennett was an adulterer, philanderer, and fraud—were true. That these rumors coincided with Joseph Smith's own polygamous project, of which the two investigators were unaware, heightened the moment's peril: while the prophet justified his own liaisons as salvific rituals, Bennett's, which had begun long before his conversion to the faith, could result in the exposure of Smith's new marriages to a critical audience. Smith decided to punish Bennett for his actions as a way to keep his own hidden. He knew this would require a tricky balance.

Much to Smith's relief, at least for the time being, the revelations about Bennett did not do much lasting damage. In an emotional and tense meeting, Smith and other church leaders confronted Bennett with the accusations, to which Bennett confessed, pleading for mercy. He was so distraught that soon afterward he attempted suicide through overdose, only to be rescued by Mormon physicians and nursed back to health. Smith accepted the mayor's promises for reform and continued to support him in his public functions, but greatly diminished Bennett's role in ecclesiastical matters. Satisfied, Hyrum Smith and William Law agreed not to make the episode public, though they grew increasingly skeptical of Bennett. The resolution also convinced them that Joseph Smith was on their side with regard to moral reform, which would leave them less willing to accept the rumors concerning the prophet that would begin circulating in earnest the next year.[43]

The confrontation with Bennett overlapped with the return of other close confidants of Smith's. In summer 1841, Brigham Young and a majority of the Quorum of the Twelve Apostles, who had spent over a year spreading the Mormon faith in Britain, arrived back in Nauvoo to great acclaim. They were astounded by how much had changed since their departure. Whereas Nauvoo only had a few dozen buildings in 1839, it now boasted over a thousand homes and a robust city charter. Smith was thrilled to have them back. The Twelve had demonstrated their leadership by bringing thousands of British converts to the city, swelling Nauvoo's population.[44]

Young's acumen as president of the Twelve was unmissable. Always confident of his abilities, Young was ready to take a larger role in the kingdom. At a special conference in August, just as he was distancing himself from Bennett, Smith elevated the Twelve to second in authority to the First Presidency. At the church's general conference that October,

Photograph of Brigham Young, circa 1850. Soon after Young returned to Nauvoo in 1841, he took a much more prominent position within the community. LDS CHURCH HISTORY LIBRARY, SALT LAKE CITY.

Young took a higher profile and gave several addresses, while Bennett, for the first time since his arrival to the city, did not speak in any formal fashion. Over the following months, the apostles took over the church's newspapers, land management, and even the church's historical records. They were now in control of much of Nauvoo's public activities.[45]

Having gained Smith's trust, the Twelve were granted access to his private projects as well. This included the new practice of polygamy. Shortly after their return from Britain, the prophet slowly presented them, often one by one, with the doctrine, with the promise that they, too, along with other leading men, would one day rule over their own polygamous families. Then, in December, a handful of the apostles spent the day with Smith as he introduced them to, according to Wilford Woodruff, "the privileges & blessings of the priesthood." Smith emphasized to them the importance of keeping the practice secret— "till Doomsday," he urged. It appears all of them agreed, as that small circle, including Young, Kimball, Taylor, and Woodruff, formed the core group of men who helped Smith manage the controversial practice. A few weeks later, Young served as officiator when Smith was sealed to Agnes Coolbrith. In his diary, Young noted that he "was taken in to the lodge J Smith was Agness." The account's awkward syntax was actually code: the second "was" served as an abbreviation for "wed and sealed." Young himself attempted his first polygamous proposal a couple months later, though without success.[46]

If Joseph Smith reacted to the Bennett episode by confidently moving forward with his domestic revolution, Hyrum Smith came away convinced that Nauvoo needed to reaffirm its morals. By the start of 1842, when the High Council transitioned to a more strictly ecclesiastical body, Hyrum saw it as an opportunity to buttress his personal mission. Tall, handsome, and firm in principles, the older Smith brother had recently been promoted to be an assistant president of the church, like Bennett, and had been ordained as the church's head patriarch, a position that meant he would provide blessings for all the faithful. Always known as someone who held firm to traditional moral values, he feared Nauvoo had lost its religious zeal due to sexual impropriety.

He told the High Council that it was time for a reformation, and that they must take action. He believed each member of the council must be a watchman on the wall, a reference to moral surveillance in Jerusalem as described in the Book of Isaiah. He wanted the council to go from house to house and make sure men were acting righteously. They were advised to make a list of those who failed to live up to the church's standards. Newly empowered, and now meeting in Hyrum Smith's office—where the patriarch kept an eye on their efforts—the High Council was ready to expand its power.[47]

Members of the council took Hyrum's counsel to heart. A month later, they penned a circular letter in which they embraced their new role as watchmen. While they were pleased with the city's prosperity, they explained, they denounced those who had slackened in their adherence to principle. There were residents, they feared, who were sowing strife and animosity, as well as spreading gossip. In an attempt to highlight their authority over that of civil courts, the High Council cautioned any saint who felt they had been wronged not to seek justice from among "the unbelievers," but rather from God's chosen vessels. In an age rampant with sin and corruption, the Mormon High Council was ready to bring judgment, even to those within Nauvoo's own kingdom. Tension between the actions of Joseph and Hyrum Smith— the former experimenting with new domestic arrangements, the latter attempting to shore up traditional values—would have widespread effects in Nauvoo over the next few years.[48]

AFTER BEING WARMLY WELCOMED by both Illinois's Whig and Democrat political parties, Joseph Smith and his city of saints had to quickly learn how to navigate party politics. If they took the wrong approach, they knew their choices could bring severe consequences. Smith justified his opposition to President Martin Van Buren, who had refused to offer the saints federal redress, for instance, in terms of personal prudence. When an elected official failed to look after the rights of one of his constituencies, he explained shortly after his trip to Washington in 1840, it was reasonable to vote them out of office. Deciding the city's political allegiance based on personal favors rather than abstract political principles seemed to be the best course.[49]

At least early on, the Mormons found that pooling their votes together would help them win friends and influence. Indeed, the Mormons learned they could exert the greatest impact in the political game if they remained willing to support any politician, regardless of party, who promised aid. They therefore agreed, as an entire community, to vote as a bloc for whoever would support them the most.

There were several politicians in Illinois anxious to take advantage of the Mormons' power. Few were as aggressive as Stephen A. Douglas. Born in 1813 in Brandon, Vermont—only forty miles from Joseph Smith's birthplace in Sharon—Douglas represented the growing number of ambitious young men who looked westward for new opportunities. Unlike Smith, who was driven primarily by religious ideals, Douglas thrived on pragmatic politicking. After migrating to Illinois in 1833, he immediately became a force within the Democratic Party. The frontier provided immense possibilities for inexperienced men who wished to skip the typical apprenticeship periods. Douglas's shortness, combined with his intensity, quickly earned him the nickname "Little Giant." He was elected to the Illinois House of Representatives in 1836, at the age of twenty-three, and became Illinois's secretary of state four years later. By the time their paths collided, both Smith and Douglas were trying to make their mark on the state.[50]

Douglas's desire for higher office meant that he was continually on the lookout for ways to broaden his support. By 1840, he understood how useful marginal groups like the Mormons could be. Along with other key Democrats, Douglas worked hard to keep Joseph Smith from falling into Whig hands, a genuine fear given Smith's antagonism toward Van Buren, and for the most part they were successful. By late 1840, there were whispers that the Democrats were influencing Mormon voting habits, including an accusation that hundreds of Mormons had, at the direction of Douglas, erased the name of Abraham Lincoln, Douglas's political rival, from the Whig electoral ticket.

Photograph of Stephen A. Douglas. Douglas was an aspiring politician within the
state who quickly befriended the Mormons in hope of gaining their support.
SPECIAL COLLECTIONS RESEARCH CENTER, UNIVERSITY OF CHICAGO.

Though merely a tenuous rumor, it was the first instance of Mormon
electoral activities arousing statewide suspicion.[51]

Douglas was one of the key proponents of Nauvoo's city charter in
December 1840, and he visited the city for the first time the following
May, just after being appointed to the state supreme court. Accompanied by Cyrus Walker, a prominent lawyer representing the Whig
Party, their trip to Nauvoo symbolized the state's continued bipartisan
support for the Mormons. Both were astonished by the city's development, and Douglas expressed his satisfaction that the saints were
a patriotic community. (He had yet to hear the rumors of polygamy.)
Douglas inspected the Nauvoo Legion and reassured the saints that
their militia was properly constituted within their chartered rights. He
even returned to Nauvoo as a dignified guest a year later to witness the
legion's annual parade and exulted at their impressive appearance. In

return for his support, Smith heaped praise on the ambitious politician. "Judge Douglass has ever proved himself friendly to this people," the prophet declared. Thanks in large part to Douglas, the Democrats were winning Nauvoo's sympathies.[52]

Smith's new political alliances soon proved their value when state authorities helped the prophet escape continued legal difficulties in Missouri. In September 1840, Lilburn Boggs, in one of his final acts as Missouri's governor, issued an order for Smith to be returned to Missouri to stand trial on grounds of treason. The charge was based on Smith's actions during the 1838 conflict. While Boggs was initially fine with the Mormons starting anew in another state, Smith's success in Illinois rankled the Missouri governor. Thomas Carlin, the governor of Illinois, acquiesced to Boggs's request, signing an extradition order and authorizing men to travel to Nauvoo and put Smith in custody. However, through an act of providence, as the *Times and Seasons* newspaper put it, Smith and his associates were not in Nauvoo at the time, and thus evaded arrest. The requisition drew bad press throughout the state, as many saw it as another example of Missouri's thirst for Mormon blood, as well as an encroachment on Illinois's sovereignty.

The ordeal reflected a deeper division. Though neighbors, Missouri and Illinois hardly got along, mostly due to several foundational disagreements. Two of the more prosperous western states, they represented divergent models of American settlement. Missouri, as a slave state, was held up as an example of how the "peculiar institution" could succeed in the new frontier territories. Illinois, conversely, hoped to demonstrate that America's capitalistic empire worked better when based on free labor. Illinois accused Missouri of giving the frontier a bad name by permitting extralegal justice and its poor decorum; Missouri accused Illinois of threatening social stability with their abolitionist rhetoric. Few issues created more controversy than the fugitive slave law, which required Illinois to return runaways who crossed the Mississippi. Boggs's demand that Illinois return Joseph Smith, then, fed into an existing framework of animosity.

Missouri officials were not willing to let the case rest. They took Illinois's refusal to turn over the prophet as a slight, and every day Smith was free as an affront to their authority. After further pressure, Illinois authorities reignited the extradition process in June 1841, and Smith was arrested while visiting friends outside of Nauvoo. Yet before he could be returned to Missouri, prominent lawyers in the state, including Cyrus Walker, Orville Browning, and Calvin A. Warren, successfully argued that the indictment was fraudulent and therefore invalid. The prophet obtained a writ of habeas corpus in nearby Quincy, and Douglas jumped at the opportunity to try the case and further ingratiate himself to the saints. In court, Douglas ruled the arrest warrant void due to a technicality—it was nullified when state authorities returned it to the governor after their failure to arrest Smith in Nauvoo the previous September—and Smith felt vindicated. Illinois appeared prepared to protect the saints from Missouri.[53]

The decision to shield Smith from Missouri was not made out of pure altruism. An upcoming election, in which a number of candidates hoped to earn Mormon votes, shaped how Illinois officials handled the case. Carlin, whose victory a few years earlier had depended on substantial support from new arrivals in Illinois, oversaw the passage of legislation that granted suffrage to adult men who had resided in the state for at least six months. The new voting laws meant that a large number of Nauvoo residents, including the thousands of converts who had arrived from Britain, would be eligible for the 1841 and 1842 elections, which would decide, among other things, three newly created congressional seats. Both parties knew they had to curry favor with the Mormons. For instance, Browning, who had helped Smith escape extradition and was now a candidate for the new Fifth Congressional District, visited Nauvoo and publicly praised the city, pledging his support for the beleaguered community in a passionate two-hour discourse. Illinois remained largely a toss-up state politically, and the Mormon voting bloc therefore seemed crucial.

Other Illinois residents were less sanguine about that reality. Non-Mormon neighbors quickly recognized the dangers involved in the political courtship taking place in Nauvoo. By June 1841 there was a call for a bipartisan convention in Hancock County specifically designed to organize resistance to Mormon control of county and state offices. When the attendees met on June 28, they voiced their desire to set aside previous political differences and oppose the Mormon power grab. As they saw it, Nauvoo posed a challenge that transcended traditional electoral divides.[54]

The next statewide election, to take place in August 1842, was the first big test. When gubernatorial contenders fought for support the preceding winter, Smith cast his lot with the Democratic candidate, Adam Snyder. It was a fateful decision. Smith explained in a public letter that, while he previously supported President William Henry Harrison, a Whig, that did not mean he was wedded to Harrison's party. Rather, Smith admitted he had recently been won over by Douglas, whom he called "a Master Spirit," and had concluded that Douglas's friends could also be counted as his friends. The Mormons agreed. As Smith put it, we "care not a fig for Whig or Democrat," but "we shall go for our *friends*, our TRIED FRIENDS, and to the cause of *human liberty*." To use the language of friendship was to draw from America's tradition of democratic reciprocity, a belief in citizens working together to find common solutions, and it cast their actions as safely within the boundaries of acceptable political practice.[55]

The Mormons' bloc voting, however, only confirmed the worst fears of those who were suspicious of them. The attempt to court public support to further private interests was far from new in American politics, but the flagrant nature of Mormonism's electoral coordination seemed beyond the pale. The nearby *Quincy Whig* denounced the Mormon activities as a "highhanded attempt to usurp power and to tyrannize over the minds of men." They described it as a "clannish principle of voting in a mass, at the dictation of one man," which was "repugnant to the principles of our Republican form of Government." The Mormons were seen as a menace to the nation's democratic process.[56]

For the Mormons, by contrast, bloc voting was necessary for survival. They viewed themselves as a religious minority whose rights were being trampled upon by a majoritarian culture that did not share their interests, and they refused to merely trust state authorities to intervene. The only way to protect themselves was to pool their resources and act as a unified body. John Taylor, an apostle and editor of the church's newspaper, explained that "it can serve no good purpose that half the citizens should disfranchise the other half, thus rendering Nauvoo powerless as far as politics is concerned." A divided vote within the faith resulted in fractured influence within the state. They were merely making the most of their situation. Why not dangle a thousand votes in exchange for securing long-desired protection?[57]

In 1842, even more so than the previous year, candidates for office eagerly took them up on the offer. John Harper, hoping to secure a congressional seat, wrote Smith to assure him that he had never affiliated with the anti-Mormon party. If the prophet promised him the entire Mormon vote, Harper assured Smith that he would always keep the faith's interests close to his heart. One day after writing that letter, however, Harper learned of a rumor—which was true—that he had attended the anti-Mormon convention the previous year, proving his first letter a lie. He therefore dashed off another note assuring Smith that he had, in fact, urged the attendees to take sympathy on the church, and to see that Nauvoo was a blessing for the state. Harper's reasoning was obviously desperate, but it reflected a broader desire for Nauvoo's potentially decisive votes.[58]

While the Whigs reached out in an attempt to win Mormon support for their gubernatorial candidate, Joseph Duncan, the saints held true to Smith's previously stated support for the Democrats. When Adam Snyder, whom Smith endorsed early in the process, suddenly died in May, he was replaced on the ticket by Thomas Ford, in part because he was not known for carrying anti-Mormon animus and could therefore count on the Mormon vote. One *Whig* editor denounced this as a "corrupt bargain," echoing the term for the backroom deal that had made John Quincy Adams president in 1824, through which the Democrats and Mormons "have formed a league to govern the State." It seemed like the fix was in.[59]

When election day arrived on August 1, 1842, the Mormons voted as promised. Voting in one Nauvoo precinct took place in the office of Hyrum Smith. This building's space, which was the site of both civic and ecclesiastical meetings, reflected the overlap in Nauvoo between the two realms. Eligible voters walked into the room, where they were likely confronted by their religious leaders, and then verbally declared their choices for the ten different county- and statewide races. Votes were tallied by a clerk in a ledger, counted, and reported to county authorities. Of the 457 people who marched into Hyrum's office that day, only eleven did not vote Democrat, a move that would have required openly rejecting their prophet's advice.[60]

The Mormon votes turned out to matter as much as politicians thought they would. Though there were only between 1,000 and 2,000 eligible Mormon voters in the state that saw nearly 87,000 votes cast that year, Illinois was almost perfectly divided between Democrats and Whigs, and most races, outside of the gubernatorial race, were decided by a few hundred votes. Every candidate supported by the saints, including Ford, won election. Watching from Washington, one national newspaper noted how the Mormons possessed sufficient electoral control to "make a profitable market" of their votes. Later that year, John J. Hardin, who was eyeing his own congressional run in 1843, admitted that all Illinois politicians were reliant upon Mormon support. Smith's calculation appeared to be working.[61]

The Mormons' bloc voting, while successful in the near term, would pose a greater and greater problem to others in Illinois. Thomas Ford later identified this form of bloc voting as the chief cause of animosity directed at Nauvoo. It was the Mormons' merging of religious and political unity, he explained, that invited the coming conflict. There was nothing new in the combining of religious belief with political action, of course, but what the Mormons did was to blend ecclesiastical authority and political mobilization. Even the Catholic communities were not as blatant in publicly dictating electoral preferences. What made Joseph Smith unique was his refusal to even act the part of republican persuasion. How could a democracy, which depended on citizens voting on the basis of their own free will, function when ecclesiastical leaders dictated their actions? For many Americans, the Mormons were leaving democracy behind in their quest to establish a theocracy.

Not that the Mormons would have fully disagreed. "All our wrongs," Smith declared a year later, "have arisen under the power and authority of democracy." Years of violence, political instability, and unreliable elected leaders had left the Mormons questioning the value of democratic governance. In a nation that prioritized majority rule, how were minority groups supposed to preserve their rights? Bloc voting was merely one possible solution, but it could not be the only one. To truly redeem America's experiment, the Mormons had to take even more drastic action. They would turn to God's law over the law of the land. The Mormon experimentation with political order was far from over. Indeed, with a rapidly developing city, a constant stream of new immigrants, a growing number of political friends, and an ambitious prophet, Nauvoo's innovations were only beginning.[62]

CHAPTER 3

Roots

The astonishing mixture of worldly prudence and religious
enthusiasm—of perfect system and wild imagination—of civilized
reason with ancient ideas—of religious observance and military
organization, is without a parallel in the history of nations since the
time of Mahomet. . . . Both combined religion, political, moral, and
social institutions in one mass of legislation and empire.

—JAMES GORDON BENNETT, JANUARY 15, 1842[1]

Joseph Smith's red-brick store, circa 1886. Four decades prior to this photograph
(attributed to B. H. Roberts), the second floor of this building housed Smith's private
office. LDS CHURCH HISTORY LIBRARY, SALT LAKE CITY.

When Alexis de Tocqueville traveled across the United States in the early 1830s, he noted how American democracy, especially in frontier regions like Illinois, had left the nation simultaneously both interdependent and unmoored. On the one hand, trade along the Mississippi River allowed white settlers to move farther and farther westward, yet still remain connected to America's economic system. The entirety of the North American continent seemed destined to coalesce within a national marketplace. Yet, at the same time, these new economic possibilities allowed individual citizens to break the cords that had previously bound them together. Whereas aristocracy, Tocqueville reasoned, linked all citizens together in a single, hierarchical chain of being, once that chain was broken, all that remained were isolated links. America, in short, welded people to capitalism, but not to each other. Many embraced this notion, with Ralph Waldo Emerson declaring it "the age of the first person singular." Modern America was to be built on individualism.[2]

Joseph Smith's vision for humanity, as implemented through a series of reforms in the first half of 1842, stood in stark contrast to Emerson's. Once Nauvoo had a powerful charter and began to thrive, the Mormon prophet introduced the principles of Mormonism's new order. It was time for God, according to Smith's journal, "to restore the ancient order of his Kingdom unto his servants & his people." This order included social, religious, and political implications—indeed, it was a totalizing vision meant to unify God's people into a new sort of community of a kind that the ancient prophets and patriarchs had envisioned but never built. The Mormons in Nauvoo were to establish "a kingdom of Priests & Kings" that could outlast the anarchic outside world.[3]

The engine room of this new society would be Joseph Smith's office, located on the second floor of a recently completed dry goods store. The red-brick structure, which had taken several months to build, was one of the first stately edifices in Nauvoo. The first floor was designed to be a much-needed commercial hub for the cash-strapped city, as it sought to integrate itself into regional and even national trading networks. The first order of goods arrived from New Orleans toward the end of December 1841, and the store was finally set to open the first week of January 1842.

The second floor was to serve a different purpose. A large room functioned as a meeting space for both sacred and secular gatherings, and a smaller room was Smith's private office, where he could perform his sacred work. From his window, Smith could see the Mississippi River below, and he expressed his pleasure at watching the boats pass at all hours of the day, a symbol of the region's close tether to the American economy. Yet, at the same time, Smith would try to inaugurate a different type of society that in many ways contradicted the very things the river's commerce represented.[4]

Over the first few months of 1842, from within his new office, Joseph Smith launched a series of theological, ritual, and familial innovations, and created new fraternal and sororal organizations. His work was based not only on existing scripture and past experience, but on a new scriptural translation project—the Book of Abraham—that dictated the order of heaven. The newly revealed principles found in this text were then disseminated through two institutions, Freemasonry and the Relief Society—for men and women, respectively—which promoted unity, encouraged morality, policed misconduct, and maintained confidentiality. Smith further incorporated these principles of belonging and brotherhood into a new ritualistic system that made tangible salvific promises. And finally, Smith built on this order to formalize the still-secret practice of polygamy.

Though Nauvoo was rapidly growing in size—one nearby newspaper estimated in early 1842 that there were already over three thousand inhabitants and several hundred large buildings—most of the new developments emanated from the red-brick store. Upstairs, Smith's office provided space for the Book of Abraham's completion, and the meeting room served the organizations that brought the new text's ideas to fruition. It was also in that room that a handful of women learned of, and entered into, plural marriage. And finally, the building was the clearinghouse for the city's swirling rumors concerning illicit relationships and disciplinary proceedings. Though the new structure's ground floor was little different from a merchant's office in any frontier town, events that transpired one floor above were anything but ordinary.[5]

IT WAS NO SMALL THING TO PRODUCE SCRIPTURE. Yet Joseph Smith turned out hundreds of pages of new sacred texts in the first decade of his prophetic career. Indeed, Mormonism was launched by the publication of the Book of Mormon in 1830, and within a few more years Smith had compiled nearly a hundred revelations that were then published in a separate volume. Followers believed these texts signified that God was once again dispensing sacred wisdom. Smith's last major scriptural project, however, was a revision of one of the Bible's foundational stories: that of Abraham, the Old Testament's pivotal patriarch and a model for Smith's own authoritative position.

The origins of this new narrative were striking. In 1835, when the saints were still based in Ohio, an antiques dealer named Michael Chandler arrived in their community, bearing several mummies and a handful of papyrus scrolls. Chandler was at the end of a long tour, during which he displayed and sold the artifacts in cities across the region, taking advantage of an antiquities craze that was sweeping across America as a result of stories of Napoleon's conquest of Egypt and Champollion's translation of the Rosetta Stone. But while the dealer worried that the relics were deteriorating and was therefore anxious to unload them, Smith saw in them divine worth. The papyrus, he proclaimed, contained the writings of Abraham, and his followers quickly embraced the idea. The church purchased the remaining four mummies and papyrus for $2,400, and Smith and his scribes went to

work producing what they called a new translation. Yet after producing only a few pages that narrated Abraham's earliest experiences, the
project languished for nearly seven years.[6]

Spurred by the opportunity to create a new society on the banks of
the Mississippi River, and taking advantage of his new private office,
Smith returned to his Abraham project in the early months of 1842.
New responsibilities weighed heavy on his mind. The growing city, full
of followers dedicated to his prophetic mission and organized around
priesthood leadership, required guidance. The patriarchs of old, like
Abraham and Moses, therefore provided an example for governance.

He also now had a vehicle for disseminating his revelations. Smith
took over the city's primary newspaper, the *Times and Seasons*, in early
1842, and he hoped to provide new and exciting material for it. Indeed,
the first issue under his editorial control ran the Abrahamic texts he
had dictated the previous decade. And now, from the privacy of his
new office, and with the assistance of his editorial scribes, Smith produced even more material for the Abraham project that, according to
one assistant, "reveal[ed] the mysteries of the kingdom of God." It was
a time-consuming endeavor. Smith informed his associates that the
process was taking up nearly all his energy. Between mid-February
and mid-March, he produced several pages that not only fleshed out
the ancient story of Abraham but also provided guidance for establishing the modern city of Joseph. Citizens of Nauvoo were thrilled to
receive the new counsel.[7]

The new scriptural text, which Smith dictated to his scribes, was
a bold recasting of the earth's creation. It revised the biblical account
of humanity's origins by introducing a "council" of "Gods" as the story's driving force. Even the creation was a result of priesthood leadership. The document also suggested that humans themselves were
divine: human "intelligences," or individual souls, existed prior to
the world's formation. Not only did their conception precede life on
earth, but they were eternally coexistent with God himself. This did
not mean all were equal, however. Nor was this divine order a form
of proto-democracy. The text described how God, surrounded by the

most noble spirits, "organized" the intelligences into societies that were structured around a particular authority. "These, I will make my rulers," God declares. Abraham, among others, was chosen to lead prior to his birth. Guided by these divinely appointed leaders, human spirits were sent to earth, which would serve as a temporary dwelling. The purpose of this probationary period was to determine whether they would obey divine commands. Those who passed a series of tests were promised eternal glory. Humanity, in this new origin story, is granted both divine provenance and a strict, hierarchical social order.[8]

The scripture instructed readers to liken human society to the cosmos. Just as the biblical account of Abraham promised progeny as numerous as the stars, individual souls were compared to the starry night. Abraham is shown the order of the heavens, including one particular star, Kolob, that was set to govern all those stars within its proximity. The universe flowed from this particular dispensation, he is told, each star taking its place within a hierarchical structure. Together they formed a grand chain of being. So, too, therefore, should humanity understand its role within the larger divine scheme. "These two facts do exist," God reasons: when "there are two spirits," one will always be "more intelligent than the other." God, the most intelligent of beings, stood at the top of the pyramid, with a cascade of lower intelligences below him. When properly organized, humanity formed a constellation of intelligences that matched a divine blueprint. As Smith declared a few weeks after this text's publication, humankind was saved through the accumulation of knowledge, and those who remained ignorant would be subservient to those who held more authority. Life depended on achieving not only intelligence, but power. This was a pre-Darwinian theology that in some ways prefigured the social Darwinism of the late nineteenth century.[9]

Where did Joseph Smith get his ideas? Many of those concerning eternity and physical matter reflected the influence of a popular theologian named Thomas Dick, and some of the more mystical elements echoed spiritualist figures like Emanuel Swedenborg. Smith's followers, of course, believed they came directly from the divine. Regardless of their origin, Smith's ideas were of their time. Many religions of the period labored to, in effect, answer new questions stemming from the Enlightenment. Recent scientific developments challenged traditional ideas regarding matter, spirit, and the age of the earth. How could the hand of providence be discerned in an age of scientific advance? And how could the monarchical teachings of the Bible square with a new democratic era? The Mormon response to the theological crisis was just one of many put forward in America at the time.[10]

Smith's Abrahamic epic went further than most creeds, however, in joining religion to politics. The language of astronomy, in fact, reflected this social setting. For many in the early modern period—that is, the three centuries immediately preceding the American Revolution—the heavens had represented God's order, and in the nineteenth century, that idea was under direct assault. Whereas monarchies were previously likened to galaxies, with a single star—or crown—serving as the center of cosmic order, the republican revolutions of the late eighteenth century realigned political discourse. For Americans, the heavens now represented populist egalitarianism. Rather than a central sun around which all planets rotated, political imagery increasingly emphasized the equal nature of self-governed stars held together by the republic's gravitational pull. The American flag, which featured stars of similar size and status, signified this new, democratic cosmic system.[11]

Joseph Smith's Book of Abraham was an attempt to return order to the cosmos. The heavens were not filled with autonomous bodies, but structured orbits dependent on divine control. Humanity was not composed of equals, but of people of varying degrees of intelligence and authority, and these qualities dictated how humans should relate to one another. In an American democracy that allowed citizens to determine their own path, Mormonism urged believers to fit within a set order, as defined by its prophet.

The Abraham doctrines provided rationale for further innovations in the Mormon city. Smith took the opportunity to introduce his developing world view in a Sunday oration given in the grove near the temple site on March 20, the day after the new Abrahamic verses were published.

His subject was the still-evolving doctrine of baptisms for the dead. As he had in describing his new Abrahamic doctrine, Smith used a natural metaphor to explain how God's kingdom operated. "God has made certain decreas [sic] which are fixed & unalterable," he explained, just as the sun, moon, and stars all moved according to a prescribed order. The world's synchronicity was rooted in a godly plan. For humankind to reach a similar point of harmony, it had to follow the script. God's house was a house of order, and the individualist strain of American culture threatened to jostle the divine society off kilter. If the saints wished to be sanctified and establish peace, they would have to comport themselves according to prophetic knowledge and priestly authority. Smith concluded the oration by going to the river and baptizing nearly a hundred saints who were anxious to live up to his teachings.[12]

But Smith's new Abrahamic principles explained much more than vicarious baptism. If society were organized like the stars in the sky, individuals had to know their particular place in human society. This included the recognition of priesthood authority in all matters. America was awash in confusion and anarchy, Smith argued in an editorial the following week, primarily because Americans had mistaken false prophets for true ones. How was one to tell truth from fiction? Only through priesthood authority, he assured his audience, as patriarchal leadership was the only thing that could assure individual liberation. God's true authority was the only remedy for modernity's ills. Anything less invited disorder.[13]

What was required was the fusion of ecclesiastical and civic authority. Because temporal and spiritual salvation were intertwined, argued an apostolic circular, then "if one fail[s], the other necessarily must be seriously affected, if not wholly destroyed." The public and private spheres had to be merged in order to preserve the sanctity of both. But how to codify this plan for the entire community? The answer was a series of organizations and rituals that involved both men and women and attempted to accomplish nothing less than restructuring both the city and the cosmos.[14]

ON MARCH 11, 1842, JUST AS THE WINTER FROST began to thaw, the Nauvoo Legion marched through town, from the unfinished temple on the bluff all the way to Smith's home near the waterfront. The temple, though not yet complete, was already a striking sight. "If ever completed," one visitor noted the next month, "it will be a magnificent structure." Smith, dressed in his brilliant blue military jacket and surrounded by his closest associates, led the parade. Few things gave him as much satisfaction as witnessing the city marshaled into order, with him at the helm. The next day, the City Council passed an ordinance reaffirming that every adult male was required to enroll in the legion. Those who did not enlist were subject to a court-martial, and those who failed to participate in these public parades were fined. The city's militia was meant to unite all men within Nauvoo. Cohesion was crucial to the Mormon kingdom. They were not merely marching down Nauvoo's muddy streets in makeshift uniforms, they were demonstrating the order and precision of God's kingdom.[15]

Smith was already looking for other ways to bind Nauvoo's citizens to his new vision. The very next week, on March 15, he called for another public procession, this time featuring those involved in the new Masonic lodge. The parade's path inverted that of the legion, as it started near Smith's home and finished at the temple. Like the earlier parade, it drew several thousand onlookers. The establishment of Masonry in Nauvoo was the result of a long process. Though Hyrum Smith, Joseph's beloved brother, had been a Mason back when they lived in New York, the prophet had never been inducted into the order. He had even spoken out against "secret combinations" and the "impropriety of the organization of bands or companies by covenant or oaths" during the Missouri crisis. Some argued the Book of Mormon contained anti-masonic sentiments.[16]

But once in Illinois, Smith saw a chance to use Masonry to forge important new connections for Nauvoo. Several prominent Masons, including James Adams and John C. Bennett, had helped pass the city's charter. Smith recognized that their ties to other Masons in Illinois could provide much-needed statewide networks. He was not alone. After a decade of backlash against Masonry throughout much of America, the fraternal order resurfaced in the 1840s. Over the next five decades, Masonic membership in the nation increased from a few thousand to nearly six million. The destabilizing nature of democratic culture led many to seek out civic organizations. Freemasonry was especially popular in frontier states, where people were liable to feel particularly unmoored.[17]

In turn, Illinois Masons, like the state's Democratic politicians, were keen to court the Mormons. For Abraham Jonas, the grand master of Illinois's Grand Lodge, supporting a Nauvoo lodge was a political calculation: he was planning a run for the state legislature and, like Stephen Douglas, wanted Mormon votes. Goaded by men like Adams and Bennett, Jonas granted the city a temporary lodge in October 1841, and then oversaw the formal establishment of a Masonic lodge five months later. After the opening ceremony, Jonas conferred three degrees, or ceremonial badges of authority, on each of Smith and Sidney Rigdon. The Mormon leaders received the first degree on the spot, and the next two the following day, a process that was expedited and unusual but within the order's guidelines. Both sides wanted to quickly cement their fraternal bond.[18]

Masonry proved enticing to the Mormon prophet for reasons beyond politics. The myths associated with the order held significance for the saints, as the lodge's minutes described the rituals as moving "according to ancient usage." Smith had just completed his Book of Abraham project days before the opening ceremony, and he was particularly interested in the idea that the rites of Freemasonry were rooted in ancient Egypt. Indeed, as part of his Abraham project, Smith produced translations and explanations of an Egyptian hieroglyph that seemed to represent practices associated with Masonry. One image, "A Fac-Simile from the Book of Abraham, No. 2," depicted ancient figures performing rites that signified "the grand Key words of the Holy Priesthood" passed down from the Garden of Eden all the way to Abraham. These words now found a physical echo in Nauvoo's new

lodge, where degrees were conferred through the bestowal of particular phrases, signs, and tokens.

Masonic rituals reinforced the message of the Abrahamic text and
facsimiles, namely that society was based around trust, knowledge,
kinship, and hierarchy. To Smith, they also reaffirmed his ecclesiastical authority. At a gathering on March 20, mere days after the lodge's
installation, he once again discoursed on the importance of key words,
signs, and tokens that related to the priesthood. Everything interwove
within the Mormon kingdom.[19]

Smith was not intent on merely experiencing these Masonic rituals
within a secular space. Within a few weeks, he began to recast them as
priesthood ceremonies. On May 1, he declared to the saints that there
were certain key words and signs necessary to govern the cosmos, but
that they could not be revealed until the temple was completed. Divine
knowledge was not enough—the Mormon salvation could only be
achieved through physical experience. "No one can truly say he knows
God until he has handled something," Smith reasoned, "& this can
only be done in the holiest of Holies." There was to be a new initiation
for God's priestly rulers. The Mormon temple, whose still unfinished
structure cast a shadow over Smith as he preached that spring Sunday,
would serve as the hinge of eternal governance. In Kirtland, the temple provided space for elders to prepare for their missions; in Nauvoo,
it was the space for priestly rulers to be ordained.[20]

Many religious seekers of the time fled cities in search of God in
the wilderness, and they avoided formalized worship, which they saw
as inherently Catholic. True religion, many believed, involved an individual relationship between the believer and God. Salvation was a
personal experience. To Joseph Smith, however, such an outlook only
introduced disorder. As a youth, he struggled to know whether he was
saved or not, and he expressed pain that he could not "feel" the same
conversion others had apparently felt. His message as a prophet, and
one of the reasons he drew thousands to him, was a promise of assurance. The rituals performed in Nauvoo's temple would silence, once

and for all, questions of one's spiritual standing. Salvation was made tangible. In the Mormon kingdom, the highest blessings could only be found within the walls of this consecrated building. The grand stone structure that impressed countless travelers on the Mississippi River was a beacon of God's restored authority.[21]

Instead of waiting for the temple's completion, which was still several years away, Smith chose to introduce the new initiation rituals to a small circle of advisors later that week. The rushed nature of their initiation reflected Smith's earnestness to introduce the rites to others. He recruited a number of men who had been involved with constructing the Masonic lodge, including Master Mason Lucius Scovil, to prepare the upstairs of his red-brick store in a way that would blend fraternal and sacred purposes. Just as Moses saw the face of God in a bush, Smith's followers would experience the rites of God in a prosaic setting—a merchant's store.

Smith gathered both apostles and other Mormon leaders on May 4, 1842, to inaugurate a temple ordinance they soon called an "endowment." He instructed them in what he described as "the principles and order of the priesthood," which included washings, anointings, and a ceremony in which participants received the much-discussed key words and signs. According to Smith, these keys were necessary to restore the ancient order of biblical patriarchs, and to enable saints to secure the exalted blessings of God's promised children. The endowment ritual included a processional through five distinct and symbolic phases: the world's creation, the Garden of Eden, Adam and Eve's entrance into a fallen world, contemporary society, and finally, an entrance, through a veil, into the celestial sphere. To set the mood for the last, Scovil had relied on the inventive use of curtains. The expectation was that things would be more formal once the temple was completed, when all worthy members of the faith would be able to participate. Smith spent most of the day teaching and performing these rituals, which were then repeated the next day as the initiates conducted the blessings on Smith himself.[22]

Many of the keys, signs, and tokens that these men had learned of only two months prior in Nauvoo's Masonic lodge were now transformed into elements of God's priesthood and divine order. In essence, Smith had imposed a sacred liturgy on a fraternal rite. Modern-day Masonry, the participants believed, had originated in antiquity with patriarchs like Abraham—"Masonry has its origin in the Priesthood," explained Smith's secretary, Willard Richards—but had been stripped of its true meaning in the same way that contemporary Christianity had lost its eternal truths. Any similarities between the rituals, then, were easily explained. Through the endowment, Smith was restoring the true basis for fraternal order, which would in turn reorient society around priesthood authority.[23]

But the endowment was not meant to immediately eclipse Masonry. In Smith's vision, the two worked in tandem. Smith could not extend the sacred ritual to all his followers before the temple was completed, but he could prepare them to make similar oaths through the lodge's rites. As one Nauvoo resident, Oliver Olney, put it, large numbers of saints became Freemasons because they were promised to eventually receive "Masonry in its best state"—in other words, "The fullness of the Priesthood." All Mormon men, in the end, could become priests in the kingdom, all spread along a hierarchical dynasty. Another participant, Joseph Fielding, explained that many joined Masonry because it served as "a Stepping Stone" for later rituals. As a demonstration of Smith's charismatic charm and energizing message, the number of Nauvoo Masons swelled. Within seven months, there were more Mormon Masons in Nauvoo (253) than non-Mormon Masons in the rest of the state (227). Soon, the state's Masonic leaders grew concerned, as they feared such swift growth reflected a lack of control.[24]

Two days after the original endowments in early May, Smith led the biggest military march yet in the city. The Nauvoo Legion had grown from six companies, each comprising forty-six men, to twenty-six, and a crowd of around two thousand gathered on this Saturday morning to witness the spectacle. The troops were led by Smith, in his striking military regalia, who rode at front with his wife, Emma. Regional politicians, including Stephen A. Douglas, were in attendance, and they all went to the prophet's home that afternoon for a grand feast. Smith announced that he had never been more satisfied than on that day. Others noticed his jubilation. "Brother Joseph feels as well as I Ever see him," wrote Heber C. Kimball to Parley Pratt. This was due in part, Kimball concluded, to Smith having organized a small group of confidants in whose hands he felt safe. Smith's new order was starting to take root.[25]

Whereas Smith found comfort in the occasion, however, others were alarmed. One anonymous, non-Mormon artillery officer who happened to witness the parade came away concerned. The Mormon military force, he wrote, put on a noble and imposing show, which made it all the more striking that it was led by a religious zealot. While theoretically part of the state militia, the legion was far more organized, enthusiastic, and warlike than any other military force in Illinois. What would happen if its lieutenant declared a holy war? Mormon Nauvoo, nestled in a scenic peninsula at the turn of the Mississippi River, represented a clear danger. Its residents were "accumulating like a snowball rolling down an inclined plane, which in the end becomes an avalanche." All it would take was a single rumble. "The Mormons, it is true, are now peaceable, but the lion is asleep." The lesson was clear: "Take care, and don't rouse him."[26]

THOUGH THE ABRAHAMIC TRADITION EMPHASIZED patriarchal authority, Joseph Smith's vision involved empowering both genders. Two days after Nauvoo's Masonic lodge was established, and in the same room where Smith had participated in the Masonic rites and would soon introduce the endowment, another group of Mormons founded the Female Relief Society of Nauvoo.

The organization was established as a way for women to contribute to the temple's construction. Sarah Granger Kimball, a wealthy young convert from New York, noted that several women in Nauvoo were interested in forming a women's society to more easily supply the men working on the temple with the necessary raw material. They were following a national trend. Women's societies, founded throughout the country, enabled women to both participate in as well as shape the era's reform movements. The women in Nauvoo turned to Eliza R. Snow to draft a list of principles and laws for their own organization, a list they then presented to Joseph Smith. Smith commended them for their efforts, but insisted he had something better in mind. "I will organize the women under the priesthood after the pattern of the priesthood," he said. The Mormon female society was to be part of the Abrahamic order. Beyond providing materials for men working on the temple, the women were to form a governing and policing society that could root out iniquity, build solidarity, and prepare the women for a future endowment. The organization would be a crucial institution in the Mormon quest to redeem society.[27]

The result of these discussions was a new institution that reshaped the city's balance of power. When a group of leading Nauvoo women gathered on March 17 in the upstairs room of Joseph Smith's red-brick store, referred to in the minutes as the "Lodge Room," they were met by Smith, John Taylor, and Willard Richards, who represented the governing priesthood authority. Yet the women controlled the meeting almost from the very start. Joseph Smith selected his wife, Emma, as the organization's first president, urged her to name two counselors, and told them that they presided with as much authority over women as the First Presidency did over the church. In a community where meetings and minutes were almost sacred, their decisions as a quorum would serve as a constitution, and all their decisions were to be considered law.

Their first act concerned the new society's name. Both Joseph Smith and Taylor opposed the word *relief* in the society's title, preferring *benevolent* because it was, according to Joseph, a more common term, and *relief* might give off the wrong connotation. Yet the women stood firm. Emma responded that it was precisely because *benevolent* was popular that they wanted to avoid it. They did not want to be confused with the corrupt institutions found everywhere else in America. Indeed, Emma insisted that they not be associated with other societies. Eliza R. Snow, who was chosen to be the secretary, concurred and urged them to pave their own path. Joseph eventually conceded and approved the Relief Society's name. In this instance, it was the prophet who had to be convinced to set himself in opposition to national trends.[28]

Still, the new society both reflected and rejected those broader developments. The antebellum period was rife with women's organizations that attempted to reform America's culture and restore the nation's dignity, which they feared had been lost amid a turn to individualism and worldly desires. The industrial revolution and westward expansion had opened up new opportunities for many more people to become wealthy and to leave traditional mores behind. But what would keep society tethered to godly principles? Women, seeking avenues for social influence, were anxious to take on that responsibility. As politicians in the early days of the republic increasingly removed the government from reform efforts, and politics remained a purely male arena, women were increasingly seen as guardians of virtue and protectors of the hearth.

In the cult of domesticity that dominated much of the nineteenth century, women were seen as the conscience of the nation. Most of the female-led societies that appeared, many of them focused on reforming asylums or curtailing alcoholism, were rooted in religion. In an era when the government made clear that policing the nation's morality was beyond its power and prerogatives, religious women served as saviors for a fallen society. Famously, Lucretia Mott, a devout Quaker, led the fight against slavery and in favor of women's suffrage. Mott was also part of a group of women reformers who met in Seneca Falls, New York, in 1848 to demonstrate their organized efforts. So even if Emma Smith believed that the Washington Benevolent Society, another women's reform effort at the time, was corrupt, her organization was originated in similar impulses and sought analogous ends.[29]

The Relief Society introduced an opportunity for Nauvoo's women to get involved in the city's reformation project. But whereas the women who founded it originally envisioned a straightforward charitable organization, it quickly became something more. Like the Puritans before them, the Mormons feared their community was relaxing on

"Leading Women of Zion," photograph of Zina Diantha Huntington Young, Bath-sheba W. Smith, Emily Partridge Young, and Eliza R. Snow. While this photograph was taken decades later, these four women played a major role in the Female Relief Society of Nauvoo. Huntington, Partridge, and Snow were also sealed to Joseph Smith as secret plural wives, and after Smith's death they were all sealed to Brigham Young. LDS CHURCH HISTORY LIBRARY, SALT LAKE CITY.

morals and forgetting their standards, and the women's society offered a means and a license to oversee their society. They were tasked with provoking the men of Nauvoo to act more righteously, but also with improving society by denouncing sin, regulating virtue, and punishing transgressors. Given that the state had no power to punish many sins, it was left to voluntary organizations like the Relief Society to provide moral stability and structure. Emma hoped that the members of their organization could stand pure before God, enabling them to expose the iniquity around them. It was their right—even their obligation—to maintain virtue in their City of God.[30]

Joseph Smith also had an ulterior motive for supporting the organization: he hoped it would defend his reputation as polygamy rumors began to spread—in part, by controlling the spread of gossip, as illustrated by an episode surrounding a young girl named Clarissa Marvel. At the Relief Society's second meeting, on March 24, Emma Smith accused Marvel, who had recently immigrated to Nauvoo alone, of spreading rumors about Joseph and Agnes Smith, the widow of the prophet's deceased brother Don Carlos Smith. Agnes had secretly become a plural wife to Joseph a few months before, and word was seeping out. The society appointed two women to personally interview Marvel. One, Elizabeth Durfee, objected to interrogating the girl, which she thought to be a harsh measure. Emma, however, was quick to reprove Durfee, reminding her that it was the society's obligation to root out iniquity. The investigation concluded two weeks later, when it was determined that Marvel was innocent. But while the case seemed settled, the society's leaders claimed that the ordeal was a warning to others who might spread gossip about the prophet.[31]

The society reflected Joseph Smith's developing religious vision, particularly concerning priesthood authority. He instructed the members to act according to "the ancient Priesthood," and informed them that they would be transformed into a "kingdom of priests," just like the biblical patriarchs. A month later, he again insisted that it was their privilege to receive all the blessings of the priesthood, a promise that had previously been reserved for men. The priesthood, it seemed, now transcended traditional gender barriers. Those in attendance took the prophet's words seriously. Decades later, Eliza R. Snow explained that the Relief Society could not exist without the priesthood, as it was the source of the organization's power.[32]

The term *priesthood*, then, possessed multiple, potent meanings to the early Mormons, reflecting their evolving sense of their social order. During the movement's first decade, the term mostly referred to ecclesiastical offices (separated into classes including deacons, priests, and elders) as well as ritual administration (including the right to perform baptisms). But in Nauvoo, the priesthood was radically transformed into an all-encompassing notion of how the faithful should relate to one another. In short, the priesthood not only oversaw the saints' community, but the operation of the world.[33]

This new understanding of priesthood authority held deep appeal for women who wished to play a role in the saints' relationship to their community. It provided them a place in the Mormon kingdom's reformation project. Women now had the authority to cleanse American society of sin and denounce the evils of the world. To be a "kingdom of priests," as Smith promised, meant establishing a refuge where God's laws could be kept alive even while Babylon burned. In this expansive definition of priesthood, all Mormons were potentially priests, and women priests possessed the distinct duty of helping return humanity to its divine stations. Rather than being passive recipients of male leadership, they were expected to help guide the church to new heights.[34]

Because Joseph Smith would often only reveal his vision of the new priesthood to a select few, and often in fragmented form, there were misunderstandings about the Relief Society's purpose and authority from the very beginning. While Joseph wished to empower Nauvoo's women to perform moral surveillance in the city, he also saw the organization as a testing ground for the temple rites that would eventually be extended to all worthy church members, male and female. The Relief Society served the same function that masonry served for men: a chance to see who could be trusted to keep signs, tokens, and teachings secret. Joseph therefore urged his wife, Emma, not to admit too many women into the order, as it could quickly become hard to manage. He hoped he could grant the society just enough autonomy while still retaining, through Emma, control. Meeting in his own store, within sight of his own office, Joseph needed the society to buttress his own agenda.[35]

The women involved, however, had their own plans. They were eager to assert their own leadership, especially once granted the priesthood keys, which they interpreted as the right to religious authority, from their prophet. Emma, confident and forthright, did not see the need for her husband's precaution. She insisted that there was no reason to maintain privacy, as transparency was central to their mission.

The only issues that deserved confidentiality were the private difficulties of individual members. She also did not believe in slowing the admission of new members: twenty women attended the first meeting, but the membership ballooned to 1,336 within two years, a majority of the city's women population, which required moving the gatherings outdoors. (Joseph did, eventually, support the society's expansion.)

But the biggest point of disagreement concerned the scope of the society's moral surveillance efforts. The prophet frequently cautioned them to be gentle when it came to identifying a member's sins; he mostly wanted the society to defend *his* character, but soon feared it might discover his own clandestine polygamous actions. However, Emma often retorted, sometimes with her husband present, that no sinner should be spared. At this point, though still unaware of the scope of Smith's secret activities, she was starting to hear more rumors. The contrast between the two Smith leaders only became more precarious in coming months.[36]

Joseph Smith must have known that empowering Nauvoo's women was a double-edged endeavor. On the one hand, his vision for social reformation required the participation of all who lived within the city; on the other, enabling them to organize and mobilize put himself and his still-developing practice of polygamy in danger. His commitment to expanding his Abrahamic project while insisting on secrecy and control put him at odds with himself. But rather than trying to reconcile the paradox, Smith was determined to continue moving forward with his radical mission.

THE ABRAHAMIC PROJECT THAT SMITH REFINED in the early months of 1842 resulted in the welcoming of Masonry to Nauvoo and the establishment of the Relief Society, but it also had profound implications for Mormon polygamy. Though it had been a year since Joseph Smith was married to Louisa Beman, and though he had added seven additional plural wives between spring 1841 and spring 1842, these unions were of a particular type, for the most part. Six of the women who were likely sealed to him—Lucinda Pendleton, Zina Huntington

Jacobs, Presendia Huntington Buell, Mary Rollins, Patty Bartlett, and Marinda Johnson—were already married. Another polygamous wife, Agnes Coolbrith, was widowed. Only Beman had never married before her union with Smith. The nature of the former marriages is hard to decipher, given the existence of these women's husbands, especially since a few of the men were faithful members of the church. There is only evidence that one of these unions, Beman, involved sex. For those who were not married to a committed Mormon, these marriages brought certainty to their place in the afterlife, as a sealing was necessary for divine advancement. But what of those who were already married to a member of the faith?[37]

Regardless, the nature and purpose of Smith's plural unions shifted in 1842. All four women sealed to the prophet in the first few months of that year, and nearly all sealed to him the year after, were young and single and fit the profile of child-rearing wives. Whereas Smith's earliest polygamous unions seemed focused on building familial ties and hereditary linkages, these new unions implied something else. As part of his Abrahamic project, Smith fashioned himself into an Abrahamic patriarch.

In expanding his family, Smith continued his cautious approach by proposing only to women whose families had deep connections to the church. But not everyone was as quick to accept the offer. Indeed, two of the women Smith approached shortly after publishing the Book of Abraham turned him down. Sarah Granger Kimball, who around the same time had come up with the original idea for a female benevolent society, rebuffed the prophet's request that she become his plural wife. Like most of the women previously sealed to him, she was already married, but her husband was not a member of the faith. According to Mormon belief, she would be considered single in the afterlife. She was also young, still in her early twenties. Smith likely assumed, given her ambiguous eternal status, that she would be open to the new doctrine.

It is difficult to know exactly how the proposal took place, given the lack of contemporary sources. However, in accounts left by other participants in plural marriage, it is possible to see a pattern in Smith's courtships. Kimball was probably approached by women who were already sealed to Smith, who informed her of the practice in a private setting. A group approach emphasized the communal nature of the practice and established a buffer between Smith and the woman he wanted as a wife. Indeed, the designated messengers were prepared to respond to the new woman's surprise. These initial meetings were often themselves the beginning of long-term commitments. Those who were sealed to Smith formed close companionships to each other that lasted years—indeed, their emotional bond to each other was in many ways stronger than their personal tie to Smith.

Sarah Kimball, however, was not interested in entering into such a union. "Teach it to some one else," she allegedly responded. Kimball had only been married to her gentile husband for two years, and still held hope that he would join the church. She was also close friends with Emma Smith, with whom she worked closely in the Relief Society, and Kimball might have worried about betraying her trust. Her rejection was measured, however, as she refrained from publicly speaking about the episode. Yet Kimball must have represented a transition point in Smith's thinking on polygamy, as she was one of the final married women to whom the prophet proposed.[38]

Kimball was not the only woman to reject Smith, and some of the others were not willing, like she was, to keep quiet about his overture. Whereas Kimball retained faith in the prophet, another young woman whom Smith approached, Nancy Rigdon, took greater offense. Her rejection must have stung. The daughter of Sidney Rigdon, a prominent member of the church's First Presidency and Smith's longest-serving counselor, Nancy came from a family that Smith believed he could trust. Further, given her status as a single woman, his proposal would not subvert an existing marriage. And yet, the proposal did not go as planned. The topic was first broached with Rigdon in a secluded space by a woman already sealed to the prophet, Marinda Hyde. To Hyde's shock, Rigdon was repulsed. She wanted the right to choose her own spouse, and she was not interested in becoming a plural wife to a man nearly twice her age. She also did not buy the theological justification for the practice, which appeared to her as mere hypocrisy. What had happened to the prophet to whom her family had sacrificed so much?

Smith, undeterred, pleaded his case directly in a letter to Nancy Rigdon. "That which is wrong under one circumstance," he wrote her, "may be, and often is, right under another." Polygamy, in other words, was covered by a special dispensation. Rigdon was not persuaded, and she reported the proposal to her father after either the first approach or subsequent letter. The elder Rigdon was furious. Could plural marriage drive away one of Smith's oldest confidants? Several weeks later, Smith dictated another letter to his counselor, trying to mend relations between himself and the Rigdon family, with whom he was no longer on speaking terms. The two men met the next day and eventually reconciled after a long discussion. But while Sidney had been mollified, Nancy was still irate.[39]

Nor was she alone. Rumors concerning clandestine relationships began to spread over the next few months, touching off Smith's largest crisis to date in Nauvoo. As senior members of the Quorum of the Twelve Apostles gained Smith's confidence, they were slowly introduced to polygamy, which widened the circle of those aware of the practice. This trend coincided with the arrival of young, faithful, and single female converts from the eastern states and British Isles. Many of these women had never wed, and others had left their husbands when they refused to join the church. This proved a potent context for a city devoted to challenging traditional boundaries.

Soon enough, stories of adultery, fornication, and other illicit sexual dalliances, many of them imbricated with polygamy, filled Nauvoo's civic and ecclesiastical courts. In May 1842, the City Council passed a resolution declaring that anyone caught in an act of fornication or in an adulterous relationship would be jailed for six months and fined up to $1,000, though Joseph Smith's control of the council meant that he and the Twelve remained safe. Simultaneously, however, the church's High Council, dedicated to Hyrum Smith's mandate that it cleanse Nauvoo of immorality, tried at least twenty cases of sexual misconduct over a matter of weeks. Some of these formal and informal relationships were attempts to follow his own priesthood leadership, while others were based wholly on rumor. It was often impossible to differentiate between the two. Joseph Smith therefore struggled to both maintain order as well as oversee his polygamous project.[40]

One of the young women caught in this maelstrom was Martha Brotherton, who had immigrated with her family from Manchester, England, earlier that year. Within weeks of her arrival, she was invited to talk with apostles Brigham Young and Heber C. Kimball in Joseph Smith's red-brick store. According to an affidavit signed by her and later published as part of a larger exposé, she was cornered in the prophet's office for an extended time while the men tried to convince her to be Young's plural wife. Though some of the more salacious details in her account were possibly exaggerated, key elements are consistent with other episodes. Smith's office was often the setting for introducing a woman to polygamy, and there were usually several people present at proposals. Further, Brotherton alleged that Young claimed he had a revelation from Smith that dictated it lawful for a man to have multiple wives, just as "in the days of Abraham." These elements all matched other trustworthy accounts from the time.

Like Nancy Rigdon, Martha Brotherton rejected the offer and immediately told her parents, upon which the entire family left the faith and the city. Rumors of the encounter quickly spread, leading Smith to

A later image of Brigham Young courting Martha Brotherton. The image depicts a much older Young, and a slightly older Brotherton.
REPRODUCED IN JOHN HANSON BEADLE, *POLYGAMY: OR, THE MYSTERIES AND CRIMES OF MORMONISM* . . .
(PHILADELPHIA: NATIONAL PUBLISHING CO., 1882), 76.

publicly dismiss them in April. He could not, however, keep the truth secret for long.⁴¹

Smith's statement on Brotherton was the first of many public denials over the next few months. Besides rumors about Young's activities, gossip circled around John C. Bennett, too. Smith had been willing to overlook Bennett's infidelities, particularly his leaving behind a wife and children in Ohio, but the new rumors were a more potentially problematic matter, as they suggested that Bennett was using Smith's example to persuade women to sleep with him. Smith pronounced "a curse" in early April on "all Adulterers & fornicators," especially those who invoked his name as an excuse for their behavior—statements that would have sat awkwardly with those aware of Smith's own recent unions. A few weeks later, Smith noted in his journal his fear that there was a conspiracy to expose him.⁴²

We do not know exactly how informed Bennett was of Smith's polygamy at this stage. Bennett had been one of Smith's closest advisors on secular matters when the prophet was sealed to his first plural wife the previous May, but Smith had kept him at an arm's distance once the revelations about Bennett's previous family came to light in July 1841. It is likely that Bennett heard about aspects of the new doctrine and then molded them to fit his own desires, in the belief that he was merely following Smith's practice. Indeed, few individuals, outside of Smith, were privy to all the details concerning the prophet's activities. Regardless of how much he knew, and how he came to know it, however, Bennett threatened to reveal an already fragile system, especially with Hyrum Smith and the High Council investigating.⁴³

Once again, there was further reason to investigate Bennett. In early May, the saints received a letter from Abraham Jonas, the Grand Master of Illinois's Masonic lodge, which cited evidence to support the claim that Bennett was "an expelled Mason." Though this wasn't new information to Smith, nor to George Miller, the head mason of Nauvoo's lodge, they were now forced to immediately call a meeting of all other leading masons in the city, to share the "revelations." Jonas informed Miller that since Nauvoo was already viewed with some skepticism by the broader Masonic community, a formal investigation was necessary. Miller took the warning from Jonas seriously, as did the others who were likely shocked at the news about Bennett. A few days later the Quorum of the Twelve, along with other leaders, decided to evict Bennett from his leadership position. Though chastened, Bennett hoped he could still win back their confidence, just as he had with Smith the previous summer. He tearfully confessed to his past activities and pled for forgiveness. He was willing to fall on his sword, he told them, as long as he could avoid public humiliation. Smith and the apostles decided to handle the matter confidentially.[44]

Privately chastising Bennett while maintaining public order proved to be a difficult, if not impossible, challenge. Bennett was mayor of the city, major general of the Nauvoo Legion, and an assistant president in the church's highest quorum. He had been the public face of the city's political ambitions for the past two years. But now Nauvoo officials had to find some way to ease him off the stage.

A delicate dance ensued. Bennett privately resigned as mayor on May 17, and even claimed in a sworn affidavit that Smith had no knowledge of his infidelities. Smith was then nominated as Bennett's replacement at a momentous City Council meeting two days later. The prophet knew he had to move carefully, especially given that one of the council members was Hiram Kimball, whose wife, Sarah, had recently rebuffed Smith's polygamous proposal. Smith likely worried that Kimball, a prominent gentile businessman who served as the city's alderman, might be reluctant to support his bid as mayor. During the meeting, Smith hastily scribbled a revelation and shared it with the entire room. "Verily thus saith the Lord," the rushed text declared, "Hiram Kimball has been insinuating evil & forming evil opinions against you with others." It chastised Kimball, and anyone else who spoke ill of Smith, and urged him to repent. Kimball, though not a member of the faith, knew how to read a room. He did not oppose Smith's candidacy, and the church's prophet was named the city's mayor. Once chosen by the council, which possessed the power to appoint an interim mayor until the next election, Smith denounced anyone spreading rumors about his private activities. The council then organized a night watch to patrol their streets and protect Smith's reputation.[45]

Bennett, who was nothing if not a talented actor, played his role perfectly before the City Council. In a display of humility, he admitted that he had erred, though he did not give details. Still hoping to escape serious censure, he flattered Smith by providing him with the moral defense he knew the prophet desired. In the scripted meeting before other city leaders, he affirmed that Smith had never given him permission to sleep with women, and that any people who claimed otherwise were "damned Liars." He swore he had no difficulty with Smith or other church authorities, and he hoped to remain a member of the faith in good standing. By taking this route, Bennett believed he could wait out the storm and eventually return to his former standing. Smith again insisted that Bennett reaffirm the prophet's reputation, to which Bennett responded that Smith had always been nothing but virtuous. Satisfied, Smith took no further action at the meeting. The mayoral transition seemed to have gone smoothly, as nobody else on the council raised an issue.[46]

But removing Bennett from office was one thing; handling the rumors of polygamy that had contributed to his downfall was another altogether. George Miller, who had been assigned to investigate Bennett, and Hyrum Smith, who was always zealous in rooting out impurity, had already uncovered disturbing facts. And Joseph's wife, Emma Smith, took these revelations about a string of sexual exploits as confirmation of her long-held suspicions about her husband's infidelity. At a Relief Society meeting held the same evening of Bennett's resignation, Emma declared that there was rampant iniquity within the city, and that she feared her own friends were not doing enough to expose it. There may have been a time when they could overlook an individual's sins, and treat them more charitably, but the day had come to confront all manner of infidelity. She specifically criticized anyone who claimed to be acting under the instruction of her own husband. Her tone and intent were clear.[47]

Over the next two weeks, much of the drama resulting from the polygamy rumors played out at the High Council, Hyrum Smith's primary vehicle for pushing reform. Hyrum's towering physical stature was matched only by his firm focus on immorality. Starting on May 21, George Miller presented the findings of his investigation into Bennett. They were extensive, and potentially catastrophic. Over the course of eight days, the council heard the cases of nine individuals. Recognizing the power imbalance in priesthood courts, all four women involved pled guilty and provided full statements detailing their indiscretions in return for retaining full fellowship; conversely, all five men insisted on their innocence and were, with one exception, disfellowshipped.

A clear narrative emerged from the women's statements. Though Bennett was not officially among the accused, his shadow loomed over the proceedings. One of the women brought to trial, Catherine Warren, accused Chauncey Higbee of teaching the same things she had heard were taught by Bennett, ideas that she had also heard were being promulgated by Smith. She asserted that Bennett had told her that if she became pregnant, he, as a doctor, could prescribe abortive medicine. Sarah Miller, another of the accused, echoed that claim. Matilda Nyman, who also admitted to intercourse with Higbee, asserted that she was told such actions were approved by church leaders. Based on the weight of the women's testimonies, Higbee was expelled from the faith.[48]

One of the reasons Hyrum Smith, Emma Smith, and others were set on rooting out Nauvoo's sexual issues was they lived in an era that was deeply concerned with rampant infidelity, especially when it came to marginalized religious movements. As a new individualistic age seemed to weaken attachment to traditional morality, some radical movements attempted new experiments that shocked their contemporaries. During the same decade when Joseph Smith was introducing his Abrahamic order, John Humphrey Noyes, a Yale-educated theologian with Christian perfectionist tendencies, was envisioning a new social order that freed men and women from the strict confines of marriage. He was also accused of adultery, and in response created his own commune in Oneida, New York, filled with believers who were all linked together through a complex marriage system. The scheme allowed sexual relations as an acceptable form of both spiritual and social practice.

Outsiders, of course, saw it as a superficial excuse for free love. To many, the Oneida Community represented the dangers of an unmoored society in need of correction. The nineteenth century was filled with numerous episodes of sexual experimentation that coincided with calls to return to more traditional domestic arrangements. Many religious groups outside the safe confines of mainstream evangelicalism were forced to prove that they were not a threat to the country's well-being, which encouraged them to better police those within their own congregations. While Joseph Smith reflected the more radical end of this debate, his wife and brother imitated the concordant desire to prove the community's respectability.

These anxieties gave context to Nauvoo's Bennett affair. Yet amid these revelations, Smith, terrified of being exposed himself, was still defending Bennett. He hoped that Bennett could leave Nauvoo, and quietly, and he feared that alienating his former associate would lead to more public attention. When Bennett confessed his activities to the city's Masonic lodge, the prophet pled on his behalf. That night, he even spoke to the Relief Society and warned that the women were exhibiting too much zeal, and that they should instead show mercy on the accused. Such an admonition to "hold your tongues" may appear strange coming from him, he admitted, but he insisted that it was the best policy. Smith reasoned that he would rather see ten iniquitous people spared than one innocent condemned. Emma Smith, however, was not convinced. Perturbed, she responded that sin should never be overlooked, especially sins against both divine and civic laws. She was not willing to make exceptions for any person in her quest for social reformation—not even her husband.[49]

Two weeks later, Joseph once again urged the ladies of the Relief Society to see that it was a mistake to seek out the iniquity in others, and that such faultfinding was a satanic tool designed to create discord. Nauvoo's women, he feared, were becoming too obsessive in their mission. But Joseph was now outnumbered. Spearheaded by Hyrum, an energetic group of leaders within the city, both men and women, was now eager to purify the church of what they believed to be a spreading virus of adultery. Joseph Smith was fighting a losing battle, as the push for moral cleansing—which he himself helped start—could not be stopped.[50]

Bennett, by this point, had become too toxic to retain the prophet's support, but he could now serve a new role: scapegoat. Joseph Smith was willing to overlook flawed colleagues, and often held on to close associates longer than others might, but the frequent questions connecting Bennett's affairs with Smith's private sealings jeopardized his Abrahamic project. One resident, Oliver Olney, knew enough to connect the dots. "If Bennett had not moved quite so fast," and instead kept the rumors controlled like Smith was able to, "all would have been well." By mid-June, it was time to cut all ties with the disgraced Bennett.[51]

At a general meeting in front of several thousand saints near the unfinished temple on June 18, Smith publicly denounced Bennett for the first time. It was now all out in the open. The city's newspaper published a litany of testimonies and accusations meant to discredit their former mayor. From then on, any rumor concerning plural marriages could be dismissed as an instance of Bennett's "spiritual wifery," a catchall term used to deny their validity. Bennett, unsurprisingly, felt betrayed. He had hoped that, as long as he privately submitted to church discipline, he could eventually return to Smith's good graces and regain his privileged position. Others, like secretary William Phelps, who had recently returned to the faith after a few years of forced exile, had shown that this was possible. But now Bennett was publicly humiliated and officially excommunicated. He fled the city and dedicated himself to writing an exposé of Smith and the saints. Nauvoo would hear from him again.[52]

———

IMMEDIATELY AFTER BENNETT'S DEPARTURE, Smith refocused his ener-
gies on organizing his society around an Abrahamic priesthood.
Rather than slowing the prophet down, the expulsion of his close colleague seemed to energize him. His secretary even noted that Smith
appeared strengthened in his resolve.[53]

Remarkably, after the revelations about Bennett and the resulting
moral fervor, there were still women in the city willing to accept
a marriage proposal from Smith. Delcena Johnson and Martha
McBride, two widows, were sealed to him that summer. But the
more notable addition to Smith's family was Eliza R. Snow. An educated and cultured woman, Snow had converted to the Mormon
faith nearly a decade before and quickly became one of its foremost
female voices. Tall, conservatively dressed, and always dignified,
Snow wrote poetry and hymns, and was chosen by Emma Smith to
serve as the secretary for the new Relief Society. Then, in late June
1842, Emma's husband had chosen her to be a plural wife. "This is a
day of much interest to my feelings," she subtly recorded in her journal on June 29, the day of the sealing. Though she did not record
details, she could not help but hint at her confusion. But even if she
could not fully comprehend them at the time, she knew the implications were immense.[54]

Why would someone of Snow's intelligence and stature accept
Smith's new patriarchal order, especially given the scandals of the previous months? Though she failed to offer explicit reasons at the time,
her life story offers some hints. First and foremost, she was deeply
committed to both the Mormon cause and the Mormon prophet. Snow
had already sacrificed much for the movement and was ready to sacrifice
more. She would later describe her faith in Mormonism as unwavering,
and the challenges it entailed worthwhile. Listening to Joseph Smith's
teachings in the Relief Society, and looking forward to the new rituals promised in the temple, Snow likely saw plural marriage as another
step in a path toward personal sanctification and transcendence.
Joseph Smith had promised the women of Nauvoo that they would
join a "kingdom of priests"—a promise Snow, as the organization's

Eliza R. Snow, photograph, circa 1852. Snow, an adult convert to the faith known for
her poetry and wit, became a plural wife to Joseph Smith in 1842.
LDS CHURCH HISTORY LIBRARY, SALT LAKE CITY.

secretary, carefully recorded in the Relief Society minute book—and
polygamy was a path to becoming queens of a godly kingdom. Paradoxically, Smith held out the promise of matriarchal power to buttress
his support for a patriarchy. For Snow, this was a promise that could
not easily be turned down.[55]

There were likely more prosaic reasons for her yearning. To the
Mormons of Nauvoo, American democracy seemed a failed experiment that only brought death and destruction to those most in
need of protection. What would happen to women like Snow, who
were beyond the typical age of courtship, in a dangerous nation that
left many vulnerable? How could American society take care of the
never-married, the widowed, and destitute? Federal and state governments refused to take responsibility, and charitable efforts were

often haphazard. Religious groups moved to bridge the gap. For Mormons, given their history, the threat from the mainstream seemed ever-present.

The crisis that preceded Nauvoo's settlement also played a role. "Description fails; Tho' language is too mean," Snow wrote in a poem in 1839, in the wake of Missouri, "To paint the horrors of that dreadful scene." A number of women had lost their houses, husbands, and children, and some claimed to have been raped. All seemed to be lost. "Thou didst pollute the holy sanctuary of female virtue," Snow wrote, "and barbarously trample upon the most sacred gems of domestic felicity!" One later oral source claimed that Snow was among those Mormon refugees from Missouri who had experienced sexual trauma that had left her unable to bear children. Though impossible to verify—in part because the cultural sensitivities of the day would have prohibited the recording of such details—the story reveals the anxiety and anger Snow felt toward the rest of society. Polygamy, therefore, provided redemption from lost opportunities and stability within a chaotic world.[56]

Snow's account in her journal on her marriage day in 1842 seemed to reflect this belief. "While I am contemplating the present state of society—the powers of darkness, and the prejudices of the human mind which stand array'd like an impregnable barrier against the work of God," she couldn't help but embrace the stability offered by Smith's marital network. She likened the chaos of the wider world to the thunderstorm that rained on her secret wedding day. "The rage of elements," she mused, reminded her of the flimsy nature of human life and the storms that tossed people to and fro. Polygamy was, at least to Snow, the force that could save her from a life of loss. She absorbed Joseph Smith's anger, and embraced his solution. America's frontier culture had failed to protect women, so it was logical to take radical action in response. She did not just want to be safe; she also wanted to help redeem a fallen world, a feeling she shared with thousands of converts to Mormonism. Her sealing allowed her to exercise a matriarchal power that could finally bring stability.[57]

The expansion of polygamy, and the increased attention to it, was a growing problem for Nauvoo. How did Snow reconcile her personal feelings concerning the prophet's private actions with his public statements and the ongoing scandal? Though a poet, even she could not put her conclusion in words. "O, how shall I compose a thought / Where nothing is compos'd?" she wrote in her diary in the autumn. "How form ideas, as I ought / On subjects not disclosed?" Smith's reformation project offered stability in an unstable world, but it still caused significant anxiety, even for those who embraced it.[58]

Though Emma Smith was still mostly unaware of Eliza Snow and her husband's other new spouses, she was only becoming more suspicious. Armed with the Relief Society, and supported by Hyrum Smith and the High Council, she was ready to do more digging. For the time being, though, Joseph had triumphed over a serious challenge to his authority, a crisis that had come close to toppling him from his prophet's perch.

While a few dozen Mormons in Nauvoo struggled with the contradictions polygamy introduced, the city was on the rise. One recent immigrant wrote home that summer that the saints had erected over three hundred brick homes over the previous few months, and many more were soon to be built. Contemplating a nation that seemed in the middle of a political crisis—with a new ascendant political party, a deceased president, and a fierce battle over the federal government's future— some could not help but think they were in a blessed position. Wilford Woodruff, fresh off his mission to Britain, where he observed a government, and a king, nearly overthrown by a lower-class revolt, observed that "the whole world is in a *hubbub* except Nauvoo we have peace & quietness here." Joseph Smith's redemptive mission, buttressed by the new Abrahamic revelation, appeared to be heading for success.[59]

CHAPTER 4

Trunk

If any citize[n]s of Illinois deny our right—let them go to hell and be
damnd.—I give up my chart[re]d right at the sword and bayonets.
—JOSEPH SMITH, JUNE 30, 1843[1]

H. R. Robinson, "Joseph the Prophet Addressing the Lamanites," lithograph, 1844.
Smith's followers viewed his outreach to Native Americans, whom they believed to
be the remnants of the Book of Mormon populations, as a key feature of their millennial mission. LDS CHURCH HISTORY LIBRARY, SALT LAKE CITY.

Mormon leaders spent the first day of 1843 preaching the gospel of their church in the legislative hall of their state. It was an odd scene. Joseph Smith and several of his closest associates were in Illinois's capital, Springfield, for a public trial that drew wide attention. Many Illinoisans gathered to see the infamous prophet. W. M. Busey, a non-Mormon spectator, reported that the public obsession was as if Smith were a foreign creature rather than a local man. From Busey's perspective, Smith was less than impressive; he described the Mormon prophet as "rather corpulent[,] round faced[,] and roman nosed." Though he tried to carry himself like a preacher, Smith otherwise had the countenance of a commoner.[2]

Busey did not remark on the adoration of Smith's followers. The saints, exuberant to be given a hearing in front of the state legislature, sang a rousing rendition of one of their favorite hymns, "The Spirit of God Like a Fire Is Burning," which celebrated their belief that the age of visions and angels had once again returned to the earth. Those packed into the room then heard from their appointed prophet and leaders. The apostle Orson Hyde, who had recently returned from a mission to Jerusalem, declared that the Mormons were not like either Protestants or Catholics; rather, they were a powerful people meant to purify the world. If the Christian church refused to cleanse itself, he warned, then God would do it through the hands of his most faithful servants. Congregants shouted "amen" in response. Springfield's congressional hall had likely never seen such a spectacle.[3]

The prophet and his followers were justified in feeling triumphant. They had strong reason to believe that they were mere days away from being vindicated by a federal circuit court following a five-month battle with Illinois and Missouri officials that seemed to put the church's future in jeopardy. Soon enough, however, Smith would face yet another round of extradition charges. But both sagas ended with Nauvoo standing victorious, in part due to the political alliances they had forged during their first three years in Nauvoo. Yet, while the Mormons achieved a number of short-term victories, they also laid the groundwork for larger conflicts.

Despite the legal turmoil, Smith's reforms within Nauvoo proceeded apace. The boundaries of Nauvoo's society continued to shift. Even as Mormons sought a place within the American nation, they were still defining the parameters of their own community. Black converts and indigenous tribes forced the prophet to reconsider the nature of their religious order. Some of the most complicated questions, however, regarded the families of Smith and his closest associates. He expanded his secretive polygamous experiment not only for himself— the twelve months between July 1842 and July 1843 were his busiest on this front—but also for others. That same year witnessed the solidification of Mormon polygamy on theological grounds: the period began with Smith dictating a revelation that also included text for the earliest plural marriage ritual on record, and the year ended with another dictated revelation that offered a formal defense of the practice.

These recorded revelations, however, belied the continued confusion and anxiety over the new practice, and they did not appease everyone. While Smith's polygamy project was meant to return order and structure to a tumultuous domestic culture, its effect was to trigger apprehension over the role and rights of women in Mormon society. From the perspective of those venturing into this new marital order, what was the best way to assure fidelity, build relationships, and secure blessings, either in this life or the next?

In these ways, the Mormons were little different from many other Americans, even as they appeared to move farther and farther away from conventional morality and to create their own distinct society. In the early 1840s, America was still a testing ground for democratic rule, witnessing legal precedents based on the flimsiest of judicial decisions and political traditions established in the wake of corrupt electoral bargains.

Politicians, reformers, and religionists questioned who belonged within their evolving empire, and who should be removed to beyond its borders. Questions of local, state, and federal authority swirled. At the heart of the many dilemmas of the era was the question of allegiance: To whom did an American owe theirs? What political parties, legal authorities, or religious leaders were worthy of loyalty? These questions were driven by a country that was still seeking to define its moral standards, geographic boundaries, and political structures.

Like the rest of the country, the Mormons attempted to answer these questions in their own way. Building on the social vision he began preaching about in the first few months of 1842, Joseph Smith moved to establish a governing structure that merged heaven and earth and united men and women into a patriarchal dynasty. The Mormons were intent on forming eternal alliances that could transcend the grave, even as they were forming political coalitions that could withstand legal threats. Many of these practices challenged the white mainstream Protestant culture that was often as inflexible as it was unforgiving. The Mormon Kingdom was not yet fully realized, but its implications were coming into focus. And just as the saints experimented with their political potential, so too did the rest of their county, state, and nation begin to perceive the danger the newcomers posed.

SITUATED IN A RURAL AREA OF HANCOCK COUNTY, Illinois, Nauvoo was largely isolated. The land between the city and surrounding towns like Carthage and Warsaw was sparsely settled and primarily filled with large farms and unoccupied territory. Unless one was traveling on county roads, it was rare to run into another human being. Which is why it was all the more shocking when a young man, walking through a dense grove, ran into Joseph Smith, the Mormon prophet, on an otherwise uneventful day on August 17, 1842.

Smith and one of his close confidants, Erastus Derby, had gone into the woods to exercise. They had been cooped up in their private hideaway for some time and needed fresh air. It was during this brief respite that they were discovered. If the passerby had been following the news, he would have immediately known the significance of this random encounter: the state of Illinois had recently issued a warrant for Smith's arrest, upon which the Mormon prophet was to be extradited to Missouri and tried as an accomplice to murder. Though the unidentified man appeared friendly and promised not to expose Smith's secret, rumors were bound to spread. And for the third time in two weeks, Smith was forced to find another hiding place.[4]

The encounter was just one small episode in a hectic summer for Smith. Just a few months earlier, he felt more secure than he had in a decade. Why did he find himself hiding out in the woods soon after? The immediate reason was an attempted assassination—not of Smith, but of one of Smith's primary nemeses. Lilburn Boggs, who had served as Missouri's governor and overseen the state-sanctioned removal of the Mormons in 1838, was resting in his home on May 6, 1842, when an unidentified assailant, likely seeking vengeance, shot him in the head and neck. It seemed to be just another example of frontier justice in a state that knew its fair share. Few expected Boggs to live.

The saints were not disappointed to hear the news. Once word arrived in Nauvoo eight days later, many rejoiced that Boggs had finally received his due. Smith had always been outspoken in his hope that God's judgment might rain down on the bloodthirsty governor, and had even once wished that Boggs's family, and his posterity, would not be spared from justice. When the Mormons learned that Boggs had been shot, they saw it as a fulfilled prophecy. "Thus this ungodly wretch has fallen in the midst of his iniquity," Wilford Woodruff wrote in his diary, "& the vengeance of God has overtaken him." Woodruff then added a crude doodle of Boggs being shot with an arrow through his head. Yet to everyone's surprise—and to the Mormons' disappointment—Boggs soon recovered from his wounds.[5]

Many observers assumed that the Mormons were somehow involved in the assassination attempt. It did not take a deep knowledge of the Mormon–Missouri conflict to suspect the saints had finally tried to seek their revenge. Within weeks, newspapers began circulating rumors that implicated Joseph Smith and his followers. Smith expressed outrage at the accusation and maintained that the saints were law-abiding citizens. But he knew that a storm was coming. A few weeks later he declared at a public gathering that God would seek judgment on all the corrupt Missouri leaders who had inflicted trauma on the church. Smith's fervor over Missouri was so intense that his seven-year-old son, Frederick, dreamt the next night that God had decapitated all the Missourians.[6]

The Boggs shooting came at a bad time for the saints. John C. Bennett, recently exiled from Nauvoo and now bearing a personal vendetta against Smith, took advantage of the situation. The second of his many exposés, published in mid-July, claimed Smith had been conspiring to kill Boggs since the previous summer. Smith, understandably worried, tried to head off these accusations by writing letters to many dignitaries, including Illinois governor Thomas Carlin and James Arlington Bennet, the prominent New York socialite, claiming that John C. Bennett was conspiring with Missouri officials to extradite the prophet. The Bennett accusation, Smith assured them, was a lie. Carlin, at least at first, agreed that Bennett was not to be trusted, but he also confessed his skepticism over Smith's innocence. The swirling rumors did not originate with Bennett, Carlin retorted, because he had heard similar tales of Smith's quest for justice for over a year, from multiple sources. While he was previously willing to overlook such remarks as "idle boasting," the governor was now forced to see the prophet's words in a new light.[7]

The Mormons acted swiftly. Nauvoo's leaders drafted a petition urging Carlin to treat skeptically any measures taken by Missouri due to the state's long history of attacking Mormons. Their beloved prophet, they argued, was a patriotic man who merely wanted his constitutional rights to be fully recognized. And as Smith could never be assured a fair trial in Missouri, they argued that he should be heard by an Illinois jury. By their reasoning, the attempt on Boggs's life was a hoax, a conspiracy to return Smith to Missouri soil for execution. The appeal was signed by eight hundred Mormon residents of Nauvoo.[8]

The city's women mobilized as well. Emma Smith, Eliza R. Snow, and Amanda Barnes Smith, representing the Nauvoo Relief Society, marched to Carlin's home in Quincy to meet with the governor. They had a petition of their own: Emma had urged Nauvoo's women to come to Joseph's defense against Bennett's accusations, and the Relief Society produced, for the governor, a bold testimony that featured a thousand signatures. A lawyer with knowledge of the meeting described Smith, Snow, and Pratt as favorably received, but not taken seriously. Carlin, despite the outpouring of support for Joseph Smith, remained noncommittal. He told the women that the Constitution dictated his actions, and that he did not believe that blaming Smith for Boggs's near murder was an anti-Mormon plot. Frustrated, the women left fearful that the saints could not rely on the governor's support.[9]

The situation soon grew worse. After recovering from his injuries, Lilburn Boggs signed an affidavit claiming he had evidence that Smith had ordered his personal bodyguard, Orrin Porter Rockwell, to assassinate him. The Mormon prophet, therefore, was an "accessory before the fact of the intended murder." The new governor of Missouri, Thomas Reynolds, immediately signed a requisition on July 22 to bring Smith back to his state for trial. Carlin was now in a bind: a governor of a neighboring state was demanding the extradition of one of his most powerful constituents.[10]

Yet, as with the previous attempt to extradite Smith in 1841, timing once again played a role: on August 1, within a couple days of Carlin receiving the requisition, he lost an election to Thomas Ford, a Democrat. Now a lame-duck governor, Carlin was free to act without concern about the Mormon vote. Convinced by the evidence, he signed a warrant for Joseph Smith's arrest on August 2 and deputized three officers to arrest the prophet in his own city. Smith's luck, it seemed, had finally run out.[11]

What happened next confused just about everyone. A neighboring county's under-sheriff, Thomas King, along with officers from both Illinois and Missouri, arrived in Nauvoo on August 8 with the warrant for Smith's arrest. Nauvoo scrambled for a response. The City Council immediately passed an ordinance that strengthened their habeas corpus laws in order to assure themselves a voice in Smith's arrest. The new ordinance declared a Nauvoo citizen's right to have their local municipal court examine the "origin, validity, & legality" of any warrant, no matter where it was originally issued, and if the court determined it in any way illegal, it could discharge the prisoner from arrest. Before he could be taken away, Smith would be tried by Nauvoo's own court.[12]

King, who held a writ signed by Carlin to take Smith in custody, was befuddled. Could a city overrule a governor? He reluctantly turned the Mormon prophet over to Henry G. Sherwood, Nauvoo's city marshal, and set out to nearby Quincy for further instructions from Carlin. The officers had arrived in Nauvoo with a direct order but left with only questions. When he heard of it, Carlin proclaimed that Nauvoo's attempt to judge writs issued by the state was not only a ridiculous and naïve misunderstanding of law, but also a gross usurpation of power. Each side accused the other of tyranny.[13]

There was a reason for the governor's rage. At a very basic level, the Mormons were interpreting habeas corpus laws in an imaginative way that did not reflect the contemporary consensus. Habeas corpus had long been seen as a bulwark of liberty within the Anglo-American tradition, a safeguard against tyranny that assured the rights of citizens. But there were always limits. First, a habeas corpus hearing was only meant to address the legality of an *arrest*, and not the merits of a *case*. That is, it could decide whether the prosecuting body followed correct process in arresting a defendant, but it could not determine the defendant's guilt or innocence. If a person was arrested under a warrant, therefore, and that warrant was later found to be illegal, they could still be arrested again under a new warrant for the same crime. Indeed, Illinois law explicitly allowed the governor to issue a second arrest warrant when the first resulted in a habeas corpus discharge. Second, a court could only hold habeas corpus hearings for cases that originated within its jurisdiction. Nauvoo's original charter had correctly granted habeas corpus rights to the municipal court over charges stemming from breaches of Nauvoo ordinances, for example.

Yet the Mormon City Council was now passing ordinances that

surpassed these boundaries. It had granted the municipal court the authority to try the merits of cases, not just of arrests, as well as of cases that originated outside its jurisdiction. These actions provided a legal buffer between Nauvoo and the rest of the state. Thomas King, the arresting officer, was understandably bewildered when he was told Smith would first require a hearing within the city before being brought to the governor. Such a process seemed to subvert the law of the land. But given that the Nauvoo Legion was ready to enforce the order, he was not willing to press the matter on his own.[14]

The Mormons did not stop there. Over the next few months, Nauvoo's City Council passed four additional ordinances that served to strengthen their habeas corpus powers. The most ambitious, passed in November, was especially bold. It declared that even if a resident of the city was arrested outside of Nauvoo, for crimes that took place elsewhere than Nauvoo, and by a warrant signed at any jurisdictional level above Nauvoo, the accused still had the right to be returned to Nauvoo for a hearing. Further, once a person had been granted habeas corpus by the municipal court, they could never be tried again for the same crime. Any officer, sheriff, or jailer who refused to obey Nauvoo's orders, the ordinance made clear, would himself be punished with a fine of between five hundred and one thousand dollars.[15]

The saints felt justified in taking these steps. From their perspective, it was fundamentally unjust for a community of non- or even anti-Mormons to issue a warrant for the arrest and extradition of Smith, who would assuredly be murdered, perhaps by a state-approved mob, once he set foot in Missouri. They initially denounced Missouri's writ as a form of religious persecution. Even if the city overstepped its authority, one Mormon editorial reasoned, it was justified because the writs conflicted with the spirit of constitutional fairness. It was clear that traditional structures could not work, given the animosity expressed by Missourians toward Smith and his followers. This was a matter of life and death.[16]

The Mormons based their arguments on a broader question concerning legal fairness. The American judicial system, they believed, promised a trial by one's *peers*. Democracy, in other words, was meant to ensure that every citizen received a fair hearing. America's judicial system was still an experiment, as religious minorities were often the victims of legal oppression. Many groups were eager to explore new avenues to secure their rights in the face of majority opposition. And as a beleaguered religious minority, the Mormons felt their only peers were within their own community. Only Mormon courts could assure a fair hearing and fair trials within a democratic society based on, as they wrote to one ally, a "devotion to mobocracy."[17]

Joseph Smith did not stay in Nauvoo long enough to see whether the city would be vindicated in this approach. Worried that the municipal court's discharge might be struck down, the prophet fled Nauvoo and spent much of the remainder of 1842 in hiding. For the next five months, he was spirited between the homes of his uncle John Smith and friends Edward Sayers, Carlos Granger, Edward Hunter, and James Taylor, all of which stood at various points on the outskirts of the city. Some of his movements proved particularly crafty. On one occasion, one of his supporters rode Smith's own horse in one direction, hoping to draw the attention of anyone tracking them, while the prophet went off in another.[18]

The state authorities grew increasingly frustrated. Unable to find Smith, officials threatened to burn Nauvoo to the ground. Smith, aware of the growing anger in Springfield, wrote to Wilson Law, recently promoted to replace John C. Bennett as major general of the Nauvoo Legion, to instruct him that if the authorities were to catch the prophet, the Mormon militia should rush to his rescue. When Smith surprised the saints by speaking at a church gathering in late August and requesting that they fight on his behalf, nearly four hundred men immediately volunteered. Women were also expected to contribute as well, and Eliza R. Snow spent the next day sewing more uniforms for the would-be soldiers. The entire town was ready to defend its prophet.[19]

Needlework was not the only way women could help defend Smith. Recently mobilized as part of Nauvoo's societal reform project, the city's women jumped at the opportunity to push for public action.

After the petition the Relief Society had delivered to Governor Carlin in late July, they again appealed to state authorities in August. Emma Smith, despite her misgivings over her husband's private activities, wrote a long letter to Governor Carlin insisting that the Mormons had not broken any laws, and that the governor's actions were only abetting Missouri's unfair persecution of her husband. Carlin, though sympathetic, responded that he was merely fulfilling his duty. Emma, unconvinced, retorted by identifying a critical flaw in Thomas Reynolds's original requisition: Joseph had not been in Missouri at the time of Boggs's shooting, and therefore could not be a fugitive from justice. In other words, she argued that Joseph could not be *returned* to a state that he did not originally *leave*. Carlin, though impressed with her argument—a sign, in itself, of the growing involvement of Nauvoo's women in civic and political matters—still refused to recognize the city's habeas corpus powers. He promised her, however, that Joseph would get a fair trial with the state.[20]

Emma was not alone in questioning the extradition order's legality. Acknowledging that he could not run forever, Joseph Smith and his associates reached out to friendly politicians and lawyers for advice on how to bring an end to his ordeal. Eventually, non-Mormons including Stephen A. Douglas, then an associate justice on the Illinois Supreme Court, and Justin Butterfield, a US District attorney, convinced Smith to try to secure a writ of habeas corpus from the Illinois judicial system. Though Missouri was redoubling its efforts—the governor increased the monetary reward for Smith's capture, and rumors spread that two dozen men were staked out in Nauvoo to capture the prophet—the relationship the saints had built with Illinois authorities were proving useful. The state's new governor, Thomas Ford, who took office in December, shared the saints' skepticism that Missouri's writ would hold up in court. Moreover, the news of these events had spread far and wide, and most observers throughout the country saw the extradition attempt as another example of Missouri lawlessness.[21]

Given these positive signs, Smith decided to trust the system. After further consultation with external advisors, he voluntarily surrendered in Nauvoo on December 27 and set off to Springfield for a hearing. The prophet's journey among Illinois's gentiles brought no shortage of tense exchanges. When he arrived in the nearby town of Paris and tried to obtain lodging for the night, the local tavern keeper claimed nobody in the town was willing to rent the Mormons a room. Emboldened by the support he had received from powerful state politicians, Smith bristled at the disrespect. He insisted they were going to stay in the town regardless of any opposition. "I have Men enough to take the town," he spat, and "if we must freeze we will freeze by the burning of these houses." The residents backed down. Smith arrived in Springfield the next day, where he received a mostly warm reception, including from Nathaniel Pope, the judge who would preside over his case, who remarked on his surprise at how ordinary the saints appeared. Smith, knowing how to act the part, did all he could to assure the authorities that the Mormons were not to be feared. Both sides were playing nice.[22]

Smith's hearing was a public spectacle. Droves of people crowded inside and outside the courthouse to see the famed prophet. Among the audience was Abraham Lincoln's new bride, Mary Todd, as well as numerous reporters from newspapers throughout the region. Butterfield, who represented Smith, opened with a quip: "I appear before you today under circumstances most over and peculiar," he declared. "I am to address the 'Pope' (bowing to the judge) surrounded by his angels (bowing still lower to the ladies) in the presence of the holy Apostles in behalf of the Prophet of the Lord." After spirited arguments, the verdict was anticlimactic. The extradition order was deemed to be based on flawed logic and was overturned. As Emma Smith had earlier noted, there was no evidence that Joseph was in Missouri at the time of the crime, and was therefore not a fugitive from the state.[23]

If the prophet had been only mildly concerned going into the hearing—though he did confess to his close friends that he would rather die than return to Missouri—he and his followers were still certainly relieved with the outcome. Pope was friendly toward the saints, to the point that lawyers in the courtroom joked that he would be baptized within six weeks. But the judge did offer somber advice: "refrain from all political electioneering," he urged. Smith responded by insisting that the church never interfered with electoral politics, but instead allowed all of its members to follow their individual conscience. While not a straightforward answer, Smith's response reflected his ability to appease.[24]

The outcome was seen as not just a victory for Joseph Smith, but for the entire Mormon community. On their way back from Springfield, Smith's close friends Wilson Law and Willard Richards composed a joyous hymn titled "The Mormon Jubilee," which called for jubilant celebration. They praised their lawyers, Judge Pope, and even Governor Ford. They sang the song several times over the next few days, including at a big celebration on January 18, 1843, when hundreds of saints danced inside the prophet's own home. Not satisfied with Law's fifteen verses, Eliza R. Snow wrote eleven more of her own, which were also passed around and sung by the attendees. The party lasted long into the night. At least for the time being, the saints' faith in both Illinois's authorities and habeas corpus was reaffirmed. Even Smith confessed his surprise at how kindly he was treated.[25]

The prophet's belief that he was fully vindicated, however, left him with an unrealistic view of his own influence as well as Nauvoo's power. And indeed, much to Smith's chagrin, his legal problems were far from over, and his deep disappointment with America's democratic system would soon reemerge.

JOHN C. BENNETT'S ASSAULT ON THE CHURCH was not limited to the legal realm. In his series of salacious exposés, published in a nearby newspaper, the *Sangamo Journal*, he attempted to reveal Joseph Smith's clandestine domestic arrangements. "Joseph Smith, the great Mormon seducer," he wrote in his first essay, "has seduced not only hundreds of single and married females, but more than the great Solomon." His hyperbole backfired, leading most casual readers to dismiss his accusations as outlandish. And in truth, Bennett did not have the entire picture of Smith's polygamy, especially after he was distanced from the prophet in summer 1841. Bennett, like most of Smith's inner circle, combined firsthand knowledge with secondhand rumor. His desire for both vengeance and book sales resulted in writings that were more sensational than reliable. He did, however, succeed in causing a stir.[26]

During the second half of 1842, many saints around Smith, including his growing number of wives, began to have difficulty distinguishing his system from that described by Bennett. Few people were as conflicted over the new practices as Orson and Sarah Pratt. One of the original apostles of the church, Orson—short, slim, and with wild hair—had spent the previous two years on a mission in Britain, where he succeeded in converting thousands to the faith. But rather than returning to a hero's welcome, he instead faced an impossible dilemma: he found that Sarah was among the women Bennett alleged was sealed to Smith. Nauvoo residents, quick to defend their prophet, responded by claiming that it was *Bennett* who started the affair with the apostle's spouse. Sarah, for her part, sided with Bennett and accused Smith of unwanted advances. Deeply disturbed by the situation, Orson contemplated ending his life. He penned a suicide note in which he declared himself a ruined man, and said that he had no hope for the future. Not only was his marriage in shambles, but now he was forced to choose who was deceiving him—either the prophet he had followed for twelve years, or a wife to whom he had been married for nearly as long. He was unwilling to accept either possibility.[27]

When Orson Pratt's note was discovered, Smith ordered all of the city's men to devote their day to finding the missing apostle. The search lasted several hours before they found Orson perched on a log several miles down the river, dazed and confused. They spent the next few weeks trying to bring the distressed soul back into the fold, though Brigham Young feared Pratt was verging on insanity. When Pratt refused to sustain a church-wide resolution on July 22 to reaffirm Smith's virtuous character in the wake of Bennett's accusations, the prophet decided to cut him loose. The apostle was excommunicated the next month. Yet, despite the drama, Smith continued on with his polygamous activities. And while he was only sealed to one woman in the ensuing months, that union proved crucial to his larger project.²⁸

Sarah Ann Whitney, a seventeen-year-old girl with brown hair, grew up revering Joseph Smith. Her parents, Newel K. and Elizabeth Ann Whitney, had been closely connected to the prophet since the very beginning of Mormonism. They converted in Kirtland, Ohio, within a year of the church's founding, after which Newel, a solemn man, became the church's second bishop and Elizabeth became known for speaking in tongues. In Nauvoo, Newel remained within the faith's leadership circles and was one of the first to receive the endowment rituals; Elizabeth, for her part, was one of the founding members of the Relief Society. They were among Mormonism's first families, ecclesiastical royalty, and some of the prophet's closest friends.

Yet in Smith's expanding theological vision, there was still another possible linkage between them. In late July, Smith proposed a sealing between himself and Sarah Ann, in a plural union. This union's timing, in the wake of Bennett's expulsion and Orson Pratt's excommunication, appears reckless, in retrospect, given the increased scrutiny of Smith. The age difference also highlighted the power disparity between Smith and the girl. Yet it revealed the fervency with which Smith embarked on his societal reformation.²⁹

Elizabeth later cast this "trial"—the sealing of her teenaged daughter to a man twice her age—as something that was only endurable due to her firm assurance of God's support. She claimed that after Smith proposed the union to them, she and her husband prayed for a sign, and both asserted to have received it. She knew that Smith's proposition required rejecting traditional marriage customs, but concluded that it was a worthy sacrifice on God's altar. But she did not arrive at that conclusion initially. Later on, she admitted that she had originally rejected the proposal, and wrote that "she cried about it but the Prophet at last obtained her consent." Her emphasis on Smith *obtaining* her consent, rather than her *giving* it, reflected her torn feelings. As a close friend to Emma Smith, Elizabeth likely feared her acquiescence could be seen as some form of betrayal. Nor was Elizabeth the only family member to have doubts. Smith asked both her and Newel to keep the marriage secret from their son, Horace, whom the prophet feared would cause trouble. This was a hard strain on a family that had already sacrificed much for the faith.[30]

The clandestine sealing of Joseph Smith and Sarah Ann Whitney took place on July 27, 1842, only days before Smith went on the run from state authorities. It is the only polygamous sealing from the period that left a paper trail, in the form of a written record composed by the participants. The extraordinary document, framed as a revelation, exhibited the dynastic theology upon which polygamy was based. It was written in the voice of God and instructed Newel Whitney on how to perform the nuptials between Smith and his daughter. In some respects, the wording reflected common marital rites, including the direction to preserve themselves solely for each other—an odd guideline for a polygamous union. But in many ways the ritual was radical and unique. The sealing promised honor, immortality, and eternal life to the entire Whitney household. The union was a family ordeal. Sarah Ann would form a link between the Smith and Whitney families, based on "the lineage of [Smith's] Preast Hood," and would serve as assurance of salvation for Newell and Elizabeth, their ancestors, and even their eventual progeny. As he had done in his address to the Relief Society that same year, Joseph Smith expanded his definition of priesthood authority to encompass the family units on both earth and in heaven.[31]

These unions involved, in many cases, great personal sacrifice. As part of Smith's reforming mission, where society was patterned after priestly connections, these polygamous tethers were a counter to an American culture centered on individualism and mobility. Salvation was found not through individual advancement, but through ecclesiastical linkages. Though Sarah Ann Whitney rarely spoke of her struggle, one of her closest friends, Helen Mar Kimball, did. Like Whitney, Kimball was a teenager sealed to the prophet in a union that seemed more focused on familial connections than personal fidelity. Indeed, it was Helen Mar's father, apostle Heber C. Kimball, who proposed the marriage. According to his daughter, he had a strong desire to be attached to the prophet, and therefore offered her up. Helen Mar initially found the idea repugnant. But the benefits, at least to her father, were clear. As with the Whitney family, Smith told the Kimballs that this sealing would ensure salvation and exaltation for the entire family. Helen Mar eventually agreed to become "one Ewe Lamb" when her father "willingly laid her upon the alter." Like the patriarch Abraham, the Kimballs and Whitneys were willing to sacrifice family to secure God's favor.[32]

It is difficult to conclude that these teenage girls had much say in rejecting their fathers and the demands of their prophet. Those outside the faith would have seen the arrangement as an abusive trade between men: Joseph Smith promised salvation to Newel K. Whitney and Heber C. Kimball in exchange for access to their daughters. Neither Sarah Ann Whitney nor Helen Mar Kimball, however, described the unions as in any way physical. Perhaps, as was common, though not always consistent, in later polygamous Mormon unions, Smith put off consummation until the wives were adults. Regardless of whether he did indeed have sex with either young woman, the Abrahamic order upon which the unions were based, which required large progenies, implied that such relations would be expected in the future. Whitney and Kimball, not yet eighteen, were now sealed for eternity to a man in his mid-thirties. In return, they, their parents, and their extended family were granted celestial blessings in the next life.

Smith relished his new relationships. Especially once he was on the run from the Illinois authorities, he craved the moral support of his expanding family. At times this led to paradoxical appeals as he reached out to different parties. While in hiding, only three weeks after his sealing to Whitney, Joseph wrote a letter to his first wife, Emma, proposing a possible escape after which they could live together, somewhere beyond the reach of worldly political matters. Two days later, he asked Newel, Elizabeth, and Sarah to visit him at his "lonely retreat." He knew the risk involved, however, as Emma was still unaware of these associations. They must be careful, Smith cautioned the Whitneys, not to come when Emma was present. He provided precise instructions for how to avoid detection: Newell was to knock on a specific window, and Smith would open the door if Emma was not within. Smith admitted that this was a "heroick undertaking" on the part of all involved. He urged the Whitneys to burn his letter as soon as they finished reading it.[33]

Clandestine reunions were not the only, or even the most difficult, struggle for Sarah Ann Whitney. Her sealing to Smith changed the course of her entire future. Even though she was initiated into the Mormon church's inner circle, and linked forever to the faith's prophet, it was not clear to her how she could proceed as the secret wife of an already-married man. In an era when a woman's circumstances depended on finding a suitable mate, Whitney's choice was made for her. Even Smith realized that she needed some form of support. In early September, only three weeks after the proposed secret meeting while he was hiding from authorities, Smith deeded her a lot of land only one block from his own home. It was rare for a woman to own land in Nauvoo, and the written deed had to be altered to strike out every instance of *his* and replace it with *hers*. This transfer of land, signed by Smith (as trustee-in-trust for the church), Newel Whitney (as a justice of the peace), and William Clayton (as Smith's clerk), represented an early attempt to provide stability for plural wives. The next year, shortly after her own sealing, Helen Mar Kimball received a similar piece of property not far from Sarah Ann Whitney's.[34]

Joseph Smith spent most of the fall of 1842 in hiding, and the new polygamous unions came to a halt. That did not mean the scandalous concept was far from the city's mind, however. Smith worked hard to distance himself from rumors that coursed through the city. "Altho' I do wrong," he proclaimed to the Relief Society in late August, "I do not the wrongs that I am charg'd with doing." Nauvoo's women proved to be some of his staunchest supporters, working with other prominent citizens to publicly defend their prophet. For some, the efforts caused significant dissonance. When the city's newspaper published a statement from the Relief Society's leaders dismissing Bennett's claims, the signatures included those of Elizabeth Ann Whitney, Sarah M.

Cleveland, and Eliza R. Snow—two of whom, Cleveland and Snow, were secretly married to the prophet, and the other of whom, Whitney, was the mother of another of his wives. Snow expressed her anxiety in poetic form. "From the mass of confusion can harmony flow? / Or can peace from distraction come forth?" she wondered. "From out of corruption, integrity grow? / Or can vice unto virtue give birth?" Her parents, however, were unwilling to tolerate the paradox. A nearby newspaper published several accounts of Mormons renouncing their faith, and the Snows were among them.[35]

Others saw the scandal as an opportunity. One nearby non-Mormon resident, Udney Hay Jacob, suddenly found himself attracted to Mormonism. Jacob had previously been a staunch critic of the faith, and several years earlier urged the American government to exterminate the church before it proved to be a nuisance. His feelings had softened by 1842, however, especially after several members of his own family were baptized. And when Jacob learned they might share his previously held opinion that polygamy was a solution to America's social ills, he arranged for Nauvoo's press to publish an excerpt from a long manuscript he had written, titled "The Peacemaker," that November. Its central argument was that American society had become too permissive of female agency. Women laughed at men's "pretended authority," he claimed, and hissed "at the idea of your being the lords of creation." Polygamy, Jacob concluded, was the only way to restore the patriarchal authority necessary to stabilize American culture.[36]

It is supremely strange that, amid the Bennett controversy, Mormon officials saw fit to publish a work that explicitly defended polygamy. While the pamphlet's title page listed Joseph Smith as the printer, it is impossible to know the extent of the prophet's familiarity with the text. At a basic level, Jacob and Smith did share overlapping critiques of their surroundings: they both feared American democracy had resulted in a society characterized by confusion and instability. They, along with other primitivist patriarchs like Robert Matthias in New York, believed that the dissolution of male control was the root cause of the nation's problems.[37]

But the two would-be reformers disagreed on other foundational issues: where Smith's system provided a way for women to choose a new spouse and become connected to priesthood leadership, Jacob denounced divorce as a misbegotten tool of female liberation. Indeed, Jacob's system permitted women far less say than Smith's, as the Mormon system, at least as later defended by its female practitioners, emphasized a woman's choice to form eternal familial units, even if priesthood pressure curtailed consent. Jacob's pamphlet prompted an outcry in Nauvoo, and Smith distanced himself from his work by claiming it had been printed without his knowledge. It seems possible that Smith attempted, by publishing Jacob, to win over more Mormons to the idea of polygamy. If that was his plan, it failed—but that failure did not stop him from pressing forward, albeit privately.[38]

WHILE IN SPRINGFIELD AWAITING HIS HEARING in late December 1842 and early January 1843, Joseph Smith learned a number of important lessons in American law. Over the course of a week, he huddled with his attorney, Justin Butterfield, to discuss their best approach to the case. By this point, they knew that the prosecution's only hope was to argue that the circuit court had no right to try the extradition order, so they prepared to prove the authority of federal judges over interstate matters. The best precedent they could find for the argument, Butterfield decided, and one that would drive a deeper wedge between Missouri and Illinois, was the fugitive slave law. When states considered the extradition of those who had escaped slavery, he reasoned, it was the federal government that held jurisdiction; similarly, when considering the extradition of one state's citizen, the verdict had to belong to the same authority.

In court, Butterfield made the argument persuasively, invoking the accepted racial hierarchy of the time: if the lowest of the nation's residents, an enslaved African, had the right to appeal to federal courts, then so too did a white man. "Has not my client," Butterfield reasoned, "the Rights of a negro?" His appeal also hinted at the complex and evolving status of state and federal power. Nathaniel Pope, the judge, agreed with this reasoning, in part because it vindicated the authority of his own bench and was a blow to slave states like Missouri.[39]

As Mormons considered their place within the broader American nation, they also reconsidered the boundaries of their own community. Most directly, Smith's discussions with Butterfield likely prompted his new reflections about race and society. Amid his legal preparations, Willard Richards asked Smith's opinion on "the situation of the Negro." It was a significant question. The early 1840s witnessed a rise in both abolitionist activities in the North and pro-slavery agitation in the South. Despite the "gag rule" in Congress, according to which politicians surreptitiously agreed not to debate the politics of slavery, the "peculiar" institution became the country's most pressing topic. In the Mormon church's nomadic experience, it had been headquartered in both free and slave states. Illinois, though a free state, produced both the antislavery politician Abraham Lincoln as well as the popular sovereignty advocate Stephen A. Douglas.[40]

Nor was slavery the only racial issue of the time. Just a few years after the forced removal of Native tribes from the South to the Southwest, Americans continued to wonder whether white and Indian communities could live together. Indeed, the land the Mormons attempted to develop across the Mississippi River in Iowa reflected evolving practices with regard to the Indians. It had previously been made up of "half-breed" tracts set aside for the children of Anglo-American and indigenous parents, but was now seen as primarily reserved for white inhabitants. That region remained home to a number of Native tribes still trying to maintain a place in a nation increasingly centered on white supremacy, and their chiefs at times visited the Mormons to form diplomatic relations, but many white Americans believed the Natives' days were numbered.

How Joseph Smith and his followers address this dilemma reflected much about how they fit into their surrounding society. Everywhere the saints looked, they were confronted with America's racial intersections as white colonialism marched on apace. Yet Smith believed that the restored gospel was powerful enough to overcome racial distinctions and create

a sanctified society based on skin color. But there were boundaries
to this optimistic belief, because as Mormons tried to find ways to fit
within their culture, they often compromised on these idealistic values
and instead echoed the segregationist policies of their neighbors. Nauvoo's quest for a united family, therefore, simultaneously challenged
and reaffirmed the exclusionist policies of its time. The city served
as a malleable space with regard to race, and the Mormons' ideas and
practices proved them to be a threat to the mainstream white Protestant majority.

Elijah Able, the black convert who had been serving as a carpenter
and undertaker in Nauvoo, was probably on Smith's mind in Springfield when he discussed the place in his society for those of African
descent. If one were to visit Cincinnati, where Able was currently
preaching, Smith told Richards he would find an educated black missionary proudly representing the faith. Able was evidence, at least to
Smith, that racial uplift was possible. Enslaved status was merely a
product of circumstance, he explained, and the roles of blacks would
be quite different had they been born to privilege. Yet while Smith
said that, if he were in charge, he would place blacks on a path for
"national Equalization," he also confessed a desire to segregate all citizens according to their race—there were limits to his racial universalism. He had also planted the seeds for future conflict. The Book of
Abraham, published the previous year, claimed that the descendants
of Ham—a cultural code name for those with African ancestry—
were "cursed" with regard "to the priesthood." But the tether between
priesthood authority and racial lineage remained tenuous, at least for
the time being.[41]

These were far from mere theoretical questions, as Nauvoo was
home to a growing number of nonwhite residents. The city was originally envisioned as a gathering place for converts from all races and
backgrounds, and the surge in immigration to Nauvoo from other
states and nations created a melting pot. Unlike in Missouri, where
their Yankee sensibilities vexed their slaveholding neighbors, once in
Nauvoo the Mormons had more room to welcome freed persons of

color. At the very least, they hoped to join in Illinois's antislavery culture. Smith, for instance, encouraged slave owners who converted to the faith to free their slaves once they arrived in Nauvoo.[42]

Indeed, Joseph Smith had been consistently opposed to slavery, even if at times his opposition was not urgent. He never embraced the radical message of immediate abolitionists, one that he and many other white northerners feared would disrupt the nation even more. Despite Smith's appeals, however, the black population in Nauvoo never exceeded more than one or two dozen people. And of the few black residents, at least a handful did not arrive there by choice. Slavery was still tolerated, to a limited degree, within Illinois until 1848, and some Mormon converts took advantage of the legal loopholes, such as they were. Among Nauvoo's residents were John Burton, who was enslaved to Susan McCord Burton Robinson, and Lambson, an enslaved boy of Henry Jolley. It is likely that a few other young slaves, owned by Bryan Ward and Jane Hardin Nowlin, also lived in the city. At least two additional families may have visited the city with their slaves, though they did not settle in it. Even if he refused to acknowledge it, Joseph Smith's City of God was tainted by the sin of slavery. The presence of these enslaved servants belied the saints' universalist language.[43]

A small number of free blacks trickled into Nauvoo late in 1843. Jane Manning, who was born and raised in Connecticut, led a group of African American converts on a long and arduous journey from New England to Nauvoo on foot. Many were anxious to hear her conversion story. Dissatisfied with her New Canaan Congregational Church, Manning later recalled, she found the radical message of Mormon missionaries persuasive and fulfilling. Joseph Smith's gospel, she believed, allowed her to exercise spiritual gifts like speaking in tongues while simultaneously offering a form of fellowship. She was also drawn to the interracial nature of Mormonism, which did not segregate people due to their color of skin. She and her family eventually joined the faith and set off for Zion.

Once she arrived in the city, however, she was disappointed to discover more "hardship, trial, and rebuff." There remained one source

Photograph of Jane Manning James, circa 1862–1873. James was one of the few African Americans to join the Mormon faith and migrate to Nauvoo. GEORGE A. SMITH PHOTOGRAPH COLLECTION, LDS CHURCH HISTORY LIBRARY, SALT LAKE CITY.

of comfort: the Mormon prophet himself. When Manning shared her story with Smith, he slapped the knee of another man present and declared, "Isn't that faith?" Smith even offered her lodging in his house (which doubled as a hotel), hired her as a servant, and reassured her that she was now among friends. At least in Manning's retrospective account, Nauvoo provided a refuge from the racial strife in America.[44]

Manning became further integrated into Nauvoo's society due to her close proximity to the prophet. She was even exposed to aspects of his polygamous project, as she lived in the same home as some of Joseph Smith's wives. Manning later claimed that Joseph and Emma proposed that she be adopted into their family, but she turned them down because she did not understand what the offer entailed. The details of the proposal have not survived. Around the same time, however, Smith granted Manning a patriarchal blessing, invoking her sacred ancestry and promising her a blessed future. Because Manning had African ancestry, her blessing, like the one given to Elijah Able a decade before, was distinct from most others. Most Mormon converts, due to their Anglo-European ancestry, were assigned lineage going back to Ephraim; Manning, on the other hand, was deemed a descendant of "the lineage of Cainaan the Son of Ham." Nevertheless, she could still be redeemed, as the blessing promised that the same God who governed the times and seasons could also change her racial "mark." The blessing, which was conveyed in a written document, reveals that when Mormons spoke of overcoming racial distinctions through the gospel of Christ and the redemption of Zion, they meant that blacks and other people of color would have to become white.[45]

Nauvoo's residents were also in constant contact with nearby indigenous tribes. Mormons continued occasional proselytizing efforts and outreach to neighboring Native communities, and they received Native groups in turn. Joseph and George Herringin, brothers who were of both Shawnee and European heritage, resided in Nauvoo, as did Lewis Dana, a member of the Oneida tribe. Integration into the Mormon community and gospel provided these young men opportunities increasingly denied to Native Americans by Protestants. Though Christian missionaries in the early republic had hoped to redeem their "red" neighbors, their efforts were largely failing to attract converts, not least because those efforts were often paired, wittingly or not, with aggressive land grabs.[46]

Nauvoo's relationship with neighboring tribes invited suspicion from other whites. The saints were often accused of forming treasonous alliances with Natives that called into question both their allegiance as American citizens and their honor as white Americans. John

C. Bennett touched on this theme in his exposés, when he insisted the saints could never thrive on the American frontier because the land was set aside for "white folks, and not *Mormons.*" Bennett warned that Smith was conspiring with Native chiefs to overrun white settlements in the West. These accusations worried those in Nauvoo, as it put into question their ability to be patriotic Americans. Living on the edge of the American nation, both geographically and culturally, led Mormons to be especially concerned about their social standing as they attempted to balance theological desires for racial integration with complicated appeals for white citizenship.[47]

At times it was a particularly treacherous balancing act. An encounter with the Potawatomi Indians in 1843 proved a turning point. On April 18, three Potawatomi leaders, including Chief Apaquachawba, visited Nauvoo to ask Smith for help. The summit took place in Smith's own home, and a large group of Mormons gathered outside. Smith celebrated the occasion by slaughtering a prized ox. Once the meeting commenced, however, only a few representatives of either side, along with the interpreter, were invited into Smith's dining room. Beyond specific complaints concerning cattle thievery, the tribe was, according to the interpreter, dissatisfied with the way their land was consistently under threat from white settlers, and they hoped Smith would help them. Tribal leaders flattered the prophet by promising to see him as their father and deliverer, and invited the saints to join an alliance with them and nine other tribes. While sympathetic, Smith responded that he could not offer any assistance due to federal regulations that only government officials could work with tribes. He had learned that such alliances drew the ire of state and federal authorities, in addition to the distrust of non-Mormon whites in general, who generally saw Indians as a menace.[48]

Despite Smith's demurral, at least one participant was alarmed by the exchange. The meeting's interpreter, identified as "Mr. Hitchcock," originally refused to attend the meeting due to his distaste for Mormon leaders, and the actual proceedings seemed to confirm his views. He grew increasingly frustrated as the Native delegates made it clear that they saw Smith as an authority figure. He informed the chiefs that this was improper, and that they should instead contact federal authorities. The Potawatomi, however, were outraged at Hitchcock's suggestion, and instead promised to return to Nauvoo in the spring without him. Hitchcock, indignant, quickly reported the details of the meeting to the local Indian agent, Henry King. King forwarded the information to John Chambers, the territorial governor of Iowa, to warn of "a grand conspiracy" that was "entered into between the *Mormons and Indians* to destroy all the white settlements." This was a serious charge, and similar rumors continued to swirl for the next few years.[49]

Smith, for his part, tried to avoid further complications. When he wrote a letter to the Potawatomi leaders in August, likely expecting the text to be read by state authorities, he emphasized his unwillingness to perform any tasks that were contrary to federal law. He still insisted that the Mormons were friends of the Potawatomi and shared their interests, but beyond that, he balked at any formal alliance. He reserved the right, however, to exchange more information through his appointed agent—the implication being that this correspondence would be more confidential.[50]

The Potawatomi visit to Nauvoo captured some of the tensions, including racial tension, within Mormonism's societal mission. Mormon theology drove its followers to reach out to people increasingly seen as existing beyond the boundaries of white American Protestantism, and pragmatic alliances with other fringe groups were a way to secure much-needed support. And the fact that the Potawatomi reached out to the Mormons displayed a belief that they viewed the saints as strategically significant and potentially amenable to cooperation. But such entanglements also brought new dangers. On the violent and unruly frontier, where the realization of the American people's manifest destiny depended on firm loyalty to the nation, a close relationship between marginalized groups could be seen as treasonous. And Smith, finding himself in an increasing tenuous position due to his electoral maneuvering, did not want to arouse suspicion.

JOSEPH SMITH'S VINDICATION IN THE CIRCUIT COURT in Springfield in early January 1843 freed the prophet to move ahead with his reforming mission within Nauvoo. The missionaries he had sent east returned with reports that John C. Bennett's national tour had failed to raise a substantial anti-Mormon coalition, and the rumors of polygamy had failed to stick. Even Bennett's hold over Orson Pratt proved fleeting. In early January, Bennett wrote to Pratt and Sidney Rigdon, who he assumed were ready to permanently turn against Smith, about a plan to capture the prophet. Yet, instead of joining the conspiracy, Pratt immediately took the letter to Smith and thereby returned to the prophet's favor. He was rebaptized and restored to his apostolic post on a bitterly cold January 20, as the saints chipped away large chunks of ice in the Mississippi River in order to perform the ritual. But while Orson was able to reconcile himself with Smith, his wife, Sarah, forever maintained her belief that it was Smith who aimed to break up their marriage. They eventually divorced decades later.[51]

Meanwhile, Joseph Smith pushed forward with new plural unions with such speed that once again appeared, to some onlookers, as reckless. He was sealed to around a dozen plural wives between January and July 1843, the busiest polygamous period during his years in Nauvoo. Following the pattern established the previous summer, most of these new brides were young and single. Several were sisters. In March, Smith was sealed to Emily Dow Partridge, aged nineteen, and Eliza Maria Partridge, aged twenty-one, daughters of Edward and Lydia Partridge. The unions added to an already entangled web of relationships. Edward, who had served as the first Mormon bishop a decade earlier, had died in 1840. After his death, Lydia married William Huntington, whose daughters Zina and Presendia had been sealed to Smith in 1841. Lucy Walker, aged seventeen, and Almera Woodward Johnson, aged thirty, also came from families with deep Mormon roots, and were among those sealed to Smith in this stretch. But not all of Smith's new plural wives were already connected to him. Ruth Sayers, in her mid-thirties, was married to a non-Mormon man; she and her husband had provided Smith shel-

Sudcliffe Maudsley, portrait of Elizabeth Partridge. Partridge, along with
her sister, was sealed to Joseph Smith
during a slew of plural marriages in
early 1843. PIONEER MEMORIAL MUSEUM,
INTERNATIONAL SOCIETY OF DAUGHTERS OF UTAH
PIONEERS, SALT LAKE CITY.

ter from state authorities the previous August. Like Nauvoo, Smith's
polygamous net captured all sorts.

Though they were silent at the time, nearly all of these women later
emphasized the difficulty that came with Smith's proposal. Several of
the younger wives were originally approached the previous summer,
likely around the time of Whitney's sealing. Emily Dow Partridge and
Lucy Walker both remembered being asked during the spring of 1842,
but they waited until the next year, when they turned nineteen and
seventeen, respectively, to agree. As before, Smith typically used an
intermediary, like Agnes Coolbrith, an older woman already sealed to
the prophet, to first broach the idea of the union. The sealing's justification was often linked to polygamy's potential for stemming the
world's anarchic tide, as well as binding families in an unbreachable
string that would last the eternities. Smith's promises of eternal salvation, of course, did not ease the difficulty the unions presented to
these women. Eliza Maria Partridge admitted that Smith's proposal

was a terrible trial, but also that she still had the utmost confidence in him. Priesthood sealings required sacrifice but promised spiritual and temporal stability. It was a high price to pay.[52]

Even as Smith added new wives, his prior relationships required more and more attention. As the secret wife to the prophet, Sarah Ann Whitney posed a problem, given that, despite her high social status, she would have to turn down suitors. Perhaps the young bride also felt regret. As a reminder of her promised reward, Smith provided her a personal blessing on March 23, 1843, nearly eight months after the initial sealing. Written in Smith's own hand and on ornate paper ceremonially decorated to match its significance, the blessing promised that God would crown her with glory throughout eternity. Further, perhaps taking into account her brother Horace, who Smith worried would be enraged over the clandestine union, the blessing promised that any member of their family would be saved in this eternal unit, regardless of how they conducted themselves. In an era when Americans of all denominations worried about the state of their own souls, and the souls of their families, the entire Whitney dynasty was promised a heavenly reward. To Sarah Ann, the written blessing must have been bittersweet: it represented both the life she gave up as well as the lives she helped save. The document remained in her family's possession for over a century.[53]

Still, the problem remained: to the public, Whitney appeared single, and her refusal to consider potential suitors was bound to raise suspicion. A solution was put in place the day after she turned eighteen. Her aunt, Caroline Whitney Kingsbury, had died giving birth the previous October, leaving her husband, Joseph Kingsbury, a widower with a small child. Smith proposed a civil union between Whitney and Kingsbury, which would successfully take his young bride off the market.

But what could he give Kingsbury in return for serving as a public proxy for Smith's private marriage? Smith offered him the chance to be sealed to his deceased wife, Caroline. "Thy companion Caroline who is now dead," Smith promised in a separate blessing, "thou shalt

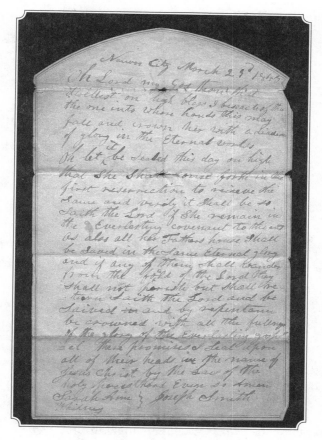

Joseph Smith's blessing of Sarah Ann Whitney, March 23, 1843, in Smith's own handwriting. Perhaps the only document related to polygamy that was personally written by Joseph Smith. Whitney kept the blessing, which promised salvation to her whole family, her entire life. LDS CHURCH HISTORY LIBRARY, SALT LAKE CITY.

have in the first Reserection." By helping Smith handle a difficult situation, Kingsbury was rewarded as the first Mormon sealed to a deceased spouse. The sealing was, in a way, an extension of existing practices, given the popular ritual of baptisms for the dead. But Kingsbury's sealing was the first time the doctrine of vicarious ordinances was expanded into the marital realm. Kingsbury jumped at the opportunity. The "pretended marriage" between him and Sarah Ann, as Kingsbury put it, took place within a month of Smith's proposal to him.[54]

Though Joseph Kingsbury was only sealed to one woman—his marriage to Sarah Ann Kimball was only valid in the civic sphere— the sealing to his departed wife opened new theological possibilities. Soon enough, the connection between plural marriage and sealing to deceased spouses, introduced on pragmatic grounds, became a driving idea in Nauvoo. For a man whose first wife had died, but who was now married to another woman, the doctrine provided an avenue through which he could be eternally united with both spouses. The practice offered simultaneously a triumph over death and an expansion of familial fidelity.

It also helped persuade one of polygamy's most significant skeptics: Hyrum Smith. As the prophet's brother, and presiding patriarch over the entire church, Hyrum was second in authority only to Joseph himself. Yet he had remained in the dark concerning polygamy. Due to Hyrum's strict, traditional sense of morality, evident in his visceral reaction to the John C. Bennett scandal, Joseph had been hesitant to reveal the practice to his brother. Teaming up with William Law and William Marks, and often using the High Council as his vehicle, Hyrum was devoted to weeding out what he believed was rampant immorality, including polygamy, in the city. As Hyrum said about polygamy in spring 1843, "If an angel from heaven should come and preach such doctrine," you "would be sure to see his cloven foot and cloud of blackness over his head." William Clayton even recorded rumors of a plot, designed by Hyrum, to capture any men involved in the practice. Joseph was under increasing pressure from within his own family.[55]

Joseph saw that emphasizing the eternal nature of marital unions was the best way to win over dedicated opponents like Hyrum. Only those unions sealed through this new priesthood power, Joseph Smith proclaimed on May 16, could survive death. The prophet preached the same idea again and again, including at a general meeting five days later. Hyrum, unable to confront his own brother, finally decided to go to Brigham Young and beg for the truth. Young acquiesced and explained how the practice would allow Hyrum to be sealed not only to his current wife, Mary Fielding, but also to his deceased wife, Jerusha. Rather than a scandalous excuse to justify fleeting trysts, then, polygamy could forge eternal relationships, for the good of all. That was apparently enough for Hyrum, who finally accepted that not only were the rumors true, but the practice was justified. Though a quick conversion, Hyrum never looked back.[56]

It was a turning point, both for Hyrum and for Nauvoo more generally. In a private gathering the next Monday, Hyrum Smith and Brigham Young were both sealed to their living and dead wives: Mary Fielding served as proxy for Jerusha Barden, and Brigham's current wife, Mary Ann Angell, stood in for the deceased Miriam Works. For Joseph, his brother's conversion removed one of the biggest threats to his larger project, which still remained largely private.[57]

It was around this time that Joseph Smith also took the risk of telling his wife, Emma, about his plural unions and the doctrine behind them. Prior to this, he had concluded that the only way to preserve their relationship was to keep the practice secret. His private letters and diaries, even during the periods when he was actively courting new polygamous wives, continued to express a deep and sincere affection to his first wife. At least in Joseph's mind, there was no contradiction between his loyalty to Emma and his other marriages.

There are no contemporaneous records that captured Emma's initial response to the revelations, and we do not know when, exactly, she heard them. In fact, her understanding seemed to evolve over the course of 1842 and 1843, which suggests that Joseph did not tell her everything all at once. It appears that sometime in mid-May 1843, she agreed to Joseph being sealed to four women: the Partridge sisters, whom Joseph had already wedded two months previous, and the Lawrence sisters, teenage orphans over whom Joseph had been an appointed guardian. All four girls, ranging in age from seventeen to twenty-two, already lived in the Smith home, and Emma probably felt a warm connection with them. She also likely assumed that the sealing solely related to the eternal world, with no carnal implications for the present. Joseph and the Partridges went through the motion of a second sealing on May 23 in order to hide from Emma the existence of the first. Within a week, then, Joseph Smith had seemingly converted two of his closest relations—his brother and his wife—to polygamy. Two days after Hyrum was sealed to his current and deceased wives, Joseph and Emma were sealed for eternity in a ritual that sacralized their already-existent marriage.[58]

Yet where Hyrum would be a stalwart defender of the practice, Emma's support proved tenuous. On the same day she witnessed her husband being sealed to four other women, she also discovered these were not his first plural unions. Emily Dow Partridge later claimed that Emma expressed immediate regret after the ritual. "From that very hour," Partridge wrote, "Emma was our bitter enemy."[59]

She did not have to look far for more incriminating evidence. The same day of the Partridge sealings, Emma discovered Joseph and Eliza R. Snow together, behind a locked door. Enraged, she attempted to burst into the room to confront them. Emma now worried that these sealings were more than just spiritual in nature. In July, she angrily confronted Snow, her former confidante and close friend. Snow reflected in her diary that darkness now reigned over Emma's heart. Emma, of course, believed she was merely seeking justice. Things did not improve the next month, when Emma discovered what appeared to be love letters written by Snow and addressed to her husband. At one point, Joseph was worried Emma might seek revenge by starting her own affair with the prophet's close friend, William Clayton. "She thought that if [Joseph] would indulge himself she would too," Joseph warned Clayton, though it appeared there was not much to the rumor.[60]

In July, after several tumultuous weeks, Hyrum Smith believed he found a solution to the problem. While discussing the issue in Joseph's office on the second floor of the red-brick store, he urged the prophet to dictate a revelation detailing the doctrine of polygamy. Surely, he believed, Emma could be convinced when she understood the doctrine in its entirety. William Clayton served as Joseph's scribe, as the Mormon prophet dictated a 3,300-word revelation "on the order of the priesthood." Building on the theological developments from the previous year, the revelation justified the unions by harking back to the ancient patriarchs "Abraham, Isaac, and Jacob." The text was the culmination of Smith's Abrahamic project, in that it presented polygamy as "the works of Abraham." Smith and his close associates were to fulfill this patriarchal tradition, and thereby bring structure to a chaotic world.[61]

Indeed, the document emphasized authority and order. "Behold," God decreed, "mine house is a house of order," and "not a house of confusion." The revelation also vindicated the priesthood's governing power. It declared all covenants, contracts, bonds, oaths, and alliances not performed by the priesthood to be inadequate and invalid. The rewards for those who were sealed by this priesthood authority, on the other hand, were clear: all those who were sealed, both men and women, would inherit thrones, kingdoms, principalities, powers, and dominions. But this divine destiny was strictly gendered: husbands received power and authority over worlds without end, while wives produced the "seed" that expanded their husband's dominion. This vision of the afterlife reaffirmed a patriarchal structure on earth, and expanded it forward indefinitely. In an American society where many reformers were striving for equality, mobility, and representation, the Mormon cosmos countered with a dynastic vision centered on authority, hierarchy, and dominion.[62]

Smith's revelation failed to convince its primary audience. After three hours of dictation, Hyrum raced across the street to the prophet's home to meet with Emma. But instead of finding a willing convert, he encountered only resistance. Hyrum returned to Joseph and informed the prophet that he had never received a more severe scolding in his life. Emma, Hyrum related, insisted that she did not believe a word of the new revelation. Unsurprised, given the events of the previous months, Joseph remarked, "I told you, you did not know Emma as well as I did."[63]

The next day, Joseph and Emma had one of the most difficult conversations of their marriage, to little avail. At Emma's request—and after

Joseph had copies made—she was allowed to express her frustration by destroying the document. Their relations did not improve. A month later, Emma threatened Joseph with a divorce. In an attempt to mollify her concerns and assure her protection, Joseph signed over sixty lots in Nauvoo to his wife and their children, a substantial amount for any individual, as well as a riverboat that they had hoped would someday be a source of financial stability. Yet Emma did not back down at all until Joseph promised not to take any more plural wives that fall. With one exception, he remained true to his word.[64]

Yet the circle of polygamists in Nauvoo continued to grow. Joseph Smith himself had married around six more women that summer, prior to his confrontation with Emma, and his closest advisors entered into similarly numerous unions of their own. Few fully understood the implications. Vilate Kimball had earlier witnessed her husband, Heber, sealed to another wife, and her teenage daughter, Helen Mar, sealed to the prophet. Now that others were being brought into the practice as well, some of the new plural wives turned to her for comfort and guidance. Yet, she admitted in a candid letter to Heber, she hardly understood polygamy herself, and therefore urged the distraught women to go elsewhere for solace. Vilate worried that her friends and neighbors might be moving too fast. The familial system that was supposed to bring order seemed to be bordering on chaos.[65]

MUCH LIKE JOSEPH SMITH'S DOMESTIC ARRANGEMENTS, Illinois state politics remained murky in 1843. In the wake of Smith's trial in Springfield, many assumed the prophet would take a step back from the political arena. Nathaniel Pope, the circuit court judge who dismissed Missouri's extradition order, certainly advised him to do as much. For a time, Smith took the counsel to heart. He published a notice in one of Nauvoo's newspapers signaling that he would decline any attempt by state politicians to win his endorsement. "I think it would be well for politicians to regulate their own affairs," he reasoned, "that I may attend strictly to the spiritual welfare of the church." These words fit what most Americans expected of religious ministers.[66]

Not all were convinced. One non-Mormon resident of Nauvoo, Sylvester Emmons, wondered if Smith was sincere. Emmons wrote Smith to ask for his blessing to run for mayor. Surely, Emmons reasoned, if Smith was ready to leave the political sphere, he would not serve another term as the city's chief executive. Emmons assured Smith that, if elected, he would preserve the church's prosperity by promoting its interests. Given the unlikelihood that a non-Mormon could receive enough support to win the mayoralty, Emmons was probably merely testing Smith. Regardless, Smith ran for reelection the next week, winning in a landslide. Despite promises to the contrary, his political career was far from an end.[67]

Even after their recent success in Springfield, the saints retained their wariness of state and federal authorities. Their most pressing issue was maintaining Nauvoo's sovereignty as outlined in the city charter. In his inaugural address as governor the previous December, Thomas Ford admitted to an interest in modifying Nauvoo's charter to bring it in line with other cities in the state. The saints took Ford's words as a threat, and they soon learned the governor's sentiment was shared by many. William Smith, the prophet's brother and Nauvoo's elected representative in Springfield, warned the church that repealing the charter had suddenly become a common subject for debate in the state legislature. Joseph likened such an act to highway robbery. Fortunately for the saints, a combination of goodwill resulting from Smith's habeas corpus hearings and the pressing urgency of other state matters meant discussions of Nauvoo's charter never progressed beyond rhetoric. The final attempt at a bill failed in mid-March 1843, just before the legislature adjourned until December. The crisis, at least for a moment, appeared over.[68]

The more immediate threat came once again from Missouri, which tried again to bring the Mormon prophet to justice. In June, the Missouri governor indicted Smith for treason against the state, based on his actions during the 1838 conflict. Thomas Ford, though sympathetic to Smith in some ways, and though he desired the Mormon vote, was committed to the laws of the land. He issued an arrest warrant for the prophet on June 17, 1843. The wheels were once more in motion for a legal clash.[69]

Again, actually apprehending Smith proved difficult. Joseph Reynolds, the sheriff of Jackson County, Missouri, was assigned the task, and was accompanied to Nauvoo by Harmon T. Wilson, the deputy sheriff of Hancock County. Smith was nowhere to be found, as he and his wife had left to visit Emma's family in nearby Dixon, Illinois, several days before. News of the warrant energized the city. "How long must the innocent be harass'd and perplexed?" wondered Eliza R. Snow. When Smith received news of the warrant the next day, he and his wife decided to once more go into hiding.[70]

Shrewder than their predecessors, Reynolds and Wilson posed as Mormon missionaries, gained an audience with Smith on June 23, took him captive at gunpoint, and, after securing fresh horses, were ready to set off for Missouri. Yet the prophet's friends and followers once again rushed to his defense. Neighbors physically blocked the officers from leaving, which allowed Smith to quickly obtain legal counsel, secure a writ of habeas corpus, and sue Reynolds and Wilson for false imprisonment. The two arresting officers were then themselves arrested by county officials, while Smith remained in their custody. The perplexed and intertwined company set out for Quincy, a seat of the circuit court, to hear Smith's writ of habeas corpus.

They never made it. The citizens of Nauvoo, including the Nauvoo Legion, sprung into action. The city teemed with men ready to fight for their leader, and a posse of eighty set off by foot, and another fifty by water, all armed. This, they believed, was why the Nauvoo Legion existed. The men soon found their prophet and, at gunpoint, brought the group to Nauvoo where Smith received a grand celebration on June 30, accompanied by a military escort, a band, and exquisitely dressed ladies on horseback. The crisis had become a spectacle. They proceeded to a formal dinner at Smith's home, where, as a demonstration of hospitality, Reynolds and Wilson, confounded by the whole ordeal, were seated at the head of the table.

After the meal, Nauvoo's municipal court, as expected, discharged

Smith with a writ of habeas corpus. Just like the previous August, the men who had been tasked with bringing Smith to Missouri left Nauvoo bewildered and empty-handed. The Mormon prophet once again escaped Missouri's justice.[71]

The episode reaffirmed to the saints that they had found the legal mechanism to preserve their freedom. Smith proclaimed to a large gathering how thankful he was to be tried by Nauvoo and not Missouri, as only the former could bring true justice. He went further than ever before, however, in declaring that Nauvoo's city and municipal authorities had as much power as state and federal courts due to their city charter. The "secret" to governance, he explained, was that Illinois had "ceded unto us our vested rights" and could never "take them from us." Nauvoo, in his mind, was sovereign, as it possessed unlimited power, while circuit, state, and federal courts were limited in their purviews. Any attempt to infringe on that authority would result in bloodshed. Democracy, especially in Jacksonian America, promised both equal protection and direct representation. The only bodies that could back up that promise, Smith believed, were city governments and municipal courts.[72]

Though Smith had embarrassed them as a group, Illinois politicians were still anxious to make the most of the situation. The lawyer who helped Smith escape extradition in Dixon, Cyrus Walker, had served as a friend and informal advisor to the saints for several years. But now he was running as the Whig candidate for Illinois's sixth congressional district, and he believed he could use the Mormon vote. Walker traveled with Smith back to Nauvoo on June 30. While there, Smith declared during his speech that Walker had supported his release, and the prophet pledged him his support in return. The city's newspaper followed in praising Walker for his actions and tenacity. Walker, understandably, interpreted this to mean that he had secured Nauvoo's vote. The Democrats immediately began speaking of foul play. One Democratic newspaper even accused the Whigs of conspiracy: it seemed quite a coincidence, they noted, that Walker was "miraculously" within a few miles when Smith was arrested.[73]

Walker was not the only politician to seek the backing of the Mormons, however. Though he had just signed an arrest warrant for
Smith a few weeks previous, Governor Ford, a Democrat, quickly came
around to the saints' defense. He had previously chastised the saints for
believing the Nauvoo municipal court held authority over state writs,
but now he chose not to speak out against Smith's equally dubious discharge. He also refused Missouri governor Reynolds's request to forcibly remove Smith with an armed militia. Instead, he dispatched a close
friend, Mason Brayman, to investigate whether Reynolds's accusations
that Smith had committed treason in Missouri held any merit. Brayman spent a few days in Nauvoo, collected a handful of affidavits, and
concluded that the Mormons were not to blame. After conferring with
Ford, Brayman insisted to Smith that the writ for his extradition was a
dead letter, and that there would be no more attempts to remove Smith
to Missouri. At the same time, the Mormons' delegate in Springfield
reported that Ford's party, the Democrats, were talking of reaffirming
Nauvoo's charter, including its innovations in habeas corpus, a message that was reiterated when Joseph P. Hoge, the Democratic candidate for Congress, visited Nauvoo in late July.[74]

This placed Smith in a difficult dilemma. On the one hand, Cyrus
Walker, the Whig, had not only been a personal friend for several
years, but he had been instrumental in keeping Smith out of Missouri.
On the other hand, Joseph Hoge represented a Democratic establishment that supported Nauvoo's rights and charter. For whom would the
saints vote? Smith genuinely struggled with the situation. He hedged
during a July 4 oration, coyly proclaiming that he never influenced
how his followers voted. Onlookers, of course, knew otherwise, and
they were keen to receive a signal from him.[75]

In the event, Smith tried to appease both sides and ended up satisfying neither. He maintained his personal commitment to vote for
Walker, but allowed his brother Hyrum to direct the Mormon vote to
the Democratic candidate, Hoge. In a move that confused many in
Nauvoo, in mid-July, Smith declared that he could no longer prophesy,
as Hyrum possessed the birthright. Though he later claimed that he

only said it "ironically," Smith had seemed to validate Hyrum's prophetic authority and diminish his own. In a carefully choreographed
dance, Hyrum announced on August 7, a day before the election, that
God wanted the people of Nauvoo to vote for Hoge. Joseph followed up
by claiming that while he had personally promised his vote for Walker,
that decision was purely based on old friendship, not revelation. Further, he added, "I never knew Hyrum to say he ever had a revelation
and it failed." The implications were clear: Nauvoo would support
Hoge and the Democrats.[76]

Not everyone who witnessed the spectacle was pleased with this outcome. William Law, a counselor in the First Presidency and close confidant to Smith, was outraged. Still hoping the saints would support the
Whigs, Law denied the validity of Hyrum's revelation and reaffirmed
Joseph's support for Walker. Smith, however, would not be stopped.
He publicly chastised Law, denounced him for attempting to dictate
the prophet's feelings, and forbade him from speaking on his behalf.
Law, wounded, stepped down. His problems with the Smith brothers
would only fester.[77]

For a brief moment, Smith's solution to the dilemma appeared
to work. Democratic candidates, including Hoge, received an overwhelming majority of Mormon votes on August 8. One nearby newspaper estimated that Nauvoo voted for Hoge by a margin of 1,083 to
90. Other Mormon communities in western Illinois produced similar
tallies. Smith's elaborate ploy to fulfill his personal promise to Walker,
maintain the link between prophetic authority and democratic elections, and still rig the vote for the Democrat Hoge, was laid bare. Non-
Mormon observers took note. One woman in attendance at that August
7 meeting rightfully identified this interplay as a "political ruse."
Another onlooker described "a deep game" played by the Democrats
and Mormons, in which the former would "screen Joe from justice,"
and the latter would "secure their vote." Smith's plan was successful in
the short term, but it would do lasting damage to his cause.[78]

To Nauvoo's neighbors, Smith's actions breached the delicate balance between religious and political authority. Mormonism's bloc

voting in the past had appeared problematic, but it could at least be justified: a minority group was supporting candidates who represented its interests. The electoral machinations in August 1843, however, invited further suspicion and scorn. The separation of church and state, to the extent the principle actually held sway in the early republic, was primarily seen as a safeguard against this very type of backroom dealing. The founders had assumed that religious belief would play a role in political action, but a democratized society required a line to be drawn between private conviction and clerical influence. The tenuous American experiment in self-rule and democratic governance was too delicate to survive a growing religious body that voted based on the dictates of a prophetic leader rather than individual conscience.

The episode proved a turning point in Mormonism's relationship with Illinois. No politician could again trust Smith and his followers. A nearby resident wrote that because the Mormons had dominated the previous election, there was now a "considerable stir"; some people believed they could be forced to move out of the county. Things never improved. Thomas Ford later wrote that after the fateful election of August 1843, both political parties were determined to drive the Mormons from Illinois. Smith and his followers may have originally appeared a heretical but benign phenomenon, but they now seemed to be a threat to the democratic process. And Smith's heresies only became more pronounced.[79]

CHAPTER 5

Branches

I feel that I have opposed a base error and that the eternal God
is on my side, and if I am persecuted it is because I vindicate principles
of virtue and justice.

—WILLIAM LAW[1]

Nauvoo Mansion, Nauvoo, Illinois. Constructed to be Joseph Smith's primary residence as well as a hotel, the stately structure—originally painted white—was completed in 1843. This photograph was taken decades later. LDS CHURCH HISTORY LIBRARY,
SALT LAKE CITY.

The last few months of 1843 were among the most troubling William Law ever lived through. He had already had an eventful life. Born in Ireland in 1809, Law, who possessed a small frame, round face, and brown hair, migrated to Upper Canada with his family about a decade later. After meeting and marrying Jane Silverthorn in present-day Toronto in 1833, the two were introduced and converted to the Mormon faith by apostle John Taylor in 1837. Law quickly exhibited his leadership abilities by serving as presiding elder over the local congregation for over a year, before leading a group of converts to Nauvoo in 1839.

The new disciple was not disappointed when he arrived. "Bro Joseph is truly a wonderful man," he wrote fellow convert Isaac Russell shortly after meeting Joseph Smith for the first time. Law kept a close eye on Smith, worried he might actually be a fraud, but soon concluded he was everything Law hoped he would be. Smith was similarly impressed with Law, and soon elevated him to the First Presidency, the highest council in the church, which typically only featured three men. By all accounts, Law proved to be a reliable counselor to the temperamental and spontaneous prophet. He was talented, a man of means, and a reminder to critics—and to the Mormons themselves—that not all of Mormonism's converts came from the lower rungs of society. He also publicly defended Smith by signing affidavits contradicting John C. Bennett's scandalous accusations and insisting that Smith had never practiced polygamy. Law eventually built a modest frame home just one block down the street from Smith's own house. He was both physically and spiritually proximate to the Mormon leader.[2]

Yet events would soon shake that allegiance. Smith's bold actions during the congressional elections in August 1843 soured Law on his beloved leader. When he tried to oppose Hyrum Smith's political maneuvering to elect a Democrat to office, instead of the Whig to whom Joseph had pledged support, Law was publicly chastised by the prophet. Smarting from this humiliation, Law was further discomfited once he learned details of Smith's polygamous unions. "Fearful and terrible, yea most distressing have been the scenes through which we have past, during the last few months," a crestfallen Law wrote on New Year's Day 1844. "Through our religious zeal we harkened to the teachings of man, more than to the written word of God." The man Law believed would revolutionize society now seemed a traitor to the cause.[3]

To William Law, Joseph Smith's political and sexual sins were inextricable. He had emerged as a tyrant who flagrantly broke the mores and laws of American society, and who had to be stopped as a result. Mormonism, under Smith, had become an insult to Law's democratic sensibilities. For others in Nauvoo, however, these same developments only reaffirmed the church's divine trajectory. The faith would soon be driven into competing camps as Smith's concurrent political and polygamous experiments entered a new and blatant stage. The medley of Mormonism's democratic dissent was reaching a crescendo.

JOHN A. FRIERSON SPENT HIS LIFE TRYING to bring order to the frontier. A native South Carolinian, Frierson was one of many easterners who relocated to the new Iowa Territory in the 1830s. As one of the early arrivals, Frierson helped establish a new society. He served in the territorial legislature, was appointed brigadier general in the militia, and even worked as a surveyor. His duties included identifying the site for the territory's new capital in 1839. He grew accustomed to building things from scratch.

Frierson moved to Quincy, Illinois, in the 1830s and became acquainted with the Mormon community when they arrived in 1839. He was moved by their history of persecution. Though he never joined the faith, he saw the saints as an embattled people who had suffered the wrath of America's mobocratic spirit. Their experience in Missouri was an outrage to democratic order, in his view. In October 1843, Frierson petitioned the congressman from his home state of South Carolina, F. H. Elmore, to consider the Mormons' plight. It was time to "put down mobocracy in our land," he urged, and for the federal government to avenge the wrongs committed against the Mormon church by the state of Missouri. The proud state of South Carolina, he believed, should lead the charge in helping the saints secure justice. Frierson was not willing to stand idly by while innocent citizens suffered.[4]

Frierson, not satisfied with just writing a petition, was also willing to directly help the Mormons. A colleague of his and fellow prominent resident of Quincy, Joseph L. Heywood, wrote Joseph Smith to volunteer Frierson's services. If Nauvoo's leaders were interested in sending another petition to Congress, Heywood explained, Frierson was the man to help them do it. The Mormon prophet readily agreed and invited him to Nauvoo. This was not the first time Smith welcomed gentile help, nor would it be the last.[5]

When Frierson arrived in the city on November 25, 1843, he was probably surprised to find a bustling town of at least ten thousand people, all in the shadow of an imposing temple that was still under construction but already two stories tall. Other guests from the period noted being struck by the "spacious fabric" of the temple on the hill that loomed over the small houses scattered on the flats, as well as the "wretched cabins" that "littered the landscape." Smith, for his part, was anxious to greet the visitor, but because it was late in the evening, they decided not to convene until the next morning. Frierson had a lot to take in.[6]

At the planned time, the men gathered in the recently completed Nauvoo Mansion. One of the largest homes in Nauvoo, it featured a Greek Revival frame structure and had two tall stories. Originally built for the Smith family, who moved in only two months before Frierson's visit, the home boasted a large wing that served as a spacious hotel. One Nauvoo resident described it as "very elegant and tastefully finished." The dining hall was intended to host large parties. There was also a secret hiding place in the attic for Joseph Smith that could only be accessed through a hidden door in an upstairs closet. Frierson was likely one of this room's first distinguished visitors.[7]

Smith presented Frierson with previous petitions the Mormons had written, including affidavits from Parley Pratt, Brigham Young, Hyrum Smith, Lyman Wight, George Pitkin, and Sidney Rigdon, all of which had been sworn before the Nauvoo municipal court the previous July. Frierson wanted all the material he could gather at his disposal. Two days later, Frierson drafted a memorial to Congress that described the church's plight in Missouri and made a plea for redress. If a foreign nation perpetrated these crimes, Frierson argued, the federal government would not hesitate to step in. So why not do the same for those harmed by fellow citizens? But the saints were not willing to let Frierson do all the work: attached to the memorial was a fifty-foot-long sheet that included 3,419 signatures. Known as the "scroll petition," the memorial, in complete form, symbolized the breadth of the Mormons' appeal for federal support.[8]

It also marked a shift in Mormon political thought. After the August 1843 elections, Nauvoo's Mormons knew they could no longer rely on state legislators or political parties for support. Their only possible support, they believed, was the federal government. But in rejecting state sovereignty, Mormon leaders were swimming against contemporary currents. Most Americans during the antebellum period, especially during and after Andrew Jackson's presidency, believed that political authority resided at the local level. The democratic promise of the young republic implied that sovereignty ruled best when it resided closest to the people.

But what happened when local residents felt their rights were being trampled upon by their neighbors and the state refused to intervene? Several political observers, including Alexis de Tocqueville, had noted this threat, and Americans were beginning to recognize its danger. The most prominent advocates for a stronger federal government were the abolitionists, who saw that only the federal government could free enslaved African Americans. But their cause itself remained a minority position in the 1840s. Indeed, it would not be until the Civil War that the nation shifted the balance of power toward federal control. But the Mormons were already making similar arguments.[9]

Nor were the abolitionists or the Mormons alone. Some of America's earliest political founders had held similar concerns, of course. During debates over the Constitution's ratification, James Madison denounced the "spirit of locality" that he feared could undermine social cohesion. He wanted the federal government to possess a veto over state actions, but he was overruled. By the mid-1790s, Madison had embraced the Jeffersonian philosophy of state sovereignty, which eventually triumphed over the Federalist emphasis on centralized power. And although there was a brief resurgence of federal power during the presidential administration of John Quincy Adams in the 1820s, the era ushered in by Jackson and the Democratic Party enshrined, for the most part, the supremacy of state authority (even as Jackson himself used the power of the federal government to remove the Indian tribes of the Southeast).[10]

The Mormons felt that the reigning philosophy put their existence in peril. In 1843, Joseph Smith published an essay, written by John Taylor, that declared all political systems, including democratic governments, "have failed in all their attempts to promote eternal power, peace, and happiness." Even America, "which possesses greater resources than any other, is rent, from center to circumference, with party strife, political intrigues, and sectional interest." The nation was not equipped to preserve the rights of minority groups.[11]

Nauvoo residents did not just add their names to the memorial; they also, at Smith's urging, requested support from their native states. What resulted were the most fervent appeals for federal intervention in the mid-nineteenth century outside of the antislavery debate. Most of the petitions drew on tales of patriotic lineage and devotion. Together, they were a forerunner to later political theories that posited that a strong national state was critical for preserving democratic rights. Joseph Smith, with the assistance of his scribe William Phelps, wrote an appeal to the "Green Mountain Boys" of Vermont, the state of his birth. But he was just the first—Parley Pratt wrote to New York, Benjamin Andrews to Maine, Sidney Rigdon to Pennsylvania, Phineas Richards to Massachusetts, and Alphonso Young to Tennessee. The saints were ready and anxious to prove their allegiance to national heritage and ideals.[12]

While the saints had previously requested federal aid and redress, they now took a further step by appealing for federal protection. On December 8, Joseph Smith suggested to the City Council that they petition Congress to place Nauvoo under federal jurisdiction and make the Nauvoo Legion an extension of federal troops. Rather than remaining under the control of a state government, prone to corruption and prejudice, they wished to be placed under federal rule as a designated territory.[13]

These measures seemed desperate, but they were the saints' last hope. When they discussed the memorial again a week later, on December 16, Smith offered his most expansive view yet of the Nauvoo city charter. As he reasoned, in an innovative reading of city, state, and federal law, the Nauvoo charter granted them the powers of a city-state, and since states had the privilege to request the help of federal troops, so did Nauvoo. The American government was bound to respond. Months later, Smith declared that if they could secure federal protection, it would finally place them on firm footing and establish Nauvoo as an independent government. This, he believed, was their only path to survival.[14]

The resulting petition, directed to both the US House of Representatives and Senate, outlined the church's past troubles with state governance and presented Smith's radical solutions. Smith requested that the government designate Nauvoo a federal territory, outside of state authority and under the direct supervision of the federal government, at least until Missouri restored all past damages and Illinois promised to protect all Mormon inhabitants. Further, the petition requested that Smith, as mayor, be empowered to raise an army of American troops to assist the Nauvoo Legion in repelling mobs. Though bold, Smith felt confident in these demands. In his journal, he prophesied that if Congress failed to grant their petition, the entire government would be broken up and "there shall nothing be left of them, not even a grease spot."[15]

But as quick as Smith was to denounce America's political order, he lacked the patience to see if his gambit would produce the desired result. By the time the petitions were debated in Congress several months later, the Mormon prophet was already exploring new options, both mundane and extreme. His was not an agenda for prolonged legal processes; the Mormon plight was much too urgent. But the principles at the core of these federal petitions—distrust in local government, fear of democratic excess, and the need for sovereign oversight— would remain and be morphed into new forms of political protest. If the federal government failed to look after its beleaguered citizens, novel modes of governance must be explored.

EVEN AS JOSEPH SMITH AND HIS CLOSEST ALLIES were trying to gain a national audience hundreds of miles away from Nauvoo, they were also attempting to keep their clandestine activities secret from their neighbors. Polygamous unions, covert rituals, radical doctrines—the Mormon leadership's furtive effort to reform society was simultane- ously expanding and becoming more scandalous. Smith did not add many wives himself after September 1843—he seemed to have come to an agreement with his wife Emma to stop expanding his own familial kingdom—but this period witnessed many other men and women join the practice. Smith took a calculated risk every time he widened the circle of people he told about his plural sealings. But with his brother's support, he now had a dictated revelation that justified the practice, and probably felt emboldened.

The latest efforts were spearheaded by Hyrum. While a late con- vert to plural marriage, he was anxious to defend and spread the prac- tice, matching Joseph's recklessness. One of his first steps was to inform those who served on the Nauvoo High Council in mid-August. Though one of the most authoritative ecclesiastical bodies in the city, outranking even the Quorum of the Twelve Apostles within Nauvoo's borders, few within its ranks were familiar with Smith's polygamous teachings. Indeed, Hyrum had previously used the council to fight what he believed to be rampant immorality, and it had been the vehicle through which he rooted out rumors of adultery and sexual dalliances. Of course, council members were certainly close enough to the center of things in Nauvoo to hear rumors of Joseph Smith's project. For many, it was personal. Among Smith's wives by that August—he had married at least thirty by that date—were Elvira Annie Cowles (Austin Cowles's daughter), Desdemona Fullmer (David Fullmer's sister), and Lucinda Morgan (George Harris's own wife). All three of these men were on the council, and yet it is possible that the August gathering was a revelation to them.[16]

The meeting took place in Hyrum Smith's office, located in a two-story brick building on Water Street, on August 12. One of the council members, Lewis Dunbar Wilson, had heard enough rumors concerning polygamy and was therefore eager to finally learn the details. The Smith brothers could no longer dodge the question, and Hyrum elected to reveal the still-new doctrine. He briefly left the meeting, crossed the street to his home, and returned with a copy of the revelation that had been dictated at his request one month previous. The saints had been willing to abide Joseph Smith's revelatory commands before, and Hyrum was sure they would do so again. He read the text to the council and argued for its acceptance. Though his precise words were not recorded, it is likely he framed his argument within biblical

Hyrum Smith, *carte de visite*. The original sketch on which this image was based was made of Smith prior to his death.

principles. He explained to another group of men a few days later that the Mosaic law dictated that a man could marry a deceased brother's wife in order to secure eternal seed, for example. Hyrum had, in fact, married his wife's widowed sister the day before.[17]

Many in the council were shocked, and resistant. But Hyrum's authority over the group was firm. Even among those who were hesitant, most showed deference to their patriarch and leader. This was to be the new marital order for God's people. As the city's ecclesiastical leaders, they, too, were expected to practice and defend the institution. No vote was taken, however, which allowed private dissent to fester. Hyrum had spent nearly two years encouraging the council to redeem the city from immorality, and to some it now seemed he was asking them to reverse course. Three of those in attendance would eventually, and publicly, denounce polygamy and push for its eradication. But public debates for and against the practice were still in the future. At the time, the council's secretary, Hosea Stout, recorded that there was "no business before the Council."[18]

The wider the circle of plural marriage grew, the more likely it was that someone would publicly reveal it. It did not help that Joseph Smith had a penchant for trusting untrustworthy men. Smith introduced George J. Adams to the plural order shortly after Adams had been tried for adultery earlier that summer, but the new inductee failed to keep his new unions private and gossip started to spread. By September, one non-Mormon resident of Nauvoo, Charlotte Haven, wrote a relative to convey the word that Adams was openly living with two families, and that his first wife had even accepted the new arrangement. The defense for this new practice, Haven heard, was rooted in the Bible, for if it was right for ancient patriarchs, it was also "right for the Latter Day Saints." If the rumors were true, Haven believed that plural marriage would lead to the church breaking apart, "for what community or State could harbor such outrageous immorality?" The implications seemed obvious. Austin Cowles, who was present at the August 12 meeting of the High Council, agreed, and charged Adams with unchristian conduct and adultery. Cowles was most likely upset with Joseph Smith himself, as Smith had taken Cowles's daughter as a plural bride, but Adams was an easier target.[19]

Smith, always quick to defend his inner circle but also worried about gossip, did everything to curb the talk. He spoke in favor of Adams at a High Council hearing, which resulted in the accusations being dismissed. The High Council then wrote an official statement, at Adams's insistence, that he had been honorably acquitted. Joseph and Hyrum, committed to maintaining an outward appearance of control, issued their own public announcement reaffirming Adams's standing. But in publicly denouncing the doctrine, privately expanding the practice, and curtailing any attempts to expose their activities, the Smith brothers were merely inviting more conflict.[20]

Indeed, another Nauvoo resident, William Henry Harrison Sagers, was similarly tried for adultery two months later, accused of sleeping with his wife's sister. When pressed, he responded that he was merely following the prophet's example. Lacking Adams's close connection with the prophet, however, Sagers was much more of a risk to the prophet. Smith accused him of not only seducing a young girl, but using his name as cover. No man, Smith argued, had license to commit adultery, and he again blamed the legacy of John C. Bennett for causing the mess. Yet the prophet was not willing to cut Sagers off completely. If the difference between adultery and divine plural unions was a matter of priesthood authorization, Sagers's desires could still be fulfilled. Within a few months, Smith taught Sagers the doctrine of polygamy and sealed him to his sister-in-law. Sagers's first wife, Lucinda, was not as eager to embrace the new social order, however. When she publicly aired her concern the following spring, Smith likely regretted his hasty actions.[21]

Joseph and Hyrum continued to widen the circle of Mormon polygamy despite these warning signs. Most of the clandestine evangelism took place in intimate face-to-face encounters. Later Mormon reminiscences mention covert meetings on rainy days in the nearby woods, where Smith read the revelation to small groups. While fewer than ten men entered into polygamous relationships prior to the summer of

1843, at least nineteen were sealed to thirty-five plural wives over the next year. This rash expansion embodied how central polygamy was to Mormonism's societal revolution. Smith warned the new initiates that if they did not have a wife sealed to them in this life, their "glory would be clip[p]ed" in the next.[22]

Given their excitement—whether it had to do with new sexual opportunities or their eternal salvation, or both—a few inductees couldn't help but spread the word. Jacob Scott, only recently arrived in Nauvoo, wrote his daughter in January that he had become aware of "Several Revelations of great utility, & uncommon interest." Though he did not go into detail, he hinted that it had to do with marriage covenants that would take on an eternal character, and even mentioned the possibility of uniting with deceased spouses. "I intend to be married to the wife of my youth," he explained, in addition to his present wife. Then there was the case of Augusta Cobb. Originally from Boston, she was a woman of means and education willing to sacrifice much for her new faith. She found in Mormonism a message of empowerment and social disruption that matched her own radical spirit. When she returned to Boston after visiting Nauvoo, where she had quickly impressed the male leaders and learned about the polygamy revelation, she told her friend she had something "glorious" to tell her.[23]

What could seem "glorious" about Smith's polygamous teachings to a formidable woman like Cobb? Her enthusiasm seems strange to modern observers. It appeared absurd to her contemporaries, too. But Smith's earnestness in spreading the doctrine and the willingness with which his followers, including women, accepted its implications reveals something important about the era. For Cobb, a woman who felt stuck in a failed marriage, the chance to leave her first husband, who refused to join the Mormon church, and unite with a powerful patriarch was profoundly appealing. She informed her friend back in Massachusetts that she was bringing "an invitation to you from *one* of the Twelve," and urged her not to refuse. And if Cobb's friend was not satisfied with the offer to be sealed to a particular apostle, "there are *two* others," each with a higher standing, she could choose between.

Any of these unions would bring exaltation to her entire family, both alive and deceased. This was a royal promise in an age of sharp limits on women's autonomy.[24]

For dozens of women in Nauvoo in 1843, the problems that came with patriarchal rule were outweighed by the potential to forge familial dynasties. The first major push for female suffrage in America had just begun, and women were, more generally, finding a more powerful voice in matters of social reform. But they were still largely on the outside of democracy, looking in, so radical experimentation could be an outlet for their frustrations. Further, some women found stability in a patriarchal structure that promised safety and control, a refuge from a world that had become too anarchic.[25]

Women had played a crucial role in Nauvoo since its inception, and every year brought the city's women added responsibility. Smith was pleased with the Relief Society when it rallied to his defense during the public controversy over John C. Bennett, and he was no doubt relieved when several of its leading members learned about, and accepted, the new polygamous order. Their voices and actions had earned them positions of power.

As a result, starting in September 1843, Smith initiated a number of them into a new and secretive order. Building on the revelation Smith dictated the previous July, in which those who embraced polygamy were promised to "be Gods," couples were now "anointed & ord[ained] to the highest and holiest order of the priesthood." This was a new ritual that made certain the blessings that were promised in previous ordinances. Women were not only part of these anointings, but they performed several of the liturgies themselves. The crowning ritual included a husband and wife washing, anointing, and blessing each other as kings and queens of the celestial world. The work that the city's elite women had begun years before was now paying off, at least for them. Tensions had even cooled between Smith and his wife. "Emma had turned quite friendly and kind," one of Joseph's confidants recorded a few weeks later, now that they were both anointed king and queen.[26]

Thanks to this new council, later referred to as the Quorum of the Anointed, women had, for the first time, a direct voice in church decisions. The men and women who were anointed into this secret council composed the most authoritative body in Nauvoo for the rest of 1843 and the early months of 1844. Smith frequently created new councils, each based on new and radical teachings, as a way to govern an expanding faith community. This new quorum included Smith's closest advisors, primarily those in the Quorum of the Twelve, while leaving out those who had fallen out of favor, and now introducing a number of women. When together, they discussed Smith's prophetic and political agendas. In his divine mandate for plural marriage, Smith had used the plural to describe exaltation—"*they* shall be gods"—in order to capture the companionate nature of the Mormon heaven, and now elite men and women were joining together to govern Nauvoo. The new quorum required the acceptance—or, at the least, the toleration—of polygamy by its members, and in turn it promised grandiose rewards.[27]

It is puzzling that, for a practice justified by its potential to produce offspring for worthy patriarchs, so few children were born to polygamous wives during these early years. Other groups in the era that experimented with new sexual practices turned to various methods of contraception, such as disciplined withdrawal for men and crude diaphragms for women, but to the Mormons, such efforts seem contradictory to polygamy's purposes. More likely, the lack of children reflected the circumstances of the still-secret order. In a bustling city with limited housing, opportunities for romantic liaisons were few. The controversies surrounding plural marriage likely led to constant anxiety for its practitioners. A number of Smith's own wives surreptitiously lived in his home, which often doubled as a boardinghouse for women without parents or spouses. Observers would have become more suspicious if a boarder became pregnant. There is circumstantial evidence that there was a specific house in which a number of Smith's older spouses lived, but Smith's younger wives were not becoming pregnant either.[28]

The growing circle of polygamous families not attached to Smith had to search for solutions of their own. One participant later remi-

Portrait of Heber C. Kimball and Vilate Kimball. The Kimball family was one of
the first exposed to Smith's polygamous teachings, as Heber was sealed to several
women, and Helen Mar, Heber and Vilate's daughter, was sealed to Joseph Smith.

PIONEER MEMORIAL MUSEUM, INTERNATIONAL SOCIETY OF DAUGHTERS OF UTAH PIONEERS, SALT LAKE CITY.

nisced that there was a home, somewhere outside Nauvoo, set aside
for troublesome arrangements. When Vilate Kimball, wife of apostle
Heber C. Kimball, reported in June that the plural wife of their mutual
friend had become pregnant, she confessed a hope that the woman
had more faith than she herself possessed. Vilate knew the risk, as
exposure would invite public censure. For the moment, however, the
new society maintained its secrecy. They were a community within a
community.[29]

The experience of William Clayton, one of Smith's secretaries, demonstrates the complexities of the secret practice. One of the more earnest
disciples in Nauvoo, Clayton fluctuated between attraction and fear when
pondering polygamy. His first wife, Ruth Moon, approved of his marriage
to her sister Margaret. But theirs was hardly a harmonious relationship.

Margaret struggled with the new circumstances and often voiced her displeasure to Clayton. She and Ruth's mother discussed her plight between themselves, too. That they all lived under one roof added to the drama. Undeterred, Clayton contemplated marrying a third Moon sister, Lydia, though he was turned away when Joseph Smith informed him of a revelation that men could only marry two women within one family. Smith, in fact, had considered taking Lydia as his own plural wife. Lydia eventually turned down both men.

Clayton's family expanded in another way, however: Margaret became pregnant, one of the few cases of a plural relationship producing a child during Joseph Smith's lifetime. Smith counseled Clayton to keep her sequestered at home and not let anyone know of her condition. If anyone raised trouble, however, Smith would publicly scold and excommunicate Clayton, but then privately rebaptize him and return him to his previous position. Throughout it all, Clayton was eager to maintain his wives' affection, their mother's approval, and his prophet's validation. It was an impossible balance.[30]

Despite the best efforts of the new quorum's members, word crept out about both the unions and the revelation that justified them. John C. Bennett acquired a copy of the new revelation within months of its drafting, as he wrote about its contents in an October letter that appeared in an Iowa newspaper. Reports also appeared in the church's small settlements outside Illinois regarding visiting elders who were accused of teaching polygamy. Smith and his counselors closed ranks. When they received word in January 1844 that a missionary, Hiram Brown, had taught polygamy in Michigan, they published an editorial denouncing his actions and cutting him off from the church. But problems continued to arise. The next month, a series of poetic editorials in a nearby newspaper accurately, if sarcastically, revealed key information concerning the practice's participants. The texts were likely written by Francis Higbee, one of the growing number of Nauvoo residents who opposed the prophet. Their primary objective was to unmask Smith's doings. Soon the whispers traveled even further. Flora Drake, a recent convert who moved to Nauvoo with her sister,

Saphronia, received a letter from relatives in Michigan that casually asked whether they had been "married to Joseph Smith" yet.[31]

The greatest opposition came within the church's own ranks, from Higbee and others. William Law, though a counselor in the First Presidency, was one of the last members of Nauvoo's elite circles to be introduced to polygamy. He had been part of the group, along with Hyrum Smith and William Marks, who had worked to expose the secret rituals the previous summer. After Hyrum converted to the practice and became its most ardent defender, Law felt further isolated. But Hyrum was confident that, with the revelatory text in hand, even Law could be convinced of its truth. At some point in the early autumn of 1843, Hyrum provided Law with a copy of the revelation on the condition that he would keep it secret and only discuss its contents with his wife, Jane. The Laws were confounded. Their beloved prophet, whom they had defended against accusations of sexual impropriety before, was indeed engaged in clandestine plural unions. Hoping it was a mistake, Law rushed to Joseph's house, only fifty yards from his own. Smith assured him that the revelation was indeed authentic.[32]

The Laws struggled with the new revelation for months. Jane missed a number of meetings of the Quorum of the Anointed in late September and early October—she and William had been provisionally admitted earlier that fall—perhaps a sign of her uneasiness. On the one hand, the Laws found the idea of polygamy repugnant. Yet, at the same time, they were drawn to Smith's teaching concerning the eternal nature of marriage. On October 9, Smith declared that those who failed to be married under the doctrine of priesthood authority would be ministering servants in the next life to those who had entered the covenant. The Laws feared that would be their destiny. Yet the doctrine of eternal sealings was inextricably tethered to Smith's polygamy revelation; for the prophet, the acceptance of plural marriage was a prerequisite for sanctifying one's marriage through priestly ritual. Because they had not yet embraced polygamy, William and Jane Law could not be sealed together for eternity, a fact that chafed both husband and wife. Meanwhile, they heard more of Joseph Smith's fervent public denials. "No man shall have but one wife," he emphasized at one gathering. The cognitive dissonance was potent. Previously close confidants, the Laws now appeared to be outsiders.[33]

Joseph Smith grew impatient with the Laws' reluctance. On October 11, he, along with Hyrum, invited William Law to have dinner at the John Benbow farm, an estate owned by one of Smiths' closest friends outside the city. It is difficult to know whether Jane was present, though it is possible that some of the Smiths' plural wives were. The trip followed a pattern of private tutelage in discreet locations, aided by the presence of other inductees, that the prophet had used with a number of polygamy's first inductees. Once safe from prying eyes and ears, Joseph and Hyrum shared many details concerning their plural unions, many of which were likely new to Law. The meeting quickly became heated and lasted longer than expected. Law was outraged to learn whom Smith had already taken as wives. Included in that group, Law now realized, were the Lawrence sisters, both teenagers, over whom Smith had been appointed legal guardian. This, to Law, was a step too far. Neither William nor Jane Law ever fully reconciled with the prophet after that fateful dinner. When considered alongside Smith's legal and political activities, which Law similarly denounced, the time for quiet acquiescence was past. Smith not only lost one of his closest allies, but he had now created a powerful enemy.[34]

ALL THE WHILE, NAUVOO'S NEIGHBORS became increasingly agitated over Mormon actions in the August election. Whigs felt betrayed, given Smith's promise to support their candidate, and Democrats, though they had secured the Mormon vote this time, understood that Nauvoo would be an unreliable ally. One group of Iowa citizens denounced the Mormons as "a politico-religious body" who refused to assimilate to democratic culture. "True to their clannish, sectarian and ambitious spirit," the Iowans warned, "we have seen them turn the elective franchise into mockery." The Mormons' actions seemed unprecedented. Mormons, they argued, had forfeited their rights as citizens by voting according to prophetic command.[35]

Many Illinoisans and other non-Mormons were especially frustrated with Smith's ability to continually escape arrest due to Nauvoo's inventive use of habeas corpus. Something had to be done. A large, bipartisan meeting took place in Warsaw, Illinois, on August 19 to determine the best course of action. Several weeks later, a committee was organized to draft resolutions aimed at the Mormons. These claimed the Mormon prophet had exhibited a "shameless disregard" for the law. His repeated reliance on Nauvoo's municipal court was a betrayal of justice and seemed to render him above the law. He was nothing more than a despot, the committee claimed. It urged the governor to take action and revoke Nauvoo's charter. At another meeting on September 6, the group vowed to solve the Mormon problem "peaceably, if we can, but forcibly, if we must." Their frustration now bordered on violence. Public speakers warned of Mormonism's militant spirit and extralegal justice. It was time, some determined, to take action in their own hands.[36]

Tensions escalated that winter. When two Mormons, Daniel and Philander Avery, were arrested for alleged horse theft in Missouri, it seemed Nauvoo's worst fears had become a reality. They heard rumors that Missouri had once again ordered Smith's extradition. Smith dashed off an appeal to Illinois governor Thomas Ford, pleading his innocence and begging for aid. Ford assured Smith that he supported the Mormons, but the saints were tired of waiting on outside help. They denounced any extradition orders as part of a "foreign process" that merely enabled kidnapping. The City Council passed an ordinance on December 8 dictating that any person who attempted to arrest Joseph Smith based on any Missouri charge would themselves be arrested on the spot, tried by Nauvoo's municipal court, and, if guilty, sentenced to life in prison. Not even a pardon from the governor could free the offending party, unless Nauvoo's mayor consented to it—an unlikely outcome, given that Smith himself was mayor.[37]

Nor did Nauvoo's council stop there. Two weeks later, it resolved that each and every writ issued outside Nauvoo must first receive approval by their mayor before being executed. Anyone who tried to circumvent the city's authorities was also risking imprisonment. The Mormons were no longer willing to tolerate, to any degree, the actions of those working to arrest their prophet. Parley Pratt proposed that they petition the federal government for an ordinance requiring that, if Missouri were to mount an invasion on Nauvoo, federal troops would be compelled to come to Mormon aid and follow Smith's order as general. In the meantime, they resolved to enlarge the police force by forty deputized officers, all under the prophet's direct command. Once these new men were appointed on December 19, Smith declared the church's new motto: "We will be at peace with all men so long as they will let us alone." The saints refused to be bullied.[38]

The motto was not all that the new policemen heard that day. Smith urged them to keep watch on Missouri, but also to understand that the true threat came from within Nauvoo itself. The prophet said that he was particularly worried about a secret assassin—a "Brutus," someone who pretended to be his friend but was intent on revenge. Smith heard from Orrin Porter Rockwell, who had recently returned to Nauvoo after being incarcerated in Missouri for several months, that the Missourians were conspiring with someone within the church's leadership. Already worried about betrayal, this rumor fed Smith's fears. At first, he accused Sidney Rigdon, counselor in the First Presidency, but soon shifted his suspicions elsewhere. If any of the new policemen were offered a bribe by someone in the evil cabal, he announced, the city would pay double if they instead turned the conspirator over to authorities. The gathered policemen, perhaps surprised to hear of this threat, were eager to prove their loyalty.[39]

It did not take too much imagination to guess the alleged traitor: within a few days, William Law was told he was suspected to be Smith's Brutus, and that his life was in peril. Though Law had been, up until that point, silent about his rift with Smith, word of his discontent had spread, and some of the policemen knew that Law was opposed to plural marriage, even though it was still largely secret. When Law confronted Hyrum Smith on January 2, 1844, about the threats against Law himself, Smith feigned astonishment and called a City Council session the next day to determine the truth.[40]

What ensued was a confusing investigation within the City Council that was reflective of a community in which rumors, secret orders, and misleading proclamations circulated without many avenues for reliable confirmation. As Nauvoo's leading men gathered on January 3 for a special session to parse out a series of accusations, some of the city's most pressing issues that had been hidden were revealed. Law alleged to the council that he had been warned by a policeman that there was an order for his removal from the city. Both Smith brothers, present at the meeting, dismissed the accusation as ludicrous and pled with Law to reveal his source. After prodding, Law admitted he heard the rumor from Eli Norton, a member of the High Council.

Norton was then summoned before the council, and under pressure admitted that he had heard the threat from Daniel Cairns, a member of the police force. Cairns, when questioned, pled that he had to keep all his instructions confidential, though he eventually confessed he had been ordered by city leaders to keep a look out for dissenters. Upon further prodding, it became clear that Smith, when he addressed the police force, had made his instructions as clear as possible: there was a distinction between "the Law of God," which was to be followed, and "another Law," of whom they were to "take care" in a discreet manner. Shaken by these allegations, the council adjourned for two days.[41]

When they met again on January 5, the council was confronted with even more shocking information: William Marks, who served as president of the Nauvoo stake, an ecclesiastical office that looked over congregations within the city itself, claimed that someone had started a fire at his house. Marks had recently joined William Law in his opposition to polygamy, so the crime seemed related to the current investigation. One resident of the city, Leonard Soby, reported that he had overheard policeman Warren Smith (no relation to Joseph or Hyrum) saying that the church had enemies, including Law and Marks, and if they caused any problem he was authorized to have them "popped over." Warren Smith, when questioned by the City Council, did not deny the accusation, but rather claimed he was fulfilling the prophet's counsel. Though Joseph Smith's speech to Nauvoo's policemen had prompted these episodes, he insisted that his only desire was personal safety. Hyrum, for his part, then likened the actions of these police-men to "an old Dutchman" and his ox:

> Soby makes me think of an old Dutchman, who had an ox the first animal he ever owned in his life, and he broke him to ride, then he filled a sack with rocks and laid it on the ox's back and got on himself and told his son to hide by the roadside and when he came along to jump out and holloa boo, as he wanted to know how well his ox was broke, The Son did accordingly; the ox was frightened and threw the old man off. "Father" said the son "I did as you told me." "Yes" said the old man "but you made too big a boo."

The lesson was clear: Smith was not to blame if others took his words too far.[42]

Even more alarmingly, the City Council debates soon centered on polygamy, a topic that had heretofore been successfully avoided in this setting. Law claimed that his problem with Joseph Smith had to do with the latter's "Spiritual wife system." That such accusations were now presented openly in a council meeting revealed that the secret had become, at least for a certain elite segment of Nauvoo, an open one. Law felt confident enough to accuse Hyrum Smith of presenting the plural marriage revelation before the High Council the previous August. Joseph, frustrated that he was losing control of the discussion, responded that any man who failed to keep a secret, like Law, could never be trusted. The prophet was rightly concerned that his secret practice might be finally exposed.

Things became so heated that they wrapped up the debate before it resulted in violence, and the council meeting ended on superficially conciliatory notes. Cairns and Smith were dropped from the police force, and Law assured those in attendance that he, at least for the moment, did not want to start any trouble. "Joseph had nothing to fear from me," he told the council, "[as] I was not his enemy." (He later added in his journal that he "did not say I was his friend.") Joseph

Smith, satisfied, refused to bring any charges. In his diary, Smith attempted to downplay the episode. Of Law's accusations, his secretary wrote that they "proved to be all about nothing at all"; Marks's, meanwhile, represented "another Tempest in a tea pot." Yet these words concealed deep antagonisms. Neither the Smiths, Laws, nor Marks were satisfied to end things there. The fight was only beginning.[43]

The night between the two council hearings, in a rare moment of tranquility, Joseph Smith had a private dinner with his wife, Emma. They had just moved into their large new home a couple months earlier, but had already started renting out rooms to guests in order to bring in needed income. The Smiths retained a dining room on the main floor that doubled as a room for entertainment and family gatherings. William Phelps observed the quaint occasion and remarked that Smith should follow Napoleon Bonaparte's example and, despite the large company of men under his command, always eat at a table just large enough for him and his wife. Emma, however, knew better. "Mr Smith," she retorted, "is a bigger man than Bunaparte," and could never eat without his friends. Joseph quipped it was the wisest thing she had ever said. It was a warm moment in an otherwise trying week.[44]

Yet Smith feared his circle of trustworthy friends was shrinking. His penchant for conflict made the comparison to Bonaparte even more apt than Emma likely meant. Within the Laws' home, only a block to the north, William and Jane Law were already plotting their own resolution. The same evening the Smiths had their quiet dinner, Law wrote about the "indignation in [his] heart."[45]

"WHAT WILL BE YOUR RULE OF ACTION, relative to us as a people?" The question appeared a simple one, and the Mormons wanted an answer from anyone with eyes set on the American presidency. The 1844 presidential election seemed a wide-open contest. Mormon leaders therefore sent the above query to each of the five leading candidates in early November 1843. National pundits took notice. Because the Mormons acted "with perfect devotion at the nod of their prophet," observed one Washington newspaper, Nauvoo could exert disproportionate power on state and even national matters, especially when two ascendant parties were battling for control. Mormon democratic principles had boiled down to pragmatism: who was going to help them recover what they had lost in Missouri, and who would promise to aid them in the future? This was an earnest question, especially since the saints could no longer rely on Illinois for protection. Perhaps their only support could come from the federal government, including the White House.[46]

Of the five presidential candidates the Mormons contacted, only three responded. That in itself was a coup, and a sign that Smith had a reputation. Yet none of them promised assistance. "If I should be elected, I would strive to administer the government according to the constitution and laws of the union," explained John C. Calhoun, one of the architects of state supremacy. However, Calhoun continued, Nauvoo's problems did not fall under federal jurisdiction. Similarly, the Whig Henry Clay, known as the "Great Compromiser," and Lewis Cass, a Democratic candidate, claimed they could not enter into any engagements, or make any promises, prior to taking office. Though respectful, nobody was willing to stick their neck out for the saints.[47]

Smith was unsatisfied with these excuses. "*I am surprised,*" he responded to Calhoun, that the men who held such prestigious government positions could have such a "fragile" understanding of the Constitution. When a federal government could not prevent a state from oppressing its citizens, the states had now become more powerful than their parent government. The cart was pulling the horse. Smith urged that "the States rights doctrine," rather than preserving the liberty of Americans, is "what feeds mobs."

Smith urged Calhoun to recognize the "sublime idea" that Congress, with the president as its leader, was as "Almighty" in its sphere as Jehovah is in his. The legislative and executive branches of government, in other words, had the authority to act like God in protecting its children. The federal government Smith envisioned was one powerful enough to overturn local injustices, but to Calhoun, who built his reputation on state sovereignty, it must have appeared as heresy. While the correspondence led only to further frustration for the Nauvoo faithful, it drew chuckles from a broader audience. John C. Calhoun, previously seen as the front-runner, had hit the end of his campaign, joked the *Warsaw Message*, because "Joe Smith has declared against him." To non-Mormon observers, the Mormon prophet was a national joke.[48]

If the existing candidates refused to represent the Mormons, then it was left for Smith to do it himself. Nauvoo's leaders met in the upstairs office of Smith's red-brick store on a cold morning on January 29. In the building where he had introduced new sacred rituals and societies, Smith now plotted to take over American politics. Willard Richards moved to reject the Whig and Democratic parties, form an individual ticket, and nominate Joseph Smith as a presidential candidate. Tired of pledging allegiance to non-Mormons, the men in the room decided it was time to promote someone from within. Smith responded that, if elected, he would protect the rights and liberties of all American citizens, including those on the margins of society. The mood was triumphant. In celebration, a visitor from Quincy, known as Captain White, offered a toast: "May all your enemies be skinned, and their skins be made into drum heads for your friends to beat upon." Just as ominously, White added that he hoped Nauvoo would become the center of America's government.

The Mormon candidate would call for national unity above partisan bickering. The people were sick of Whig or Democratic presidents, he reasoned—it was time for an *American* president, untethered from partisan obligations. Smith ordered William Phelps to draft a campaign pamphlet, and his advisors began organizing a vast electoral push to get Joseph Smith's message distributed nationally. Though it is impossible to gauge how serious a contender Smith believed himself to be—he may have envisioned his candidacy more as a means of garnering attention and sympathy for the Mormons—he was committed enough to draft a list of potential cabinet appointees. At the very least, the campaign energized both the prophet and his followers, as the opportunity to perform on a national stage heralded the next stage in the Kingdom of Nauvoo's work.[49]

One reason Smith and his close associates might have believed he had a real chance of being elected was that 1844 was a year of transition. The incumbent, John Tyler, a Whig, was not a gifted politician and could not call on wide support. He assumed office only after William Henry Harrison died shortly after his inauguration in 1841, and Tyler, like most vice-presidents of the era, was a tenuous consensus pick. In fact, his own party did not support him and planned to run a different candidate, and the Democratic Party, with which his policies were more accurately aligned, was equally hesitant to cast its lot with him. Henry Clay and John C. Calhoun were the most prominent candidates, and both had been campaigning for two years (if not their entire careers), but Calhoun pulled out of the race as his support dwindled by the end of 1843. Replacing him at the head of the Democratic ticket was former president Martin Van Buren, who had rebuffed Mormon appeals for help four years previous.

There were numerous contentious topics of debate. Western expansion, Texas annexation, and, increasingly, slavery divided national politics and promised a contested race. It could only help Joseph Smith's cause that Illinois appeared to be a swing state. While the Democratic ticket won its votes in 1840, Henry Clay wondered if Illinois could back the Whigs in 1844, and the party mobilized in the state. The Mormons were ready to take advantage. "It appears," noted *New York Herald* editor James Gordon Bennett, "that the Mormons are preparing to regulate matters so as to control the presidential question in the ensuing election." The saints would play their voting game on the national stage.[50]

Smith would run on a platform emphasizing executive power and morality. When wielded correctly, a Nauvoo newspaper declared in a lengthy editorial, a strong executive branch was a great blessing for all citizens, as it could balance the nation's competing and divergent interests. That is, only the president could preserve the peace when states oppressed marginal groups within their borders. When the editorial called the president "the mouth-piece of this vast republic," the author was granting power to the executive office that had rarely been wielded, at least in local matters, for nearly two decades. The editorial denounced Clay because he belonged to the "old school" of state sovereignty, and they could not trust Van Buren, either, due to his previous refusal to support the Mormons. Since neither party had put forward a suitable candidate, it was time to cast their lot with someone they could trust: their own prophet. Even if they were throwing away their votes, the Mormons reasoned, it was better to do so on a worthy individual. One resident explained in a later memoir that his "object was to vote for a man whom we know to be our friend," as previous politicians had proven "faithless and untrue to their trust."[51]

After a month of planning his next steps with his closest advisors, Smith was ready to make a public announcement and publish an electioneering pamphlet, *General Smith's Views on the Powers and Policy of the Government of the United States,* by the end of February. He chose to be identified by his military, rather than his ecclesiastical or mayoral, title, as his primary issue was the apparent inability of the United States to assure liberty for all its residents. He called for the eradication of slavery, the end of debtor's prisons, and the protection of religious minorities. America could not celebrate its national ideals until *all* citizens experienced freedom. Dividing the nation into classes, races, religions, and parties, he argued, led to unrest. To overcome this partisan and sectional spirit, the federal government had to take an activist role. Smith insisted that "unity is power," a political phrase common with Whigs, but he tried to transcend partisan divides with much of his rhetoric. Throughout Smith's proposals ran an emphasis on using the government as a social good for the nation's inhabitants, most especially the marginalized, poor, and oppressed.[52]

Smith's political energy was not buttressed by a firm historical knowledge. As part of his campaign, he invoked out-of-context quotes of founding presidents. Nor did the Mormon prophet have a firm grasp of recent presidential history. Rather than seeing Andrew Jackson as the man who dismantled the American system put in place by his predecessors, Smith claimed that Jackson's administration had occasioned the *"acme"* of American prosperity. It was a puzzling statement for someone who believed in strengthening federal power, including by creating a national bank. (Many observers of Smith's campaign noted his reliance upon Whig policies, and one even jokingly referred to him, after Clay's faltering, as "the true Whig candidate for president.") But Smith's praise for Jackson reveals two key features of his political approach. First, the popular image of Jackson as a powerful outsider who brought change through force of will fit Smith's own model of frontier governance. And second, emphasizing Jackson's success allowed Smith to blame Martin Van Buren for America's decline. "Thirst for power, pride, corruption, party spirit, faction, patronage"— these were the vices Smith attached to the president who had turned him away only four years previous. For Smith, personal reputation was as important as political policies or party affiliation. John Tyler, to him, was not much better than Van Buren. It was time for another strong, spirited, and outsider candidate to go to the White House—another Jackson for the new age.[53]

The Mormon candidate's proposals were radical, but consistent with his broadly populist message. He called for Congress to be cut in half and its members to be paid the same salary as ordinary farmers. He asked citizens to petition state legislatures to pardon convicts and reform the penitentiary system, as "rigor and seclusion" could never transform an imprisoned man into a good citizen. Only murder should result in long sentences. Given his firsthand experiences of the excesses of the American legal system, Smith wished to save others from them. He further suggested that the nation sell off enough public lands that the profits, combined with the money saved from reducing congressional salaries, could pay off slave owners and abolish slavery once and for all. Smith embraced manifest destiny, calling for the annexation of Oregon and Texas, and for furthering expansion efforts in Canada and Mexico.

The relationship between the federal government and ordinary citizens also required an overhaul. Because of the Mormon experience in Missouri, Smith believed common citizens should retain the right to bypass their states and petition for federal aid in instances where the

governor himself might be "a mobber." From this perspective, the federal government's first allegiance was to the people, not the states. It
was time, Smith argued, for America to arise, like a phoenix, fly over
the ruins left by Van Buren and Tyler, and recapture the spirit of an
earlier age. The platform was a prophetic vision for his country. The
church printed 1,500 copies of the pamphlet and mailed them to politicians and newspapers throughout the nation.[54]

Organizing the campaign became a holy mission for Nauvoo's Mormons. Smith solicited ideas for a running mate at the next meeting of
the Quorum of the Anointed, mixing, as he often did, sacred rituals with
political machination. They decided to invite James Arlington Bennet,
a recent convert and friend of Smith who lived in New York, to be their
vice-presidential candidate. His reputation and place of residence—
not to mention the fact that his baptism as a Mormon was not well
known—made him an enticing candidate. Willard Richards, Smith's
secretary, implored Bennet to join the cause, arguing that Smith was
the "greatest statesman" of the nineteenth century. Before they could
receive a response, however, they heard that Bennet had been born in
Ireland and was therefore ineligible. (This information turned out to
be false.) Their next choice, a non-Mormon colonel in Kentucky named
Solomon Copeland, whom Wilford Woodruff had befriended during
his missionary work in the region, also proved a dead end. Smith tried
to temper expectations. He insisted to his followers that he cared more
for his prophetic office than he would for any presidential election. But
he nevertheless continued to defend his campaign in public meetings.
The Mormons have as much a right to push candidates as any citizen,
he once boasted, and he expressed his confidence that with their orga-
nizational skills, anything was possible. "When I look into the Eastern
papers & see how popular I am," he exclaimed, "I am afraid I shall be
president." Smith never lacked confidence.[55]

The Mormons were always extremely optimistic when gauging popular opinion. Reactions elsewhere to Smith's announcement reflected
a mix of amusement, puzzlement, and, in the cases of the Mormons'
immediate neighbors, outrage. The *Warsaw Signal*'s Thomas Sharp,

who resurrected the paper in early 1844 with the sole purpose of opposing the Mormons, responded with scorn, concluding that Smith was the "greatest dunce" he had ever encountered. But the derision was not limited to Illinois. Even Smith's hometown paper in upstate New York, the *Wayne County Sentinel*, mocked the "Hero of Stafford street"—a sarcastic nickname based on the Smith family's Palmyra address—for descending from the clouds of heavenly revelation and entering the dirty world of electoral politics. Many saw his platform as either a superficial cousin of the Whig platform, a humorous publicity stunt, or as the work of a delusional man. But Smith's supporters refused to be deterred. John Taylor, editor of the *Nauvoo Neighbor*, made sure to excerpt the most positive—or, more accurately, the least negative—coverage. And Smith defended himself against the accusations that his proposals were too idealistic. He made clear that he was willing to stand up for the downtrodden despite the backlash.[56]

Some of the most important reactions came from within Nauvoo's city limits. A growing number of vocal critics had emerged, led by William Law. At the March 7 public meeting where Smith detailed his presidential ambitions, the prophet called for a vote on whether the city was willing to support his candidacy. The tally was unanimous in Smith's favor, with one exception: Charles Foster, a prominent Nauvoo physician who, unlike his brother Robert, was not a Mormon and was increasingly concerned with his mayor's activities. Polygamous unions, secret rituals, and now national political aspirations—Smith seemed out of control, and it was time to take a stand. Smith and Foster then engaged in a verbal sparring match that ended with Smith, acting as mayor, fining Foster ten dollars.

Smith's most loyal followers were quick to stand up for their prophet. John Taylor, the apostle who never lacked for words or convictions, compared those who were afraid to back Smith to ostriches who stuck their heads in the sand, and asserted that true saints would never be cowards in the face of opposition. He had drawn a line in the sand: the faithful must be willing to stand behind Smith or suffer the consequences.[57]

CHAPTER 6

Fruit

Governments must have originated from some place—if from heaven
they ought to pattern after heaven.

—CHARLES C. RICH[1]

George Loyd, "Joseph Smith Addressing the General Conference, 1844," colored
lithograph. In April 1844, Joseph Smith pronounced some of his most daring doctrines of his prophetic career, including that men could become gods. LDS CHURCH
HISTORY LIBRARY, SALT LAKE CITY.

R alph Harding, like many in the eastern states, was alarmed by the news coming out of Nauvoo. The *New-York Observer*, for instance, warned that Joseph Smith was becoming more dictatorial every day. Though Harding lived in Massachusetts, similar reports were appearing in Boston's newspapers. But the issue was personal for Harding: his son Dwight had recently converted to the Mormon faith and moved to Nauvoo. Indeed, the Harding family was part of a Massachusetts community in the early 1840s that was vexed by the proselytizing success of the Mormons in their region. The *Salem Gazette* expressed astonishment that "this superstition has found many converts in our vicinity," including "men of reputable character." Drawing converts from the western frontier of American society, the edge of civilization, was one thing, but stealing members of educated and stable families in Massachusetts was quite another. The Mormon threat was more menacing than expected. And the problem was not going away.[2]

Harding's worry only grew after receiving a letter from his wayward son. It was the first time he had heard from Dwight in several years, and he was hopeful for good news. The letter, however, was disappointing. It not only reaffirmed his belief in Joseph Smith as the Mormon prophet, but revealed that Dwight Harding had descended further into madness: he was now urging his father to support Smith's presidential candidacy. Ralph was outraged. He chastised Dwight for urging his family "to vote for Jo Smith for President of the united states," and assured him that their neighborhood was not foolish enough to contribute to such a misguided effort. Ralph made reference to a Baptist preacher who had just returned from visiting Nauvoo and regaled their part of Massachusetts with stories of Smith and "all his armies," hell-

bent on conquering the country. Ralph Harding felt justified concluding that what Smith and the Mormons desired was to seize "the power
into their own hands" so that they could "rule this nation." Harding
now worried his son was part of a treasonous cabal trying to overthrow
American democracy.[3]

Events between March 1844 and when Ralph Harding wrote his son
several months later made clear that the Mormons had decisively broken with mainstream American society. Conflicts, especially relating
to polygamy, escalated, and many within and without Nauvoo fought
back against Joseph Smith's new patriarchal regime. His opponents
included his own wife, Emma, who once again used the Relief Society in a crusade against clandestine activities within Nauvoo. But the
Mormon prophet was undeterred. Indeed, even after declaring his
campaign for the presidency, Smith's public and private opinions only
became more extreme.

In the Mormon prophet's mind, it was time for their social project to expand beyond Nauvoo, and for the Kingdom of God to encompass the entire world. For many of his followers, this was an exciting
fulfillment of prophecy, the moment that the biblical patriarchs had
long expected. For their neighbors, it was the logical conclusion of the
dangerous trajectory that began soon after Mormons set foot in Illinois. The ensuing debate displayed fault lines and fissures embedded
within America's democratic establishment.

JUST AS JOSEPH SMITH LAUNCHED his presidential campaign in 1844, he
faced new problems at home. His creation of the Female Relief Society
in 1842 simultaneously empowered women and granted Emma Smith
control of a formidable, and quasi-autonomous, vehicle for reform.
Emma believed the organization was dedicated to, among other pur-
suits, governing the city's morality. The society was to "watch over
the morals" and "be very careful of the character and reputation" of
the city, she declared at their first meeting. Any new accusations concerning polygamy were a threat to societal purity. While Emma had
learned of the practice in 1843, she vacillated between tacit resignation

and outright rejection over the following months, even as her husband became even bolder with his activities. She was consistent, however, in publicly calling for moral conduct on behalf of the church and its leaders. While her efforts reflected the broader American anxiety over moral purity, her cause was sacralized in Nauvoo. Anything less than perfect morality would lead to the failure of their noble experiment.[4]

Another wave of polygamy accusations hit in the first few months of 1844. Each allegation threatened to make the practice public. Perhaps one of the most prominent and threatening accusations came from one Nauvoo resident, Orsamus Bostwick, who claimed he knew about Hyrum Smith's multiple "spiritual wives," with whom he alternated sleeping every night. Bostwick also alleged that there was a thriving prostitution ring located just around the corner from the temple. This untoward business, he explained, was not only known by church leadership but had been initiated with their oversight. Bostwick was immediately brought before the city court and fined fifty dollars. But there was still risk of further damage. Bostwick's lawyer, Francis Higbee, promised to appeal the decision to the circuit court, which was in nearby Carthage and therefore outside Mormon control. Joseph Smith feared that a spectacle in that town would stir up a mob, and so he called a special conference a week later, in the grove next to the unfinished temple, where he could publicly speak on the matter. Standing in front of as many as eight thousand congregants, Smith openly questioned why men like Bostwick should even be tolerated within their city, and he disparaged the lawyers, journalists, and other agitators who provided him a platform. It was time to silence the dissent before it became too boisterous.[5]

Bostwick's accusations prompted a renewed effort by Mormon leaders to distance themselves from accusations of "spiritual wifery." Though Joseph Smith had denounced Bostwick in public, that was not enough for Emma, who had once again set herself to stopping her husband's secret transgressions. She had earlier urged William Phelps, one of Joseph Smith's clerks and ghostwriters, to pen an explicit defense of the Mormon community's virtue. Phelps completed the document and read it aloud at the large gathering on March 7, where it was received with two hearty "amens" from the audience. But its usefulness was not yet exhausted. Emma then made the speech her own by editing it, presenting it before the Relief Society, and publishing it under her and her secretary's names in the *Nauvoo Neighbor* with the new title "Virtue Will Triumph." Her version denounced any and all attempts to deviate from traditional standards and morals, especially concerning marriage. For those who were tired of looking past the clandestine polygamous activities of the city's leading men, the document proved a powerful weapon. It was both ironic and fitting that Emma used something produced by her husband's own secretary to attack his secretive institution.[6]

Emma wanted the entire Relief Society to hear the document read aloud and to approve it. The society had not met during its winter hiatus, and it had been much longer since Emma had presided over a meeting. She quickly reasserted her position within the organization, regardless. To assure that everyone could attend, the society repeated the same meeting four times over the span of a week, and each instance featured Emma reading the document and the audience granting its unanimous approval. Like many pamphlets produced by women reformers of the era, the text insisted on their right to express outrage against any sexual impropriety and called for radical reform. Any enemy of female chastity, it declared, had no place in their houses, their churches, or their community. And while it praised Joseph Smith for defending Hyrum against Bostwick's accusations, it expressed "unqualified disapprobation and scorn" for any Nauvoo resident who veered from traditional morality. While Joseph may have approved the document for publicly defending his reputation, in Emma's hands it became a direct condemnation of his covert activities. It closed by explicitly condemning polygamy, bigamy, and adultery as ills that could destroy any society. There was little room for artful dodging. Though the document was short enough to be read aloud in less than ten minutes, the meetings lasted two hours each, and little of the discussion was recorded. Emma Smith had a lot to say, albeit discreetly.[7]

At the last of the four meetings, on March 16, Emma was even more forceful in her denunciations. While she again attacked John C. Bennett's "spiritual wifery," the shorthand for the illicit and unauthorized practices of the city's former mayor, she added that similar ideas taught by anyone in the name of Joseph Smith were equally unacceptable. Emma was tired of diverging public and private notions of morality. She exhorted listeners to follow Joseph's teachings as they appeared *"from the Stand,"* a sharp contrast to what he might say in private. She made clear that she could use no stronger or more direct language to make her point. This was the most forward Emma had ever been in publicly challenging her husband. While Joseph and other male leaders looked at outward threats and sought to reform the world through political campaigning, Emma envisioned a necessary internal regeneration to cleanse their community. Neither hope would be fulfilled.[8]

The four meetings of the Relief Society in mid-March 1844 were the society's last recorded gatherings in Nauvoo. The prophet refused to scale back plural marriage. As public pressure grew, Joseph Smith blamed, in turn, his wife, her society, and the document she had commissioned and then spoke aloud. When dissenters skewered Smith in nearby presses and helped organize efforts to expose Smith's activities, the women in Nauvoo proved an easy scapegoat. In late May, he declared he had never had any problems until the Relief Society commenced their reformation mission. He saw to it that this agitating thorn was removed from his side by publicly subverting their authority within the city.[9]

But the problem, which was of Smith's own making in multiple ways, was not going away. Not only had he introduced and expanded the polygamous practice that was now causing alarm, but he had also originally cheered the Mormon women who mobilized on behalf of the society. When he needed their help, as in the early public disputes over John C. Bennett or during the extradition attempts, the Relief Society proved immensely efficient in coming to his aid. But once he found himself in his wife's crosshairs, the association threatened to become a nuisance. An organization originally conceived to bring unity to the city was now an embodiment of its fracturing. Once granted the ability to weigh in on societal issues, the women of Nauvoo could not be easily constrained. Further, the Relief Society itself was divided: some were loyal followers of Smith and participants in the plural unions, while others were either ignorant of or opposed to the practice. Given this division, Smith started to feel he could no longer trust his wife and the women who were faithful to her cause.

Meanwhile, rumors continued to spread. Those eager to attack Joseph Smith's secret relationships were gathering evidence. Thomas Sharp, whose *Warsaw Signal* was increasingly dedicated to exposing the Mormons, was now armed with firsthand accounts. The week after Smith and the Relief Society publicly denounced and denied the practice of polygamy, Sharp published an anonymous letter from someone who had attended the trial of Harrison Sagers the previous November. Sagers had been accused of adultery, only to have Smith dismiss his charges and then authorize him to be sealed to the same woman, Phoebe Madison, with whom he was accused of cheating on his wife, Lucinda Sagers. But if Smith believed that was the end of the episode, he was sorely mistaken. The *Warsaw Signal* correspondent noted that Sagers had been tried not for teaching polygamy, but for teaching it "*too publicly.*" Mormon leaders immediately went on the defensive. Hyrum Smith wrote a circular letter addressed to saints within and beyond Nauvoo, once again denying that the city's leaders practiced polygamy, and vowing that anyone caught teaching the doctrine would be cut off from the church. By then, though, the coded language and calculated denials were stretching thin.[10]

Lucinda Madison Sagers, Harrison's wife, did not buy the Smith brothers' defense. Although Harrison escaped adultery charges in November and was now sealed to Lucinda's sister, he did not escape Lucinda's wrath. She refused to accept the new polygamous order and was willing to confront her ecclesiastical leaders with their own words. On April 13, she appeared before the High Council, in a meeting that took place in Joseph Smith's red-brick store, to launch her accusations. Since the Mormon leadership threatened to excommunicate all persons who practiced polygamy, Lucinda explained she was there to notify them that her husband, Harrison, was guilty of that very crime. She assured the council that she had proof, including firsthand testimony of a witness who related how Harrison claimed his salvation rested on obtaining two wives. Armed with the anti-polygamy language of her leaders and evidence of her polygamist husband, Lucinda had cornered the Smiths with their own words and Harrison with his own actions.

If the council had heard this case a year earlier, when Hyrum Smith was urging them to be an anti-corruption force, Lucinda might have found a receptive audience. Yet the High Council, at Hyrum's insistence, determined that since Harrison had already been tried the previous November, they could not try him again. Harrison was once again acquitted. But Lucinda refused to give up. She warned the council that if the laws of the church would not punish her wayward husband, she would take it up with the laws of the land. She soon joined William Law and other Nauvoo residents who were weary of the private actions and public denials. They were ready to bring Mormon leadership to justice.[11]

JOSEPH SMITH, FOR HIS PART, WAS READY to bring justice to the world. Just as one council, the Relief Society, was failing him, the Mormon prophet was already envisioning another. This council would be more explicitly political than any he had established before. It aimed for nothing less than the construction of a new form of governance altogether. Humanity's salvation, Smith believed, was to be found outside America's political tradition.

Envisioning novel, secret, and increasingly important councils was a common pattern in his life, as Smith frequently created new organizations in order to match his evolving understanding of leadership and theology. Yet the latest council truly was different from those that came before: rather than an assembly that would oversee Mormon activities, the new council was destined to rule the world. Created in March 1844, Smith called it, simply, "The Kingdom." It was the culmination of his increasingly bold vision and represented the climax of early Mormonism's political ambitions.

It also spoke to the Mormons' anxiety about democracy. God had given humanity the freedom to establish nations and kingdoms, but their efforts had resulted in political and social strife. Division plagued human society. The solution was an all-powerful, divine ruler. Smith declared at a general meeting on March 7 that, while the Mormons believed in republican governance, such a system only worked when those in charge ruled with righteousness. The next day, he explained to the City Council that whenever the voice of the majority no longer followed God's law, democracy was doomed to fail. In those situations, he reasoned, "Aristarchy," or the governing by the "wisest & best" men, should replace it. The world needed a kingdom with God as its sovereign and God's appointed people as its officiators.[12]

The immediate impetus for the Kingdom was the need to explore other potential sites for Mormon settlements in case the saints were expelled from Nauvoo. But it soon evolved into something more. Smith's presidential campaign required a vast army of electioneering missionaries. The Mormons also planned to send more, and more radical, petitions to Congress. A coordinating committee seemed necessary. Further, Smith had lost faith in the Quorum of the Anointed as a governing body, as it featured several women, including his wife, whom he could no longer trust. He had also lost faith in the First Presidency, now without the once-reliable William Law but still featuring the still-unreliable Sidney Rigdon. The Kingdom, then, would help run his campaign, and at the same time, it filled a leadership vacuum.

Even though Smith had consistently centralized authority in his own position and extended his executive reach, he often felt most comfortable when he could also boast of having legislative support. He would rule as a divinely appointed monarch, but only with a strong parliament of priesthood bearers. This continuous struggle between autocratic and democratic impulses had shaped his evolving conceptions of authority. The result was one of the most radical political organizations in nineteenth-century America.[13]

On March 10, Smith gathered some of his closest advisors to hear from a handful of missionaries who returned with news of a colonization possibility in Texas. It was at this meeting that they decided to organize a new council. Smith's diary for the day merely stated their intention to send men to Texas to convert the republic's president, Sam Houston, and amend the Texas Republic's constitution so that it featured "the voice of Jehovah." But their plans were much grander than that. William Clayton, who was chosen to be the council's clerk, enthusiastically wrote in his journal that they had discussed many bold and glorious ideas for divine rule. It was yet another exciting time.[14]

The new council was officially founded the next day in the assembly room of Henry Miller's Nauvoo home, just two blocks north and east from Smith's Mansion House. The large room had frequently been used for Masonic meetings, and while this gathering also featured the city's elite men, its purpose was quite different. Rather than cementing a fraternal order of brotherhood, they implemented a new form of political sovereignty. "All seemed agreed," the minutes recorded, "to look to some place where we can go and establish a Theocracy either in Texas or Oregon or somewhere in California." Smith moved that the council, then comprising twenty-three men, be organized according to eternal principles into a government of God. Their government would bring order to a disorderly world.

Participants were selectively chosen based on their loyalty and merit. Voting on new resolutions must be unanimous, Smith insisted, as "the most perfect harmony" must prevail. Their new council would not look like the divided halls of Congress. The council was a blend of Smith's ecclesiastical experiments, which were centered on a shared yet unified authority, and his political theology, in which God's voice dictated the parameters of democratic participation. Even the name of the council was given through revelation: "Verily thus saith the Lord," Smith dictated on March 14, "this is the name by which you shall be called[:] The Kingdom of God and his Laws, with the keys and power thereof, and judgement in the hands of his servants." The organization would eventually be colloquially known, however, as the Council of Fifty, based on the number of participants—or, more simply, "the Kingdom." The purpose, practices, and even the name of the council were divinely appointed.[15]

The number of men inducted in the council grew every week. No women were invited to join, however. The new organization was to be formed "after the pattern of heaven"—the same phrase Smith had used at the Relief Society's founding two years previous. This particular pattern, however, revolved around male priesthood. Though Smith had previously approved the admission of women to the Quorum of the Anointed, which had served as the city's governing body since late 1843, only men could participate in this new political council. The timing of the Kingdom's founding was significant, as the same week the Relief Society was holding its meetings denouncing the evils of polygamy, Smith was establishing a new organization rooted in patriarchal authority. The men were specifically directly not to share details with their wives. As a result of the public controversies over polygamy, Smith had given up on his brief experiment with ruling bodies that included women.

The physical structure of the new council, during its meetings, suggested a strict order. Participants were seated in a semicircle, arranged from oldest to youngest, with Smith the lone figure in the middle as chair. Though everyone was allowed to speak on the topic at hand, the oldest spoke first. They were also bound to strict secrecy, with a warning that anyone who broke their oath would "lose his cursed head." Rather than turning toward transparency, in response to criticism, Smith concluded that the solution was to double down on clandestine authority. Smith's final council was to be the climax of the social, theological, and political developments in Nauvoo, the arena in which all of these spheres finally merged. It was also an explicit rejection of America's democratic model that triumphed equality.[16]

One of the primary goals of the Kingdom was to create a new governing document. The members appointed a committee to draft a constitution that featured those principles they felt the US Constitution lacked. Only a government that recognized God's sovereignty and priesthood authority, they posited, could weather the problems of the age. Orson Spencer, a member of the council, argued that if a government failed to perform God's bidding, it was necessary for God's elect men to bring about a correction, even if they drew accusations of treason from other Americans. Their activities, they believed, had been predicted by prophets of old. They explicitly referenced the Old Testament prophecies that foresaw the coming of a new millennial kingdom. The second chapter of the Book of Daniel, commonly treated as a political text by more militant religious groups in early America, was frequently cited. In it, the prophet Daniel explains King Nebuchadnezzar's dream in which a stone not cut by human hands destroys a manmade statue. Biblical interpreters, emphasizing God's sovereignty, traditionally identified the statue as the composite human kingdoms throughout history that would eventually be consumed by God's kingdom. In Mormon hands, however, the story predicted their latter-day restoration and eventual dominance. Smith's new council was the realization of the prophecy. God's kingdom—the Mormon theocracy—was not "cut by man," because it was divinely designed and ready to topple the kingdoms then inhabiting the world.[17]

The effort to write a new constitution was not unique to the Mormons. Many groups wondered whether a document crafted half a century before was still capable of governing in the present. A number of reformers, who believed the age required new political thinking, argued for constitutional amendments. Angelina and Sarah Grimké based their argument for an expansion of women's rights on an innovative reading of the Bible that emphasized female empowerment. Some antislavery activists, including William Lloyd Garrison, believed the entire founding document was too dated and deserved to be dismissed wholesale. These anxieties only heightened as the sectional conflict intensified. Radical abolitionist John Brown would eventually draft his own provisional constitution— a document in which the human rights of all races was ensured—in preparation for his raid at Harpers Ferry. Simultaneously, many slaveholders wondered whether the Constitution lacked the provisions necessary to suppress the abolitionists. Some southern politicians argued that one way to strengthen political order was by sacralizing it through divine rule. When the Confederate States of America created its own constitution shortly after seceding from the Union in 1861, its preamble stated that it sought to "secure the blessings of liberty to ourselves and our posterity [by] invoking the favor and guidance of Almighty God." On many points of the political spectrum, people found the authoritative nature of divine validation appealing.[18]

The saints' hopes, like those of some of their contemporaries, were buoyed as they considered a new constitutional order. The Council of Fifty provided a platform for many men to express their desires for God's kingdom. Secular constitutions, Reynolds Cahoon declared at a council meeting on April 5, were nothing more than a skeleton without flesh. As no nation recognized divine rule, Brigham Young concurred, every government lacked the mandate to properly rule humanity. The only solution was to turn to the example of Moses and his sacred monarchy. In these ways, the saints were planning to go further than even someone like Garrison, who did not seek theocracy as a solution to the problem of slavery.[19]

Yet members of the council were not ready to forgo republicanism altogether. At an April 11 meeting, Joseph Smith paradoxically explained that the "political title" for the council was still "Jeffersonianism" and "Jeffersonian Democracy," a claim that would have made Jefferson, had he been alive and present, blanch. But how could theocracy be squared with democratic principles? To Smith's mind, it was all about priorities and allegiances. Saints would work with the freedom granted them by divine rule, even if they were subject to revelatory correction. When asked why a council should labor to draft a constitution when a prophet could merely recite God's will, Smith explained that he envisioned theocratic and democratic principles blending: delegates were to gather as much information as possible, debate it as a council, and then God would reaffirm their actions. Citizens of the kingdom, in other words, were "to get the voice of God and then acknowledge it, and see it executed." It was stretched, if not broken, reasoning, but it was a sign of Mormonism's malleable political theology.

Smith even revised the common American mantra of "*Vox populi, Vox Dei*": rather than meaning "the voice of the people is the voice of God," Smith instead insisted the phrase meant "the voice of the people *assenting* to the voice of God." Yet at other times they were quite explicit in rejecting democratic conventions. At one point, apostle Erastus Snow moved "that this honorable assembly receive from this time henceforth and forever, Joseph Smith, as our Prophet, Priest & King, and uphold him in that capacity in which God has anointed him." The motion passed unanimously. Even if Smith lost his bid to be president of the United States, he could console himself with the position of king of God's empire.[20]

Yet Smith was careful not to let this monarchical rhetoric go too far. Though he was appointed "Prophet, Priest & King" at the morning meeting on April 11, that afternoon he delivered a discourse more traditionally republican in nature and centered on religious liberty. His new council would rule the world under the auspices of God's priesthood, but Smith insisted that they should always include non-Mormons within their ranks, as the kingdom was separate from the church. Smith even initiated three non-Mormons into the council. He declared his intent to allow any citizen to think and worship as they please, as long as they worked within the boundaries of divine law. That citizenship in the kingdom required allegiance to Smith's prophethood did not seem to throw off that balance, at least in his view. To him, it was the only way to preserve order and reserve the religious liberties to the saints that he felt they had been deprived of. Smith became so animated during his discourse that he swung around a twenty-four-inch ruler and broke it in two. In response, Brigham Young said, "as the rule was broken in the hands of our chairman so might every tyrannical government be broken before us." The world was theirs for the taking.[21]

The culmination of these early council meetings came on April 18, when the members presented a draft of the new constitution. The document was long on indignation but short on details. It featured a rambling preamble that summarized much of the political debates within the council to that point. "We, the people of the Kingdom of God," it declared, recognized that "all power emanates from God, that the earth is his possession, and he alone has the right to govern the nations and set in order the kingdoms of this world." No other government acknowledged God's authority as lawgiver, king, or sovereign, and all governing bodies were therefore bound to fail. Secular republicanism failed to ensure universal rights, but rather introduced "cruelty, oppression, bondage, slavery, rapine, bloodshed, murder, carnage, desolation," and all the other "evils" that plagued the world. The inevitable result were corrupt rulers like Missouri governor Lilburn Boggs, who trampled upon the liberties of the oppressed.[22]

After this preamble, the constitution featured three articles: the first declared God the ruler of all mankind, the second reaffirmed the authority of God's prophet and priesthood, and the third dictated the necessity of righteous judges. While the language at times borrowed from outside sources, and while the draft emphasized the rights and liberties of all citizens, the document's structure was clearly drawn from the patriarchal tradition of the Old Testament. Even so, Joseph Smith judged the draft insufficient in its attempt to capture revelatory power. He explained that any written constitution would be too rigid to contain the word of God and the flexibility required by prophetic leadership. A week later, he dictated a revelation declaring that the council itself would serve as a living constitution. God's kingdom would be governed by priesthood leadership rather than according to a sacred text.[23]

This decision reveals an important and distinctive element of the Mormon protest. Americans of the time venerated the idea of founding texts, even if they, like Garrison, rejected the US Constitution. After all, the Constitution, in setting out the contours for fair government, was a correction to the British tradition of a "living" (that is, unwritten) constitution centered on parliamentary action and monarchical control. Without a set of stated and agreed-upon principles meant to disperse authority, many Americans believed, control of government and society would be concentrated into too few hands. The US Constitution's dispersal of sovereignty throughout the general population of citizens democratized control and enabled civil justice.

But to the Mormons who feared that democratic sovereignty had become synonymous with mob rule, a return to strict hierarchy and concentrated power was appealing. Smith's preferred title for his role in the council—he called himself the "proper source"—hinted at his theory of power. While the code name had primarily been used previously to emphasize Smith's authoritative role over doctrinal and ecclesiastical matters, it now took on a political import. To those in the Mormon council, what made a theodemocratic government function was the full authority of its leader. Councils and democratic participation were important, but only inasmuch as they revealed and enacted priestly wisdom. Even if the entire council disagreed with Smith, Brigham Young argued, it did not matter, because Smith was the font of divine knowledge. The core democratic principle that elected officials represented the interests of the citizenship was misguided. They had not "*elected* [Smith] to be our Prophet, Priest and King," Young explained, but rather "our prophet has *chosen* us, and what this people receives through him is law." One participant in the same meeting, David Yearsley, wondered aloud, "How can a man be elected president when he is already proclaimed king?" It was a good question.[24]

Again, though, Joseph Smith was not ready to fully break with the American democratic tradition. He envisioned the council functioning as a shadow government, "the head" of the American political body, with Washington as "the tail." They would still work within the system—at least for the time being. This was Smith once again tempering the Mormon message even after he started it on a new radical course. The Kingdom's rhetoric always outpaced its reality. At times, the council served as a release valve for Smith's radical ambitions, a space in which he could envision drastic solutions to their problems. At least during his lifetime, however, the council never sought to enact any of his most radical proposals.[25]

When William Clayton returned to his home after debating the new constitutional document, he exuberantly recorded in his diary that it had seemed as if heaven had already begun on earth. At least at the rhetorical level, Mormons involved with the council were ready to roll back some of the most significant elements of American democracy. They wanted to infuse government with divine origin and meaning, and they knew that such a proposal promised an angry response. A year later, after a flurry of violence, William Phelps said that "the greatest fears manifested by our enemies is the union of church and state." Phelps chose to embrace the accusation: "I believe we are actually doing this and it is what the Lord designs." The Mormon Council of Fifty was a radical rejection of America's political culture and religious order. In its view, the separation between church and state had only inaugurated chaos and degeneracy. It was time to reinstate God's kingdom, the only authority equipped to bring harmony to a fractured world.[26]

IN THESE SAME HEADY WEEKS in the spring of 1844, Joseph Smith began to contemplate whether God's empire would be best suited to the western frontier, or the land beyond it. At the same time that Mormon leaders sought to redeem America, then, Smith considered a future for the Mormons outside of it. The idea alone of another migration seemed tragic, given the Mormons' previous expulsions from Missouri and Ohio. But tensions were increasing within the state, and the saints had to be prepared.

The Mormons had been considering new homes for their faith for some months, if not years. Several men were assigned on missions to the Republic of Texas, a nation that had recently broken off from Mexico, and they had returned by the end of October 1843. Intrigued by their positive reports of a warm welcome, Smith immediately sent more missionaries south. The Mormons also considered sending men to Oregon, which was jointly managed by the United States and Britain. Assigning proselytizing ministers on missions had been common since the church's founding, but these exploratory missions were different, in that they were focused on finding sites for new Mormon settlements. The church's focus was split: they wanted to cement their place in Illinois and at the same time secure fallback options outside the state. The city petitioned the federal government's executive and legislative branches, asking for sponsored immigration to either Texas or Oregon. Even if Nauvoo was to remain the center of the Mormon kingdom, it made sense to establish other colonies as a safeguard.[27]

The concept of manifest destiny, or the belief in America's inevitable march across the North American continent, was not far from American minds in 1844. The Texas region had long been a fascination. It had been part of the Spanish Empire until Mexico won its independence in a decade-long revolution that ended in 1821, and then the region was immediately filled by Americans anxious to take advantage of the land. (Indeed, many had had their eyes on the territory since 1803, as some argued that it was included in the Louisiana Purchase.) The influx of immigrants who sought autonomy—and wanted to overturn Mexico's antislavery laws—eventually climaxed in a new rebellion and the creation of a Texas Republic in 1836.

The new republic, never intent on remaining independent, immediately petitioned to be admitted to the Union as a new state. The question of slavery and a fear of angering Mexico, however, paralyzed Congress for nearly a decade. Yet Texas's allure was strong. The region had become an economic hub, and the territory was rich with cotton and livestock. Federal officials began secret conversations with Texas leaders in 1843, and statehood finally became a national issue during the following year's presidential election. Because the area had been primarily settled by immigrants from slaveholding states, southerners salivated at the thought of strengthening their slave empire. Even some northern politicians envisioned Texas as crucial to making the United States a continent-spanning power. New York journalist John L. O'Sullivan famously proclaimed it was America's "manifest destiny" to expand across the entire continent.[28]

This hope infused Joseph Smith's presidential platform. His campaign pamphlet argued that the nation should immediately annex Texas, and also consider further expansion into Canada and Mexico and even into all unsettled regions of North America. The entire continent, in his mind, should be one national family. Smith was aware of the opposing point of view. He had read Senator Henry Clay's vehement rejection of Texas's annexation on the grounds that it would extend the Slave Power, and felt the need to address it in his first public speech as a candidate on March 7. Slavery, he reasoned, was *precisely* the reason Texas should be annexed, because the federal government could sell much of the land and use the money to liberate all of those enslaved within its borders. This proposal was unrealistic—and naïve in its understanding of federal finances—but it was one of many moderate appeals to end the peculiar institution. Smith understood that some would oppose his emancipation scheme on the grounds that it would lead to interracial mixing, a great fear of many white Americans. To satisfy these concerns, Smith proposed to let Texas's newly freed blacks emigrate to Mexico, "where all colors are alike."[29]

The possibility of settling Texas became an even more immediate focus for the Mormons in early March. Messengers from the church's pinery operation in Wisconsin arrived in Nauvoo with appealing ideas. Lyman Wight and George Miller, longtime members and leaders of the faith, had most recently been in charge of harvesting lumber for the church's building projects in Wisconsin. Their experience now led them to turn their gaze to the South. Conversations with local tribes in Wisconsin opened their minds to possible settlement options in the Texas Republic. According to Wight and Miller, the "Lamanites"—a shorthand, based on the Book of Mormon, for Native Americans—were anxious to join the gospel and, if they received support, would be willing to relocate to the Southwest, where they believed they could receive a warm reception from the Cherokee and Choctaw nations. These tribes, recently resettled through the Indian Removal Act, were allegedly willing to meet with church leaders. Even as the prophet made public his plans to avoid a mixed-race society in Texas, some of his advisors were scheming to form an interracial alliance on America's borderlands.[30]

Smith called for an emergency meeting to discuss these possibilities. In the very same room where the city's elites crafted Smith's campaign to become president of the United States, they began orchestrating an alliance outside its borders. They sent Lucien Woodworth to Texas to speak confidentially with Sam Houston, the republic's president. Willard Richards, Smith's secretary, knew this act would be controversial. After recording portions of the conversation in Smith's diary, Richards took care to cross out the reference to Texas and Houston and instead wrote the names backward as "Saxet" and "Notsuoh." It was a crude encryption, but one that captured their earnestness.[31]

Western settlement remained a constant topic for the Council of Fifty throughout its meetings in the spring of 1844. Its members knew that Texas, given its national attention, provided them an opening. American politicians were genuinely concerned that if they did not act quickly, the British Empire might make a move to acquire the territory. The British Parliament, it was believed, was dedicated to isolating the slave states, and if they could remove Texas from the equation, it would be an antislavery coup. At the same time, the Oregon Territory, which had been awkwardly joint-managed by America and Britain for some decades, had also become a focal point for politicians who wanted to solidify control on the continent. The fear of British espionage was a real and constant presence.[32]

Joseph Smith referred to the dilemma of western expansion in his March 7 address to the saints when he claimed America must move quickly to displace the British officers then infiltrating Texas. But they also had their eyes on the Oregon Territory. Knowing the federal government was desperate, Richards proposed that they send Congress a petition offering their services to protect the northwest region. The resulting congressional proposal reveals their bold vision, if also their naïve expectations. It requested that the government appoint Smith a military general over a company of 100,000 armed soldiers who would be ready to take control of the Oregon Territory and otherwise expand the boundaries of America's empire. Any citizen who opposed their march would be fined a thousand dollars and sentenced to two years of hard labor. In return for receiving the armed protection they long desired, then, the Mormons were willing to be enlisted in the cause of American imperialism. The Pacific Northwest could be a jointly managed space for Mormons within the American nation.[33]

Excitement grew when Woodworth returned from Texas and reported that Sam Houston seemed interested in the proposal they had previously sent to him in March, though the republic's president was unwilling to make any promises. The Mormons had reason to be hopeful. To Texans, the prospect of thousands of armed Mormons joining their ranks would help alleviate the worry of an invasion by Mexico. They were especially vulnerable after their case for annexation failed in April, which left them still without the aid of the American army. Writing from Washington, Orson Hyde, the apostle who had been appointed as a political delegate, similarly reasoned that Houston would offer encouragement for settlement as long as the Mormons offered military support. Confident in their success, Hyde believed the Mormons and Texans could even invade Mexico and claim its land for themselves. Or, if Mexico left them in peace, Texas could serve as a new hub for the Mormon church, a place where southern converts could gather with their slaves and establish plantations to benefit the broader Mormon kingdom. Nor were the Mormons alone in making proposals. John Walton, former mayor of Galveston, wrote a letter on June 3 that offered the church over 265,000 purchasable acres in the eastern part of the republic and promised they would face no religious persecution. He even pledged that the church would immediately have voting power in the republic, and Smith could conceivably be elected to any office. All the Mormons had to do in return was help crush any Mexican resistance.[34]

Even before he received Walton's letter, Smith recognized an opportunity when he saw one. There was a power void in Texas's inchoate republic, as Woodworth reported that the government was working at only half-capacity. If there was no room for Mormons in the American nation, then the saints would merely make the Texas Republic Mormon. Smith instructed the Kingdom on May 3 to send fifty able men to Texas, where they would purchase homes, convert their equals, and take control of the government. Hyrum proposed that the new territory could serve as a place of settlement for the growing number of English converts. Church leaders immediately instructed those overseeing Mormon migration from Britain to consider sending as many as 100,000 converts to Texas over the next eighteen months. Three days later, on May 6, they appointed commissioners, including Woodworth, to continue negotiations with Houston. They also designated the twenty-five families who had just returned from the pineries in Wisconsin to serve as the first undercover migrants to Texas.[35]

But neither company ended up making the voyage. Church newspapers continued to share new information about both Texas and Oregon, yet the Mormons would never send settlers to either place. There were other matters more pressing than an imagined western empire.

EVEN AS MORMONS LOOKED SOUTH AND WEST for new settlement options, they also looked east in their support for Joseph Smith's presidential candidacy. Campaigning for the Mormon prophet required a missionary army nearly as large as the one needed to colonize Mexico, though armed with pamphlets instead of guns. This was not a half-hearted effort. Just a month after the campaign's public announcement in March, church leaders declared at a general conference that they needed both volunteers and resources. Hyrum Smith explained that they would approach the election the same way they approached everything else: with a massive mobilization. Two hundred and forty-four men were called as "electioneering" missionaries and sent across the United States. "Lift up your voices like thunder," Hyrum instructed them, as "there is power and influence enough among us to put in a President." Just as most of them had previously been called to spread the word of God, they were now called to spread the policies of the prophet. The missionaries were to host conventions in every state, which would choose electors for a new political party to run in the November general election. Even where their voice couldn't be heard, they hoped their words would be read—they therefore decided to establish a newspaper in New York City. All these efforts would culminate in a national convention, to be held in Baltimore, Maryland, in July.[36]

Not only were these activities remarkably well organized, but they also reflected the nation's growing commitment to party politics. In

1844, political conventions, as a practice, were less than two decades old, and Americans were only just becoming accustomed to national parties. (While there had been a form of a two-party system since the 1790s, the earliest iterations mostly rejected the identification of party organization.) The Anti-Masonic Party in 1831 was the first to hold a national convention, and the Democratic Party convention in 1840 was the first to adopt a national platform. All were evidence of the Jacksonian impulse to expand decision-making power to a broader array of delegates. Despite Mormonism's emphasis on hierarchy, and even though Smith could expect the support of all Mormons, they decided to follow national precedent. Their choice of location for a national convention, Baltimore, was an act of political mimicry: it was the same city that hosted the Whig and Democratic conventions and John Tyler's independent convention that year. Soon, Mormon delegates had spread across the nation, ready to organize individual state conventions.[37]

The saints' New York–based newspaper emphasized that their candidate was neither a southern man with northern principles, nor a northern man with southern principles, but an outsider with *American* principles, anxious to fight for the rights of all citizens. Meanwhile, the message that Smith's spokesmen shared across the nation was a mix of traditional political rhetoric and radical theology. One missionary spoke of their duty to campaign for a man he knew to be the friend of all religious people, and the only candidate worthy of the nation's confidence. The campaigners argued that a world that separated ecclesiastical and political leadership led to the alienation of the former and the corruption of the latter. Righteous men, however, were immune from the entanglements that politicians seemed to always find themselves in, and their prophet was the man to save the nation from its perilous direction. America could still be redeemed from its partisan division. It was a hard sell. "It takes nothing short of labour and the assisting grace of God," reported one campaigner, "to hunt up the honest in heart and adopt them into the kingdom." Another confessed to being "not a little chagrined" at their lack of success.[38]

Their message was also one of divine intervention. Joseph Smith was not only a righteous candidate, but a prophetic visionary assisted by God. America's problems were too serious to be solved by the squabbling that resulted from a reliance on human reason. Who better to direct a godly people than God's chosen prophet? In one of the most notable campaign images, Mormons in New York printed an advertisement that announced the Mormon prophet's platform as a divine spark to heal the fractured world. The image depicted dark clouds, which represented error and apostasy, being pierced with the divine light of revelatory command. The phrase *"Super Hanc Petram Aedificabo,"* the Latin text of first half of Matthew 18:16—"upon this rock I will build my Church"—appeared at the center of the image. Yet the latter part of the phrase, which translated as "my church," had been excised. It now implied that the "rock" was not limited to the religious sphere, but should also serve as the foundation for politics. Just as Peter had

Campaign image for Joseph Smith. The New York–based Mormon newspaper *The Prophet* published this image as an advertisement for Joseph Smith's presidential run on June 15, 1844.

been the repository for religious authority, the Mormons now believed God's commandments to Joseph Smith would be the basis for political authority. The United States was not to be saved through political compromise, but redemption.[39]

While the electioneering missionaries were tasked with convincing the general public to support Smith's campaign, Orson Hyde had an even more challenging commission: to convince American politicians to support the church's various colonization projects. If anyone was prepared for such a lofty assignment, it was Hyde. An early convert to the church and one of the faith's original apostles appointed nearly a decade before, he was a portly figure from Connecticut who had already been on a mission to Jerusalem to rededicate the land for the gathering of the Jews. Now he found himself in an equally foreign land—Washington, DC—arguing that congressmen should deputize Smith as an officer in the US Army, give him the command over 100,000 troops, and allow the Mormon-led militia to colonize the disputed territories of Texas and Oregon. The Council of Fifty had advised Hyde not to revise or soften any of their congressional proposals—Smith directed him "not to suffer any part of the memorial to be stricken out"—and Hyde tried to follow orders. He had originally been jubilant about his prospects, and even prophesied that Congress would accept the petition. But once he reached the damp streets of Washington in late April, those hopes already seemed like a distant memory.[40]

Hyde immediately went to work nonetheless. The day after he arrived, he met with members of the Illinois delegation: congressmen John Hardin, Joseph Hoge, John Wentworth, and Stephen A. Douglas, as well as senator Stephen James Semple. They all appeared interested in the Oregon settlement, Hyde reported, but they were not optimistic about the memorial's chances. Hoge, whose election the previous August had been orchestrated by the Mormons of Nauvoo, was especially doubtful, as he believed any military effort would alarm Britain. Semple claimed that the very thing that made the proposal relevant—the current excitement over the Oregon territory—also made it ill timed, as it was far from the only petition currently being considered by Congress. The debates over northwestern expansion had become heated as northern Whigs were mostly opposed to organized and militant expansion for fear it would lead to war. Hyde proposed that the men commissioned into Smith's army be considered "emigrants," rather than soldiers, as a way to ward off those concerns. He must have been aware, however, that the sight of tens of thousands of people marching behind the Mormon prophet was bound to cause suspicion, no matter what they were called. The congressmen eventually persuaded Hyde to remove the provision that Smith be made a military officer, but the revised petition still floundered in Congress and was quickly swept aside.[41]

The Illinois delegation encouraged Hyde and the Mormons to migrate to Oregon on their own accord, however. Though they couched the suggestion as a means for Smith and his followers to finally achieve independence, and to solidify America's claim on the Oregon Territory, the politicians likely saw it as a way to rid themselves of a growing nuisance. Hyde objected to their plans by claiming that they needed federal protection from various threats, including Missourians, during their westward march. Douglas, for his part, was especially keen on the settlement possibility, and suggested that he was willing to resign from Congress, lead their expedition, and serve as their territorial governor. Though Douglas's sincerity could be doubted in many cases, his counsel was consistent with his belief in the private colonization of western lands as a way to expand popular sovereignty. He provided Hyde with a copy of John C. Frémont's *Report on an Exploration*, the most popular overview of western territories at the time, and promised to put Joseph Smith in touch with people in the region. Douglas appeared as eager to advance American colonization of the Northwest as he was to erase the Mormon problem in Illinois.[42]

After lengthy discussions with the congressmen, senators, and even President Tyler himself, Hyde came away with little optimism over the possibility of federal support. He concluded that Congress would not act in either Oregon or Texas anytime soon, out of fear of inciting Mex-

ico or Britain, and so the saints, if they decided relocation was the
correct move, should emigrate as soon as possible. It would be better
to arrive early, he reasoned, because if they waited any longer, they
might be competing with other settlers. He believed that integrating
with other populations would be difficult, given their experience in
Missouri and Illinois, so if they wanted their own, isolated kingdom,
they had to act quickly. Hyde teamed with fellow apostle Parley Pratt
to author yet another petition asking Congress for $2 million as repa-
rations for Missouri—they would refuse to give up until they received
some form of restitution, he warned—but otherwise he would wait no
longer for government assistance.[43]

Just as significant as Hyde's pragmatic conclusions were his reflections on the democratic process. Now having witnessed national politics up close, he was all the more convinced that the entire system was
a failure. Congressmen appeared to him as cowardly and naïve players
in a game of checkers, too scared to make a wrong move. They were
never able to address the most important questions facing the American people because they were too worried about losing their constituents and the approval of their parties. What was important was not
whether an action was correct, but whether it suited the politics of the
majority. Hyde denounced these "tangling alliances" that forbade Congress from seeking justice. He contrasted the flailing politicians with
the Council of Fifty, where unity prevailed due to the unimpeachable
word of the Lord. "There is more wisdom and order manifested in one
of our councils at Nauvoo," he wrote fellow apostle John E. Page, "than
you would ever see here." His experience in Washington reaffirmed
his skepticism toward secular government. A compromised democracy
was incompatible with the uncompromising nature of divine laws.[44]

But to Hyde's colleagues, his actions in Washington demonstrated
he was already infected with the democratic virus. Smith called a
council meeting as soon as Hyde's letters arrived in Nauvoo. He was
frustrated that their own delegate to Washington agreed to amend the
original petition: Hyde, after all, had removed the provision that would

make Smith an officer in the army in order to assuage the fears of the congressmen, as well as out of Hyde's sincere concern that such an action could only be taken by the executive branch. But to Smith, Hyde had compromised God's will. The Council of Fifty moved to send another memorial that should be presented to Congress without any alteration. Smith chastised Hyde for his concessions and claimed that, to accomplish anything with Congress, he must be willing to "command them as the sovereign people." Congress should be bending to *his* will, not the other way around. Though his brother Hyrum tried to calm the prophet by explaining that "there was policy in people being crafty," Joseph responded by emphasizing the importance of maintaining pure sovereignty. The council then commissioned a letter of rebuke. "To throw away that *one item*," the letter explained to Hyde, "is to throw away *the whole* Memorial."[45]

When he received the rebuke, Hyde quickly replied and apologized for tarnishing the council's dignity. He then brought the unaltered memorial back to Illinois delegates as well as to John Tyler. It failed again. Congress, including the Illinois delegation, did not give it much consideration, and Tyler insisted it would exceed his constitutional limits. Meanwhile, Smith had nearly given up hope of working with the American government. Richards reported to Hyde on May 25 that their only chance to redeem the nation was Smith's election to the presidency. After meeting once more the following week to discuss a mission to Native tribes, the Council of Fifty adjourned indefinitely. Much would happen before it would meet again.[46]

The late-winter and early-spring months of 1844 were the zenith of Mormonism's expansionist thinking. Even as Nauvoo's leading men faced increasing resistance to polygamy, including from women within the city, they cultivated grand plans. They campaigned to elect their own prophet as president of the American nation, plotted colonization projects outside of America's borders, and created a new theocratic organization meant to replace the American government. There was no limit to their audacity.

But their ideas ran aground on the facts of their situation. A grow-

ing number of people—inside and outside Nauvoo—were uncomfort-
able with their bold activities, both public and private. The Mormons
could no longer be relied upon, one neighbor wrote to Congressman
John Hardin, because, at any time and without notice, Joseph Smith
could once again "have a Revelation" that upended the entire religious and Nauvoo's society. He urged Hardin that the party must
take an explicitly anti-Mormon platform and settle the problem once
and for all.[47]

CHAPTER 7

Harvest

The reason why the Mormons and the Anti-Mormons cannot live
together is this; the mormons are governed by their religious leaders,
their fanatical prophets and priests. The religious leaders are also
their civil magistrates, and control the actions and votes of the people
with despotic sway.

—THOMAS SHARP, UNDATED EDITORIAL, CIRCA. 1845[1]

The greatest fears manifested by our enemies is the union of
Church and State. I believe we are actually doing this and it is what
the Lord designs.

—WILLIAM W. PHELPS, MARCH 4, 1845[2]

I think the result [of the conflict] will be the extermination of the
one [community] or the other.

—JAMES BRATTLE, JULY 5, 1844[3]

Carthage Jail, Hancock County, 1853. HISTORIC SITES PHOTOGRAPH COLLECTION, LDS CHURCH
HISTORY LIBRARY, SALT LAKE CITY.

James Robbins worried about the current state of affairs in Illinois. A resident of Adams County, in the western part of the state, Robbins had never seen anything like the events of June 1844. What had once been a quiet region had become a site of ominous and escalating activity. "Our roads have been throng[ed] to over flowing for nearly 2 weeks," he reported in a letter to his family on June 16. Angry groups of men were roaming from one town to another, threatening revenge against each other. Robbins worried where his state was headed. If the Mormons refused to step down, he mused, they would be forced out of the country. This would not be easily accomplished, however. Robbins knew that Joseph Smith, the leader of the beleaguered faith, commanded a militia of around four or five thousand men.[4]

The frontier was known for rough justice—often enacted through extralegal action—and the drawn-out conflict between Nauvoo and its neighbors seemed headed for a familiar conclusion. Robbins knew that blood could be shed at any moment, and he was not alone. "The feeling of this country is now lashed to its utmost pitch," reported a nearby newspaper, "and will break forth in fury upon the slightest provocation." The Mississippi River was about to turn red.[5]

Modern Americans often pride themselves on their peaceful democracy and successful—or, at least, grudging but nonviolent—incorporation of divergent cultures into the national fabric. Yet the climax of Mormonism's fraught relationship with the state of Illinois reveals the boundaries of acceptance and inclusion. It also highlighted the limits of American democracy. The Mormon community, as a minority religion, could not assure its own protection; its non-Mormon neighbors, unable to directly control Nauvoo's citizens through judicial means, turned to an extralegal process in order to reaffirm the will of the majority. Both sides recognized the tenuous nature of America's system of governance: redress came slowly, if at all, and legal protections for religious liberty were far too fragile. Sometimes, the voice of the people had to be heard outside official channels.

Robbins's fears were soon realized. "We are now," wrote Wesley Williams ten days later, on June 26, in reference to his torn community, "in a state of warfare." Williams, another non-Mormon resident of the region, reported hearing the sounds of military drums, as local troops gathered from throughout the surrounding counties to confront the Mormon threat. Conditions only grew worse from there. The very next day witnessed the start of what would be an eighteen-month period of violence between the saints who lived around Nauvoo and their neighbors who wished they lived anywhere else. At stake was whether the Mormons belonged in America. In the end, both sides would conclude that they did not.[6]

EVER SINCE HIS CONFRONTATION with Joseph Smith earlier that year, William Law had brooded. While the January 5 dispute in front of the City Council appeared to end peaceably, both sides quietly sought retribution. Law was informed later that week that he had been expelled both from the formal First Presidency as well as the informal Quorum of the Anointed. And while in public their relationship appeared amicable, their private discussions were anything but. At one point, Law told Smith that his cause was both unjust and dishonorable, to which the prophet responded in kind. Freed from his ecclesiastical duties, and now under no obligation to defend Smith, Law worked to bring an end to what he believed were Nauvoo's corruptions.[7]

Nor was he alone. Several other influential men in the city were also finally ready to challenge the prophet directly, including William's brother Wilson. Another set of brothers, Francis and Chauncey Higbee, had been members of the faith for more than a decade, but had soured on Smith's leadership. Chauncey was excommunicated in May 1842 as part of the John C. Bennett scandal—he, like Bennett, was accused of improper sexual relationships—and Francis was accused by Smith of conspiring with Missouri officials in early January 1844. Similarly, Robert D. Foster, a prominent physician and businessman in Nauvoo who had long butted heads with the prophet, was also now taking a more active role in the growing dissent. And around the same time, Joseph H. Jackson, an itinerant author who floated in and out of the city, began spreading gossip about the saints. He eventually published his own exposé in the style of Bennett's.[8]

Each of these men held a particular grudge against the prophet. Some of their grievances were personal: Francis Higbee allegedly pursued one of Smith's plural wives, and Joseph Jackson was denied a chance to marry Hyrum Smith's daughter. Others took issue with the institution of polygamy itself: William and Wilson Law believed Smith was a fallen prophet who was corrupting God's true faith. For his part, Foster saw his economic activities continually stymied by Smith's efforts to prioritize his own and the church's. But together, these men formed a formidable leadership of an organized resistance.

And unlike John C. Bennett, they had both the means and support to pose a considerable threat to the prophet. Though Jackson was a newcomer to the city, the others boasted deep roots and significant positions: besides William Law's role in the First Presidency, Wilson Law served as the major general and Robert Foster as the surgeon general in the Nauvoo Legion, and the Higbee brothers were sons of one of Smith's most trusted advisors. Their accusations could not be easily dismissed. Encouraged by the public dissent within Nauvoo, onlookers, especially from nearby Warsaw, increased their print attacks on the faith, and many urged the state to revoke Nauvoo's charter. Not even a direct appeal from the governor in January could quiet their concern.[9]

The growing discord within the city made Smith nervous. Even as he pushed forward with his public and private political activities, he redoubled his efforts to secure the loyalty of those around him. Brigham Young, noting Smith's anxiety, complained that their greatest difficulties came from those within their own community. Late in March, Smith heard that there was a conspiracy to kill his entire family. Terrified, he increased his personal security, appointed two witnesses to sign affidavits affirming the rumor, and instructed the police force to be on call. The barricade he had worked so hard to build around him, his family, and his church seemed to be crumbling.[10]

Besides the rumor of a direct threat on his life, Smith recognized the mounting opposition as a challenge to his prophetic authority. Never one to back down from a confrontation, he spent April's general conference proving he was not a "fallen prophet" by pronouncing some of his most radical doctrines yet. He declared to a rapt audience that God, perched on his heavenly throne, was nothing more than "a man like yourselves," and that "you have got to learn how to make yourselves God, king and priest," just like the divine being they worshipped. The discourse was the climax of Smith's theological development, and it left many believers astonished, as it provided new possibilities for human progression. One faithful observer noted that anyone who failed to see in Smith the spirit of prophecy "must be dark," while Law dismissed the teaching as among the most blasphemous he had ever heard. There was no middle ground.[11]

But if Smith's detractors viewed his latest theological claims as heresy, it was Nauvoo's continued judicial actions that were interpreted by the outside world as a more direct threat. While city officials were willing to walk back some of their more extreme resolutions from the previous December, Smith continued to find ways to evade prosecution. Francis Higbee, familiar with his father's handling of Smith's legal cases, was especially concerned that Smith was flagrantly breaking democratic norms. He therefore began testing Smith's defenses through a series of trials. In early May 1844, the prophet was arrested by Hancock County deputy sheriff John Parker for slandering Higbee back in January. Once again, Smith turned to Nauvoo's municipal court for help, and the court not only granted him a writ of habeas corpus but also ordered Higbee to pay the court's costs. (The county, unconvinced by Nauvoo's actions, ordered Smith to appear before the circuit court later that month.) This was merely the first of Higbee's attempts to bring Smith to justice, as his faith in America's judicial system led him to continue agitating.[12]

It was another Smith, however, who revealed the breadth of Nauvoo's rejection of American law. That same spring, a newcomer named Jeremiah Smith—no relation to Joseph—arrived in Nauvoo after escaping legal trouble of his own. He was accused of defrauding the federal government after claiming funds in Iowa that were meant for a relative with the same name. While charges were dismissed at his first hearing in February, he was caught attempting the same crime in April, which prompted him to flee to Nauvoo. The charges had nothing to do with the Mormon church, but Joseph took sympathy and instructed his clerk to prepare a writ of habeas corpus for Jeremiah in advance of any arrest warrant. The municipal court obliged not once but twice, allowing Jeremiah to evade arresting officers when they arrived in Nauvoo. Though Nauvoo's use of these writs had already been exceptionally liberal, the granting of one before an actual arrest warrant had even been issued was a new tactic, and it drew additional ire. Nearby newspapers that had previously been hesitant to criticize Mormon practices angrily denounced the Jeremiah Smith ordeal as a flagrant violation of the American legal system. Thomas Sharp, always eager to attack the Mormons, announced that Smith was now effectively *"above the law."*[13]

That did not stop various groups from trying to bring them to justice, however. In late May, Nauvoo's prominent dissenters, including Higbee, flooded the church with legal cases, including accusations too grave to dismiss. The Law brothers swore that Smith was living adulterously with his plural wives, and Robert D. Foster accused the prophet of perjury. Smith first responded to these accusations by hiding from arrest, but soon followed the counsel of advisors who suggested that he go before a county jury. He declared in front of gathered saints on May 26 that all of the accusations, charges, and indictments were part of a wicked conspiracy originating with the devil. But he assured them that he was not wearied by the attack. "I should be like a fish out of water if I were out of persecution," he noted, and claimed he would not be "near so humble if I was not persecuted." The next day, he rode to Carthage, the county seat, to meet with a county judge, but was told he would have to wait until the fall for a trial.[14]

Those aiming to bring down Smith were not willing to let the matter linger. There were now enough dissenters to organize their own church, and they started holding weekly meetings in late April, only a week after the Laws and Fosters were officially excommunicated. They also sought new recruits, sending out missionaries to teach that Smith was a fallen prophet and that William Law had been appointed in his stead. A heartened Thomas Sharp reported in the *Warsaw Signal* that the group were among the most intelligent and formidable within Nauvoo, and that their numbers were quickly growing. Some estimates placed them at three hundred attendees every Sunday meeting.[15]

This group of dissenters rejected Smith's Nauvoo experiments and harked back to a time when the faith followed more traditional American values. They denounced, in particular, Smith's practice of polygamy and attempts to unite church and state. At first, Smith reacted to the new church with dismissiveness. "I had rather be a fallen true prophet," he declared one sabbath meeting, "than a false prophet." But the dissenters' actions were ominous: rumors soon circulated that they had acquired a printing press to publish all of Smith's secrets. Smith, as much as anyone else, knew a religious war could be won with words alone.[16]

The first and only issue of the dissenters' newspaper, the *Nauvoo Expositor*, appeared on June 7, 1844. The Laws, Higbees, and Foster were all listed as publishers. It was time, the paper claimed, for a reformation within the city. Their accusations were both sweeping and meticulously detailed. They accused Smith of claiming plural wives and teaching that there were innumerable Gods. They denounced the city's use of habeas corpus, which had shielded not only Joseph Smith, but also his friends, like Jeremiah Smith. The prophet was accused of making unholy alliances with politicians, explicitly directing the Mormon vote, and merging religious and civic spheres.

Most damaging, perhaps, were the newspaper's firsthand accounts of Smith's polygamous teachings. William Law swore to an account detailing how Hyrum Smith had shared the polygamy revelation in a City Council meeting the previous August, and his wife, Jane, testified to learning about it from the Smiths in private discussions. Lucinda Sagers, who had tried on several occasions to convince the church to punish her husband for taking another wife, published a notice revealing her continued frustration. When the church failed to provide her with justice when she brought her husband before the High Council a few months previous, she decided to take it herself by exposing the iniquity. Together, the accusations and evidence put forward were intended to justify the dissenters' allegiance both to American principles and Mormonism's original teachings.[17]

Even as the issue hit the streets, Robert Foster still wrestled with conflicted feelings, given his long relationship with the prophet, close friends within the church, and financial ties to Nauvoo. The same day that the *Nauvoo Expositor* was printed, Foster went to meet Smith at the prophet's home, eager to talk in private. The prophet, however, refused him. Though a few days later Smith attributed nefarious motives to the visit—and even hinted that Foster's real purpose was to privately corner Smith and shoot him—there is reason to believe that Foster sincerely desired to make amends with the prophet.[18]

Foster was perhaps not alone in his ambivalence, even if reconciliation would have been impossible at that point. Many of the people behind the *Expositor* were genuinely reticent to harm the church and city they loved. However, in the end, they saw no other way. It was their duty, they insisted, to disclose Smith's activities. A democracy required the full knowledge of a religious community's deeds when it threatened social order. They could not be true citizens, their preamble claimed, if they merely stood by as Smith trampled upon American principles. Anything less was a dereliction of duty. And so they exercised their American right to dissent and expose.[19]

AS COPIES OF THE NAUVOO EXPOSITOR ROLLED OFF the press only a couple blocks from the unfinished temple, Nauvoo was set ablaze. Could the *Expositor* be the mechanism through which Smith's city, and the entire project it represented, would be destroyed? The prophet called the City Council into session and urged them to take action. They met the very next morning, on Saturday, June 8, and three more times over the following days. These meetings would determine the course of Nauvoo's future.

Each session lasted several hours, and the muggy weather could hardly match the heat of Smith's fiery rhetoric. The newspaper, he bellowed, was calculated to destroy any chance of peace within the city; it was destined to stir up a mob spirit, as had happened to the Mormons in Missouri. Smith insisted it was the *Expositor*'s authors, and not those they claimed to expose, who were the true villains. He accused the Laws and Fosters of adultery, counterfeiting, and even attempted murder. In response to the *Expositor*'s account of Hyrum reading the polygamy revelation to the High Council the previous August, the prophet's brother came up with a clever, if unconvincing, response: the revelation only concerned ancient days, not the present. Joseph further claimed that he had merely taught that a man had the privilege to marry again after his first wife had died, and that Law had either invented or exaggerated the rest. The idea that eased polygamy's expansion—that a man could be sealed to both a deceased as well as a living spouse—was now used as a misdirection. The prophet insisted that the accusations, if not confronted, would result in the city being burned to ashes.[20]

But what could they do about the *Expositor*? Smith had long marshaled various groups to defend his reputation, but suppressing a newspaper was something new. The saints themselves had witnessed mobs destroy their own printing press, after all. However, by Monday, June 10, Smith was growing impatient. He argued that desperate measures were required and asked for a city ordinance to legally muzzle the press. Some were shocked at the proposal. One councilman, Benjamin Warrington, urged caution. Could they not merely fine Law and Foster, and give them a chance to retract their paper's first issue? But the Smith brothers brooked no dissent. Joseph emphasized that he would be disappointed if there were a single dissenting vote, and Hyrum argued that the only proper response was "to smash the press all to pieces and pie the type." Other councilmen voiced their agreement, including one who said a fine would never work on people as nefarious as Law. Another reminded his colleagues that he had lost a child during the Missouri crisis, and he was not ready to see a similar mobocratic spirit appear in Illinois. No single voice was louder than Joseph Smith's, however. At one point, worried that his motion might not pass, he insisted he "would rather die to morrow and have the thing smashed, than live & have it go on." It would prove a prophetic line.[21]

Eventually, Warrington—and anyone else who might have had reservations—was defeated. When asked whether it was time to shut down the *Expositor*, the council gave its unanimous approval. The newspaper was declared a nuisance to public safety and condemned to destruction. Smith called upon the Nauvoo Legion to support the action. Shortly after sundown, the city marshal led the police force and about two hundred armed men down the street to the *Expositor*'s print shop, dragged its printing press into the street, and burned it. To assure its destruction, the men used a sledgehammer to smash the smoldering remains. Smith then spoke to the police and legion men and assured them that what they had just done was justified.[22]

The resulting outcry was immediate. Francis Higbee leveled threats, Robert Foster warned of vengeance, and other dissenters claimed they would tear down the temple one stone at a time. Charles Foster detailed the "UNPARALLELED OUTRAGE" in a letter to the *Warsaw Signal*, which was eager to print his words. "War and extermination is inevitable!" Thomas Sharp breathlessly responded in his own editorial. The time for appeasement was past. "We have no time for comment, every man will make his own. LET IT BE MADE WITH POWDER AND BALL!!!" At an anti-Mormon gathering in Carthage a few days later, frustrated residents, incensed that Nauvoo would trample on the sacred right of freedom of the press, passed a resolution that declared they would take their protection into their own hands. Though they had previously held hope in the judicial system, that faith was no more. The circumstances justified each citizen taking steps to "put an immediate stop to the career of the mad prophet and his demoniac coadjutors." It was time to take a stand.[23]

The events of the following week went by in a blur. Based on the testimony of Francis Higbee, a warrant was issued by the Hancock County justice of the peace for the arrest of Smith and seventeen other men for inciting a riot on June 11. As expected, the prophet convened the municipal court and claimed that the accusations were baseless and nothing less than a conspiracy against him. Once again, the Mormon-controlled court ruled in Smith's favor, concluded that he had acted with proper authority, and issued him a writ of habeas corpus on June 13. They even ruled, once again, that Higbee had to pay Smith's court fees.[24]

The Hancock official, who was justifiably outraged at the city's dismissal of the county's charges, swore he would return with further legal action. Smith dashed off a letter to Governor Thomas Ford, emphasizing that they had destroyed the press only after a prolonged and responsible discussion and had followed legal precedent. Warsaw residents had heard this story before, however. At a gathering of three hundred anti-Mormons on June 14, they passed a resolution denouncing Nauvoo's use of habeas corpus, which they argued, rightfully, was intended to consistently screen Joseph Smith from arrest. The law was no longer capable of bringing the Mormons to justice, and the people of Warsaw were willing "to exterminate, utterly exterminate the wicked and abominable Mormon leaders, the authors of our troubles."[25]

The escalating tensions were felt throughout the region. While the Mormons had previously been seen as a benign city of religious fanatics, they were now understood to be a renegade military body unwilling to follow American law. Citizens throughout the state donated arms to the Warsaw resistance in preparation for battle. If the legal system could not bring justice to Nauvoo, then Illinois's residents were ready to do it themselves. There were even rumors that 1,500 Missourians had crossed the Mississippi River to join the cause. Smith, growing increasingly worried, urged the saints to maintain their composure while he went about preparing to defend the city. He appointed twenty-four delegates to spread word of Nauvoo's peaceful intentions to the neighboring community and wrote another letter to Governor Ford complaining that there was "an energetic attempt" to "exterminate 'the Saints' by force of arms." He urged Ford to dispatch officials to investigate the situation in order to avoid an all-out war.[26]

In the meantime, things were getting worse for saints living outside of Nauvoo. Levi Williams, the commander of Warsaw's militia, demanded that Mormons in surrounding communities give up their arms and ammunition and assist the county in arresting Smith. The prophet, responding to the resulting pleas for help from the outlying Mormons, encouraged them to defend their homes and families, but if the odds seemed insurmountable, they were to retreat to Nauvoo. At no point, however, were they to forfeit their arms. Hyrum Smith wrote a letter to the Quorum of the Twelve Apostles, who were still campaigning on behalf of the prophet in the East, urging them to return home and bring reinforcements, as well as "a little powder, lead[,] and a good rifle." It was time to batten down the hatches.[27]

Meanwhile, Joseph Smith mustered the Nauvoo Legion—the city's last line of defense. Receiving supplies from friendly neighbors, the legion drilled on a nearly daily basis, with the prophet at their head. He urged them to not shed innocent blood, but still be willing to defend the city and "die like men of God." Those who did not have rifles or swords were to make their own weapons. Smith knew these preparations would not be enough, however. Hundreds of Mormon men were currently serving missions, which left Nauvoo short on manpower. Nor did the prophet believe he could rely on Governor Ford. Out of desperation, he petitioned President John Tyler, explaining that a mob of Missourians had joined with the Mormons' Illinois neighbors to eradicate every member of the faith. Smith hoped he could hold off the mobs until they received reinforcements, either from their missionaries or the federal government.[28]

Until then, anticipating the coming storm, he was willing to do what it took to defend the saints. On June 18, he declared martial law in Nauvoo—though, of course, he had no authority to do so under United States law. He instructed the legion to require documentation from anyone entering or leaving the city. Smith believed these were necessary actions, though they only invited more problems.[29]

Governor Ford, worried things were spiraling out of control, decided to investigate the goings-on in the western part of the state himself. He traveled to Carthage and instructed Smith to send delegates who could explain their case. The prophet rushed to gather as many affidavits as possible testifying to his innocence, knowing that the Laws and Fosters were doing the same. He refused, however, to travel to Carthage himself, explaining to Ford his belief that he would be murdered on the way.[30]

After weighing the evidence, Ford concluded that Smith and his Mormon majority were to blame. Not only did he call the destruction of the dissident press a gross outrage and a violation of the laws and liberties of American citizens, but he sided with the anti-Mormons in the view that Nauvoo's municipal court was exercising power illegally. He assured Smith and the seventeen others who had been indicted by the justice of the peace that they would be safe if they turned themselves in, but warned that there would be military retaliation if they did not.[31]

Fearing an impartial trial or an extralegal lynching, Smith decided to flee across the Mississippi River to the Iowa Territory in the middle of the night. "We dare not come," he wrote Ford. Before he left town, he ordered the Council of Fifty's secretary to either burn or bury the council's minutes—he knew the contents could be seen as treasonous, especially in the present climate.[32]

Once he had decamped to Iowa, Smith and his closest advisors planned their next move. Smith instructed his secretary to once again petition the federal government while he ordered his wife, Emma, to prepare for a trip to Washington. These plans did not go far, however. After receiving more assurances from Ford, as well as urgent pleas from his followers, including Emma, who worried they would be slaughtered in the prophet's absence, Smith begrudgingly organized a rendezvous with county authorities the next day, June

24, back in Nauvoo. Vilate Kimball admitted her relief at this decision, as she was terrified at the prospect of Smith leaving them "in
the hour of our danger." She concluded Smith had given himself up
in order to save their city.[33]

Alongside Smith's surrender, Ford demanded that the Nauvoo
Legion forfeit all its state-issued arms—approximately 250 firearms
and three cannons. Smith begrudgingly conceded. Nauvoo's residents
worried that this was a sign they were about to be massacred. Apparently resigned to his fate, Smith appeared solemn to those who saw
him, and confessed to his family that he did not expect to outlive the
crisis. He bade a tearful farewell to Emma and their children in front
of their home, mounted his horse, and set off for Carthage with the
other men under indictment. Upon his departure that evening, he
could not help but glance back at the city from the bluff that held the
unfinished temple. He would never see Nauvoo again.[34]

Smith's legal situation worsened once he arrived in the county seat
on June 25. Though he had agreed to be tried for rioting, based on the
destruction of the Expositor's press, he was now charged with treason
for his declaration of martial law in Nauvoo. The severity of these new
charges left him ineligible for bail. Smith, his brother Hyrum, secretary Willard Richards, and several close friends, including apostle John
Taylor, were moved to the county jail. The two-story brick structure,
which housed the jailer's family, included a cell for criminals, another
room for debtors, and an upstairs bedroom. The Mormon men were
originally placed in the gloomy cell, but were shortly thereafter moved
to the more comfortable debtor's room, which served as a hub as they
prepared their defense documents for the governor and wrote letters to
local and national authorities.

Soon after they were jailed, an organized militia as well as a mob
surrounded the building. William Law was among the crowd, and
some heard him boast that Smith would not escape the city with his
life. Smith, sheltered within the jail, confessed to his close friends a
deep anxiety about his own safety. The trial was set for later that week,
and the saints rushed to prepare. Richards drafted a list of twenty-

seven men who could serve as witnesses on the prophet's behalf. The prisoners were then moved upstairs into the second-floor bedroom, which was more spacious. All the while, the crowd outside continued to increase in size.[35]

Worried that Nauvoo might be attacked, Smith urged the governor to send troops to defend the saints, and Ford obliged by dispatching sixty men. The prophet hoped to return to Nauvoo himself, protected by the state militia, but Ford decided to leave him behind while he accompanied the troops to Nauvoo, which left fewer militiamen to guard the jail. The crowd grew restless. That Smith was held in the county jail awaiting trial on the charge of treason did not satisfy those who feared him most. They had already witnessed several occasions on which the Mormon prophet seemed to be finally brought to justice, only to escape through some legal loophole or political chicanery. Smith's opponents had concluded, according to Carthage resident Thomas Barnes, that "the law could not reach them." Nauvoo's use of habeas corpus, Smith's close relationship to political figures, and Governor Ford's refusal to acknowledge the urgency of the matter convinced them that extralegal action was necessary—just as the Mormons had decided when it came to the *Nauvoo Expositor*.[36]

On June 27, a large group of men congregated in Warsaw to bring an end to the Mormon prophet. To make clear the patriotic intention for their actions, they chose a name from American lore: they called themselves the Warsaw Committee of Safety. During the American Revolution, "committees of safety" had appeared throughout the rebellious colonies to protest threats to their rights. That belief in the legitimacy of vigilante justice—where the right to defense was considered the first and inalienable law—was now resurrected seven decades later. At the root of their critique was the frailty of their democratic system. The existing laws were "inadequate . . . to protect the lives, reputation, and property" of Illinois residents. The Mormons had succeeded in placing themselves above their constituted authorities and consistently subverted justice. Politicians refused to take any action that would cost them the Nauvoo vote, legislatures refused to set a precedent by repealing the

Nauvoo Charter, and judges refused to risk tensions by overturning Nauvoo rulings. Democracy, in other words, had proven too easily manipulated. The result was a religious tyrant. Sometimes the voice of the people, those gathered in Warsaw reasoned, transcended the laws of the land. The mob then began their march to Carthage. They were determined not to return home disappointed.[37]

Meanwhile, Smith and his fellow prisoners were in a solemn mood. By the afternoon of June 27, only the Smith brothers, John Taylor, and Willard Richards remained in the upstairs bedroom, as the rest had been dispatched to perform various tasks. They continued to write pleading letters to friends, lawyers, and politicians. Hope seemed dim. "I am very much resigned to my lot," Joseph wrote Emma that morning, "knowing that I am Justified and have done the best that could be done." Taylor, known for his powerful voice, sang one of their favorite hymns, and they sent a guard to fetch some wine to revive their spirits. When the Smith brothers were asked by the jailer if they would feel safer in the heavily protected cell, Joseph became reflective and asked Richards, who was not indicted and there on his own accord, "Will you go in with us?" His close friend responded that he had followed him thus far, and had no intention of forsaking him now. "I will tell you what I will do," Richards said. "If you are condemned to be hung for treason I will be hung in your stead." They decided not to retreat to the cell until after dinner.[38]

Their move across the hall never happened. The Warsaw mob, now totaling around 250 men, arrived in Carthage in the late afternoon and gathered in the woods just outside the jail. They painted themselves with wet powder to mask their identities, and at about a quarter after five o'clock, around a hundred men charged the jail, beat back the guards and jailer, and made their way upstairs, fully armed. Hearing the commotion, Joseph and Hyrum reached for pistols that had been smuggled in the previous day, and Richards and Taylor grabbed their canes.

The confrontation at the door to their room was brief but deadly. Hyrum was the first to fall, talking a bullet to the left side of his face and collapsing to the floor. Taylor then tried to jump out of the window, but was stopped by a hail of bullets, including one that ripped off a chunk of his hip the size of a fist. Joseph Smith, after firing several rounds into the mob, made his own attempt at jumping. By that point, however, the men had opened the door enough to take aim and fire as he approached the windowsill. Smith was struck twice in the back from within the room and once in the breast from a shooter outside. He exclaimed to heaven above as he fell through the window to the earth below.

The crowd gathered around the body to review their work. Four men then dragged Smith to a nearby well, propped him up, and shot him at least four more times. The Mormon prophet was dead.[39]

"Death of Joseph Smith." FOUND IN JOHN HANSON BEADLE, *POLYGAMY: OR, THE MYSTERIES AND CRIMES OF MORMONISM* . . . (PHILADELPHIA: NATIONAL PUBLISHING CO., 1882), 89.

The whole ordeal had lasted only a couple minutes. As the mob receded and eventually scattered, Taylor lay severely wounded in the upstairs bedroom. Richards, who escaped the attack unscathed, dragged his bleeding friend across the hall to hide in the criminal cell. Later, they discovered that Taylor's pocket watch had shattered during the commotion. The clock's hands were stuck at "5 o'clock, 16 minutes, and 26 seconds." The moment of their beloved leader's death was etched in time.[40]

NEWS OF THE SMITHS' DEATHS HIT NAUVOO like a storm. "O the ever to be r[em]embered awful day of the 27 of June 1844," wrote Zina Huntington. Along with her sister Presendia, Zina was one of the first women sealed to the prophet, in 1841. Now, three years later, she attended his funeral.[41]

Willard Richards, who had survived the attack in Carthage, tried to send word of the Smith brothers' death as soon as the commotion subsided. He downplayed John Taylor's injuries, urged the saints not to seek revenge, and dispatched close allies to deliver the message overnight. Governor Thomas Ford, who had just left Nauvoo, where he had been instructing the Mormons to remain peaceful, intercepted Richards's letter before it arrived. Worried about civil war, he rushed to Carthage to dissolve any remaining groups of angry men, gather important county records, and urge residents to evacuate the city. He also encouraged Richards to write an addendum to his message assuring the saints that the governor was dedicated to protecting them. He wanted to prevent the legion from assembling. His hope was to make it through the night without further bloodshed. The revised letter finally arrived in Nauvoo around sunrise, but not before rumors started trickling in.[42]

The anticipated battle never came. Instead, there was only sorrow. The bodies of Joseph and Hyrum Smith arrived in Nauvoo the afternoon of the twenty-eighth, borne in oak coffins on a cart pulled by white horses and escorted by thousands of mourning saints. They were taken to the Nauvoo Mansion, Joseph's home, where the family had their first look at their slain husbands, fathers, and sons. "There was the aged Mother, the wives, the children, the brothers and sisters," wrote Almira Mack Covey, a cousin to the "aged Mother," Lucy Mack Smith. "A dry eye I did not behold." (Nor was Lucy's mourning to end anytime soon: another son, Samuel, died a month later from a fever, which they attributed to their flight from anti-Mormon mobs.) Joseph's wife, Emma, sobbed uncontrollably as she was helped upright by close friends. The Smith family had already faced major tragedies in the last two decades, but the latest seemed insurmountable.[43]

The Smiths were not the only ones who were inconsolable. Zina Huntington, due to the secret nature of her plural sealing, was not granted a public role in the mourning, but she was allowed to wash her plural husband's clothes. The following day, a Saturday, the bodies were prepared and made available for public display. An estimated five thousand saints walked through the home to look upon their prophet and his brother, the patriarch, once more. While Joseph, according to William Clayton, still looked natural, the same could not be said about Hyrum, who had taken a gunshot to his face. The sight prompted immense grief. Vilate Kimball observed that the very streets seemed to mourn. A powerful thunderstorm hit that evening, and the rain continued for several days. An entire city was awash with agony.[44]

The eulogies at the Smiths' funeral on the twenty-ninth were tinged by politics. Many saints saw Smith's death as emblematic of the nation's problems. William Phelps denounced America for allowing "liberty" to devolve into "the popular will of mobocracy." Freedom was no longer assured. "Thus perishes the hope of law," mused Willard Richards. Huntington agreed. While observing the Fourth of July the following week, she noted that "drearryness [sic] and sorrow" prevented her from celebrating the nation's holiday. America's banner of liberty, in her view, was stained with the blood of the prophet. The nation's failure to protect God's chosen people would bring divine recompense.[45]

While the mourners directed their scorn at the nation, to Joseph and Hyrum Smith they exhibited only devotion. The city's two newspapers ran prose and poetry revealing the saints' passionate connection

to their leaders. Eliza R. Snow, Nauvoo's unofficial poetess and one of
Joseph's plural wives, wrote verse in memory of them:

> Now Zion mourns—she mourns an earthly head:
> The Prophet and the Patriarch are dead!
> The blackest deed that men or devils know
> Since Calv'ry's scene, has laid the brothers low.

The connection she drew between Smith's death and Jesus Christ's
crucifixion was daring, but not unique. In the official memorial for
the prophet, published in the saints' book of scripture later that year,
John Taylor was unrestrained: "Joseph Smith, the prophet and seer of
the Lord, has done more, (save Jesus only,) for the salvation of men in
this world, than any other man that ever lived in it." Mormon love for
the prophet only grew after his martyrdom.[46]

Some of Smith's opponents, meanwhile, were quick to celebrate
these events. The *Warsaw Signal* defended the vigilante killings as a
righteous cause. Was it not better to kill "the two guilty wretches,"
asked Thomas Sharp, than allow them to continue in their corruption?
Another nearby resident explained that the rights of non-Mormon citizens were under threat as long as Smith was alive. The mob, therefore,
had cause for its action. William Law confessed that he was shocked
at the murder, but concluded he could "see the hand of a blasphemed
God stretched out in judgement." If anything, he reasoned, the Smith
brothers had brought the tragedy upon themselves. Law, like many of
the other dissenters who joined forces to publish the *Nauvoo Expositor*,
believed they had accomplished their work and could now move on.
The Laws, Higbees, and Robert Thompson relocated to nearby Illinois
towns and tried to start their lives over again, this time without the
religious drama. If there was to be any further escalation, they refused
to take any part in it.[47]

But Governor Ford worried that the animosity might not end there.
While convinced the Mormons were not likely to seek revenge, he
feared those who opposed them, who were circulating rumors of a

Mormon insurrection in order to justify military intervention. Ford fled to Quincy and ordered soldiers to keep the peace between the two sides in Hancock County. In Nauvoo, word spread that there was a conspiracy to kidnap the city's top officials, and Mormon men were tasked with keeping watch throughout the night. The saints even took precautions to protect the bodies of Joseph and Hyrum Smith. Though there was a public burial at the city cemetery, the coffins that were lowered into the ground held sandbags; the real corpses were secretly buried in the unfinished Nauvoo House, out of fear that they would be mutilated otherwise.[48]

The rumors of further aggression never came true, and the greatest threat to Nauvoo came from within. Within two weeks of Joseph Smith's death, William Clayton recorded that there were a half dozen possible successors to the fallen prophet. Joseph Smith had been the linchpin holding the faith together, and there was no clear replacement. Who could take over a church that relied so heavily on the charisma of a single individual? In a religious culture that increasingly prioritized choice, change, and conversion, Mormonism's succession crisis embodied a national interest in authority as a counterweight to pluralism. The Mormon faith had been prone to fissures over its first decade, with a number of members breaking off to form their own schismatic movements. Smith had not clearly and publicly delineated a successor in Nauvoo, ensuring that the continuity problem would recur after his death. The City Council, after passing a series of resolutions emphasizing its desire to maintain peace, resolved to wait until the Quorum of the Twelve returned before charting their next steps.[49]

Many Mormons were awaiting the return of the Twelve, who were currently serving missions in the East, and letters were dispatched to call them home within days of Smith's murder. News of the martyrdom, however, arrived before the correspondence. Wilford Woodruff recorded that they obtained the "solumn & awful information of the Death of President Joseph Smith" through a newspaper in Boston on July 9. Hearing word of a riot against Catholics that same day in Philadelphia, Woodruff could not help but feel that the nation deserved to be destroyed, as any hope that democracy could protect religious minorities had vanished. Five days later, he was still musing on how the mob spirit was on the rise throughout America. Where could they find relief? After conferring with Brigham Young and a number of other apostles, Woodruff penned a proclamation for the saints' eastern newspaper, encouraging all those on missions to return to Nauvoo immediately. They had been sent out to publicize Smith's campaign, but they were now returning home to deal with his death.[50]

When the Twelve finally arrived in Nauvoo a few weeks later, they confronted the city's, and the faith's, crisis of authority. The saints were like a sheep without a shepherd, Woodruff observed, as they had no idea where to look for guidance. Rumors swirled concerning who would take charge. From New York, James Gordon Bennett mused that Smith's death sealed the church's fate, as they would never find another leader to replace him.[51]

There was at least one man ready to fill the void: Sidney Rigdon. A member of the First Presidency for over a decade, Rigdon's relationship with Smith and the Twelve had run hot and cold over the previous few years. A talented orator and still a public spokesman for the faith, he was increasingly distanced from some of Nauvoo's inner council decisions due to personal clashes with Smith and the Twelve. Yet that trend had reversed itself in the month leading up to Smith's death. While he was not one of the first inductees into the Council of Fifty, once added to the group, he was a frequent and enthusiastic participant. He delivered a roaring address at the April general conference that reminded his audience of his glory days. And when Joseph Smith's first two choices for vice-president did not pan out, Rigdon had been selected to appear on the campaign ticket, allowing him to take a prominent role in the church's most public initiative. He had traveled to Pennsylvania that summer in an attempt to claim residency so that he and the prophet could fulfill the constitutional obligation that a ticket represent two different states. But once he had heard of the martyrdom, he raced back to the Mormon capital. Once he arrived, he quickly began to build support for his own cause.

Others were not convinced about Rigdon, and none were as skeptical as Brigham Young and the rest of the Twelve. They were therefore worried when, upon their arrival to the city, they found that Rigdon had called a special meeting on August 4 to share his own revelation. Standing before a large crowd on the appointed date, Rigdon declared that he should serve as a guardian for the faith. Nobody could replace Joseph Smith, but Rigdon was ready to serve as the deceased prophet's interlocutor. Woodruff dismissed Rigdon's revelation as "a kind of second Class vision," and Young called for a special conference to convene a few days later on August 8. Everyone understood it would be a fateful meeting.[52]

From very early on, the Twelve based their claim to authority on the priesthood keys—a metaphor that represented religious authority both on earth and in heaven—that had been bestowed through new rituals over the past two years, activities in which they had been closely involved. These keys, they believed, were what set them apart from Rigdon. The problem was that very few of the ordinary saints in Nauvoo knew about these developments. Smith had often glossed over details when giving speeches, instead urging saints to wait until they could experience the temple rituals themselves. Young, however, believed the Twelve could use these temple keys to their advantage, and he argued that it was because they had participated in these rituals that they were Smith's true successors. During his first conversation with Woodruff in Boston, even before they knew about Rigdon's competing claim to be Smith's successor, Young argued that Smith had prepared for his death by providing the Twelve with the keys with which to govern the kingdom. Now it was left to them to convince the rest of the church, during a public showdown with Rigdon—who was now the faith's longest-serving leader—that these esoteric "keys" would determine the church's destiny.[53]

An estimated five thousand saints gathered on August 8 to hear the two primary claims on the Mormon leadership. Rigdon, speaking in the morning while standing on a wagon, delivered an eloquent and impassioned speech that mostly repeated his leadership history and claims to be a guardian over the church. But he was soon outplayed. After allowing the embers of Rigdon's fiery address to smolder, Young spoke that afternoon and forcefully made the case for the Twelve's governance. If the people wanted Rigdon as their guardian, he said, they were welcome to it. But a guardian was no replacement for a prophet, and Rigdon lacked the authority to govern God's kingdom. It was the Twelve, he argued, who possessed the keys to God's kingdom, and it was the priesthood that dictated who should rule. Pointing to the unfinished temple, not far from where they were gathered, Young emphasized that only the Twelve were prepared to fulfill Nauvoo's overall mission and purpose. Though the saints had not yet experienced these new rituals, he assured his audience that the Twelve, with Young at its head, possessed "all the signs and the tokens" that would get the saints into heaven. Rigdon was neither prepared nor qualified to lead the faith. In a world characterized by competing truth claims, priesthood keys were the only things that could unlock certainty.[54]

Young soon went to work securing support for his position as the designated president of the Twelve, and thereby the church. Where Rigdon looked isolated as he addressed the saints alone that morning, Young was flanked by several other prominent men. He also had two aces up his sleeve. Amasa Lyman, who had been a member of the First Presidency for the past year, theoretically held similar succession claims as Rigdon. Yet when Young called on him to address the conference, Lyman backed the Twelve's authority. And when Rigdon called on his old friend and confidant William W. Phelps to speak on his behalf, Phelps shocked Rigdon by supporting Young. Rigdon appeared increasingly stranded, and the audience noticed. Once properly positioned, Young called on the entire congregation to vote between the two options. The verdict was assured. William Clayton recorded that there were very few who went for Rigdon, and Woodruff wrote that a sea of hands supported the Twelve.[55]

Young's public role over the previous few years, and prominent position among the thousands of British converts, eased the transition. Many had become accustomed to seeing him as their leader. Henry and Catherine Brooke, recent converts from Britain, believed that Young had merely retained his previous authority, only now with the added responsibilities once held by Joseph Smith. They believed Young filled the part to perfection. Zilpha Williams agreed, and explained to relatives that instead of two leaders, Joseph and Hyrum Smith, they now had twelve, with Young as their moderator, and were therefore stronger in the face of adversity. The transition, for some, appeared seamless.[56]

Once he gained the mantle, Young eagerly ran with it. From the moment he was chosen as the new leader of the faith, he made clear his belief that the Twelve were solely authorized to regulate the church's business, and he warned he would not be patient with dissent. What happened to Smith would not happen to him. Young instructed the other members of the Twelve that his first duty was "giving every one his place" within the kingdom. Most fell in line. Given the uncertainty of the prior months and years, the church turned to one strong personality for stability, and Young was happy to fill the role.[57]

Rigdon continued to press his case over the next six weeks, with little success. He was eventually excommunicated by the Twelve in September 1844, for failing to support the new leadership structure. He left the city soon afterward, taking a small following with him. Young sought out other recalcitrants. At a general conference in October, he released William Marks from his position as stake president due to his support for Rigdon, and chastised two others, Lyman Wight and James Emmett, for pushing forward with post-Nauvoo settlement plans without the full approval of the Twelve. From the very beginning of his tenure, Young demanded loyalty, believing that his control was crucial to maintain the church's stability amid change. "If you don't know whose right it is to give revelations," Young told the congregation, "I will tell you. It is I." The saints listened. One attendee gleefully wrote how Young had purged all threats, relieving the church of a "great burden." Many were grateful for his steady hand.[58]

One way that Young sought to fulfill Joseph Smith's mission was through the expansion of plural marriage. This included becoming

William Warner Major, "Brigham and Mary Ann Angell Young and Their Children," circa 1845. This stylized family portrait, depicting the Youngs in a successful and traditional monogamous marriage, was painted at the same time Brigham was being sealed to an increasing number of wives. LDS CHURCH HISTORY AND ART MUSEUM, SALT LAKE CITY.

a steward of Smith's own plural wives. Starting in September, Young and Heber C. Kimball, his close friend and functionally the faith's second-in-command, were sealed to many of the women who were first sealed to Mormonism's founding prophet. On September 19, one month after besting Rigdon at the public conference, Young wed Louisa Beman, Smith's first plural wife. Beman was the first of at least seven of Smith's widows to be united with Young. He also married Eliza R. Snow, Zina Huntington, and Emily Dow Partridge, the last of whom bore Young a child the following year.

Many of these unions were recorded in code: "I saw Louisa B. Smith," Young's journal noted, with "saw" an acronym for "sealed and wed." Elsewhere, Young's secretary penciled "M.E." into his journal to stand for "married for eternity." In total, Young married fifteen more times over the next twelve months following Smith's death. Kimball, for his part, married at least twelve women during the same period, including six Smith widows. Among them was Sarah Ann Whitney, the prophet's young bride who continued to clutch at the blessing that promised exaltation to her and her entire family. Lucy Walker and Sarah Lawrence, two other teenaged girls who had previously been sealed to Smith, were also now under Kimball's stewardship. It is impossible to know how much say they had in these new arrangements. The two senior apostles inherited both Smith's church as well as much of his familial kingdom—indeed, their embrace of the latter served to vindicate their seizure of the former.[59]

Succession questions were just one of the Twelve's new challenges. Also of immediate concern was Nauvoo's relationship with Illinois. County elections, on August 5, had closely followed Smith's martyrdom. Governor Ford advised the saints to avoid any political activities that year, yet members of his own Democratic Party continued to court Mormon votes. Nor were the saints willing to stand aside. After forging an informal alliance with a slate of candidates who promised to back the Mormons in their pursuit of justice, Nauvoo once again voted uniformly, and successfully, to elect those they believed would advance their interests. Despondent that Mormon bloc voting did not end with Smith, Thomas Sharp and ten other prominent residents of the county signed a proclamation claiming the "old citizens" were virtually disenfranchised. It seemed the Mormons could never assimilate. Either they had to leave Illinois, or everyone else did. Young tried to ease tensions by issuing a proclamation of his own the next week that urged the saints to avoid politics, but it was to no avail. Joseph Smith's death had failed to bring a resolution to Hancock County's democratic crisis.[60]

For once, the state was ready to act. While Ford still hoped that the conflict could be settled without fully revoking Nauvoo's city charter—his annual address in December strongly urged the legislature to merely amend its offending portions—growing fear of the Mormon threat finally had tangible consequences in the statehouse. The legislature, when it gathered in December 1844, took aim at Nauvoo, but the city would not easily relent. Two of the officials the Mormons voted into office that August, Jacob Backenstos and Almon Babbitt, fought hard in Springfield on behalf of the saints, along with Nauvoo's new mayor, Orson Spencer, who made several impassioned speeches to the state legislature.

Their efforts were in vain. Even as Governor Ford, a Democrat, advised the legislature to restrain itself, and even as the Whigs were persuaded by arguments that it was unconstitutional to unilaterally repeal a city charter, the Democratic-controlled Congress had seen enough. Illinois attorney general Josiah Lamborn alerted the saints that "the tide of popular passion" could no longer be resisted. All the Mormons could do now was submit to the laws, be quiet, and wait for things to calm down. The Illinois senate passed a bill to repeal the charter on December 19, and the state assembly followed with its own version on January 24. The document Mormons believed preserved their liberty and independence was now void.[61]

It was a damaging blow. By being stripped of their chartered rights, the Mormons lost the power of self-rule, municipal courts, and even their organized militia. The death of the charter was second only to the death of their prophet in terms of its impact on Nauvoo. As conflicts with gentile neighbors continued, and as Warsaw residents reiterated their calls for the expulsion of the Mormons, the people of Nauvoo all of a sudden found themselves in an unprotected and incorporated territory. Their actions over the next year would determine whether or not their faith could survive, within or beyond the boundaries of the American republic.

AROUND THE SAME TIME THAT THE DEVASTATING news about the city charter arrived in Nauvoo, Lewis Dana returned to the city after an extended mission. Many Mormon men served missions during this era, but Dana was unique: as one of the few Native American converts to the faith, he was seen as a fulfillment of the Book of Mormon's prophecy that the nation's indigenous population would receive the restored gospel. Raised in the Oneida Nation, and a man with extensive experience as an interpreter and emissary between different indigenous groups, his conversion to the Mormon faith around 1840 was a boon to the church's efforts to reach the "Lamanite" population. He spent the next few years proselytizing among neighboring tribes in such Midwestern territories as Iowa, Michigan, and Wisconsin. Once he arrived in Nauvoo again in January 1845, a captive audience of Mormons listened to his missionary tales and believed them to be an omen for future success. At the moment when it appeared their white neighbors were rejecting God's kingdom, perhaps it was time to focus their conversion efforts on another group.[62]

Dana was likely surprised to hear a proposed solution to the city's crisis that was bandied about: seeing Native American settlements as a potential model, some Illinois citizens wondered whether the federal government could designate a Mormon reservation. The proposal did not seem far-fetched, given the current political climate. William Richards, a nearby non-Mormon resident, proposed the quixotic idea in a letter to Mormon leaders. Because he could not see how peace could ever be secured between the two sides, he asked if the government might create "a *Reserve* to be set apart by Congress for the Mormon people exclusively, which would meet the approbation of that Sect?" The saints could be assigned a twenty-four-square-mile plot of land, perhaps in Wisconsin, surrounded by a ring five miles wide separating them from any non-Mormon settlement. Anyone who entered the Mormon region would require documentation that they were members of the faith, and the reservation would be overseen by a gentile superintendent. The proposal was met with intrigue from both Mormon and non-Mormon audiences. Dana, after leaving a string of Native reservations, probably found it strange to learn that the Mormons might attempt to create one of their own.[63]

It was not the first time someone proposed that the Mormons be removed to their own distinct and segregated community. A similar solution had been offered in Missouri in 1836, when the state legislature created a county specifically designated for members of the faith; several years later, Joseph Smith had petitioned the federal government to reclassify Nauvoo as a federal territory beyond state control in 1843. Nor was it rare for the Mormon faith to be categorized as distinct from mainstream white culture. Heber C. Kimball claimed that summer, in 1845, that they were often seen as unsuitable to live among "white folks."[64]

William Richards's proposal was taken seriously enough by Brigham Young that he reconvened the Council of Fifty to consider the option. Orson Spencer was eventually chosen to distill their argument in an editorial, in which he maintained that a central pillar of democracy was the ability of "men of congenial religions or other interests" to separate themselves from the rest of society to form their own community. Put another way, only when societies were formed by like-minded citizens could democracy truly function. The "promiscuous intermixture of heterogeneous bodies for the purpose of unity & strength," he reasoned, is "distant both from pure religion & sound philosophy." He recommended segregated settlements not only for Mormons, but also for Catholics, Jews, and Muslims. Contrary to mainstream American belief, which emphasized the nation's ability to mix divergent groups together, the Mormons believed that democracy was not suited to the mixing of faiths. Spencer recommended that the Mormon reservation cover at least two hundred square miles in order to fit their expected growth.[65]

As with previous petitions to the federal government, nothing ever came of the proposal. Which was just as well, because Brigham Young and the other Mormon leaders were coming to see any alliance with the American government as untenable. Instead, prompted by Dana's promising reports, they became even more enamored with the possibility of forming an alliance with Native tribes in the West. Both Mormons and Indians, they believed, had been oppressed by America's democratic system, which seemed to make them natural, if still odd, bedfellows. Young claimed to the Council of Fifty that the nation had severed the Mormons from other citizens and made them "a distinct nation," just like Native tribes.[66]

This was not a completely new idea for the Mormons. Before Joseph Smith's murder, the Council of Fifty had sent James Emmett west to instruct the Indians to "unite together," perhaps in preparation for mass conversions. Emmett, however, turned out to be too earnest for Young's liking as he began making decisions without consulting the Twelve, and his mission eventually lost support. Yet in Dana they had another potential emissary to the indigenous armies they believed were ready to join their ranks. One Nauvoo resident, Sally Randall, heard a rumor that there were over ten thousand Natives waiting to be baptized and to join the Mormons in avenging the deaths of Joseph and Hyrum Smith. And whereas Smith had been hesitant to form official alliances with tribes due to their potential to invite suspicion, Brigham Young had no such misgivings. They assigned Dana, accompanied by several white missionaries, to travel west and build a foundation for a Mormon–Indian alliance.[67]

Mormon visions of a multiracial empire in the West challenged the contemporary understanding of manifest destiny, especially its assumption that whites would dominate the entire continent. Yet the Mormons were not completely altruistic in their approach to Native American tribes. Though they were not as willing as most Americans to merely erase Native populations from the land, as prophecies in the Book of Mormon seemed to suggest their presence would continue indefinitely, Young's vision for indigenous tribes was patronizing. He assumed the Natives were eager for his leadership, as the Mormon priesthood was the only thing that would save the "Lamanites" from becoming extinct.

Bitterness toward other white Americans remained the driving force behind discussions of a possible Mormon evacuation. The Mormons were not so much anxious to join the Indians as they were despondent that America continued to deny them their rights. Young was so vengeful that he threatened to completely close off any missionary work to the "white gentiles." In March 1845, he announced that he would cease sending out missionaries to white populations that year, and if anyone wanted to hear the gospel, they would have to come to Nauvoo. He added that if the gentiles were not willing to acknowledge their previous atrocities, they could first clean the blood off the floor of the Carthage jail. Young and other leaders continued to dream of a Mormon empire outside American boundaries—especially in California, which became the most frequently discussed destination—but their preference, still, was to remain in Illinois.[68]

Despite the fiery rhetoric from Young and others, the first half of 1845 was a period of relative peace in Nauvoo. The Mormons once again began planning to build a dam up the river, a project that promised to supply power, jobs, and stability for their community. Estimated to cost nearly a quarter of a million dollars, it was no small initiative. But the most important project remained the temple, whose unfinished structure on the bluff still overshadowed the city below. Immediately after receiving word of the city charter's revocation, Brigham Young considered promptly leading the Mormons out of Illinois. However, he quickly changed his mind and decided that they should remain and finish the temple, and even claimed to have had a revelation dictating as much. This was more than a concern over sunk costs: for Young and the Twelve, completing the temple and introducing the saints to its rituals served to reaffirm their authority as Joseph Smith's successors.[69]

Finishing the temple also remained a sacred mission. By that summer, the roof was finally completed, and the last shingles were laid in August. People from the region flocked to the city to marvel at the sight. "They seem filled with astonishment," William Clayton wrote, as it was "the most beautifull piece of architecture I ever witnessed." There was new development within the city too. More saints were moving out of their temporary wood shacks and into brick homes. Nauvoo looked like paradise, Young said in a letter to Wilford Woodruff on the anniversary of Smith's death. In fact, he could not help but report that prospects had never seemed better for the saints, as a tentative peace had descended on Nauvoo and its neighbors, and the city was also receiving renewed support from the state. There finally seemed to be peace and unity in Nauvoo—at least for the time being.[70]

One reason for optimism was that they felt they had restored a degree of self-rule. Without a city charter, Young decided to reorganize the community under the new name "The City of Joseph," in

Photograph of Nauvoo, circa 1846. LDS CHURCH HISTORY LIBRARY, SALT LAKE CITY.

honor of their fallen prophet. Young then immediately placed it under ecclesiastical rule. The town was officially incorporated the following month—at a much smaller scale—and the church moved quickly to secure control. Without an official police force, they sought to defend the city through private initiatives, which often required code words. If anyone came to the city to cause problems, Brigham Young explained, "set aunt Peggy at them and anoint them." In Young's terminology, "aunt Peggy" referred to vigilante action, and to "anoint" meant a more violent form of laying hands on someone's head.[71]

At the same time, Mormon leaders mobilized a group of men, both young and mature, who were assigned to follow any suspicious individuals and menace them until they left town. When confronted, the Mormons could respond that they were merely sharpening their knives and whistling their songs. Young called them the "whistling school." Mormons took up the cause with earnest. "It is true the boys get a little saucy now and then," wrote one resident, Dwight Webster. But whenever there was a complaint, he explained, they would merely respond, "We know your cause is just but we can do nothing for you," relishing the irony of using President Martin Van Buren's reply to Joseph Smith's petition for federal support. John Taylor defended these actions in the church newspaper, proclaiming that every Mormon could act above the law so long as they did not interfere with their neighbor's rights. Human law, he reasoned, was not binding upon God's chosen people. Taylor's blunt rhetoric was a step too far, however. Church leaders were soon forced to publish an editorial distancing themselves from it, and they disbanded the "whistling school" after a public outcry from surrounding communities. Still, Nauvoo seemed on the rise once again.[72]

YET THIS PEACEFUL TIME WOULD TURN OUT to be merely an interlude. News of the Mormons' continued political involvement and turn to extralegal force spread to neighboring towns, rekindling anti-Mormon sentiment throughout the region. From the Mormons' point of view, the ongoing failure of the state's legal system to bring Joseph and Hyrum Smith's killers to justice confirmed their suspicion that coexistence was impossible.

In May 1845, five men were tried for the Smith brothers' murders. Though Willard Richards and other witnesses named several dozen men who were part of the killing, Governor Thomas Ford concluded that the state's best chance at a conviction was to charge only the leaders of the mob: Thomas Sharp, Levi Williams, Mark Aldrich, Jacob C. Davis, and William N. Grover. Mormon authorities decided not to participate, for fear of only stirring up anti-Mormon anger. The Council of Fifty claimed anti-Mormon gentiles were spreading rumors of a Mormon conspiracy to take vengeance that would justify state-sponsored expulsion, and therefore forbade anyone from leaving the city. But even holding back, the Mormons did not expect a fair result. Young openly opined that he expected the accused to be acquitted, and he was proven correct. The jury concluded that the five men could not be convicted for merely fulfilling the wishes of an entire community. Apparently vigilante justice could be vindicated through majoritarian opinion.[73]

Though not surprised, Mormons were still crestfallen. One noted that the whole proceeding was nothing more than "a perfect mob court." Nor did they feel they could appeal to the federal government for help, as they had now lost all faith in America's democratic order. The Constitution, wrote Amasa Lyman, was "a damned wrotten thing, full of lice, moth eaten, corrupt." America, as a political experiment, had failed.[74]

With hopes of legal justice dissolved, the possibility of moving west became more real. Lewis Dana and the other missionaries sent to explore an alliance with Native tribes had not brought back much information, but there was no more time to wait. Brigham Young moved beyond sending exploratory missionaries and began organizing a mass migration. Immediately after the verdict was handed down, Orson Spencer, still acting as Nauvoo's civic leader, informed Ford that most of the Mormons would relocate within eighteen months. Two months later, Young confided to Wilford Woodruff that they hoped to establish western settlements within a year. At the end of August 1845, the Council of Fifty debated various proposals and concluded that three thousand men would travel first to the Rocky Mountains before eventually moving on to the Pacific coast. At that point, they had their eyes set on the San Francisco region. The days of Mormon settlement in Illinois were numbered.[75]

Their migration to the West would not be fully by choice, however. Despite pleas from Governor Ford, Mormons refused to stay out of state politics. Their participation in the August 1845 election, where they once again successfully elected all their desired candidates, made their gentile neighbors all the more agitated. They were not privy to discussions within Nauvoo, of course, and many feared the saints were digging in. But without state support, they once again turned to extra-legal violence. Levi Williams, one of the men charged with leading the mob that killed Joseph Smith in 1844, now led men from Warsaw in attacks on outlying Mormon settlements. Writing during one of these assaults, Solomon Hancock and Alanson Ripley reported that the mob had burned a half dozen buildings. Within a few days, that number jumped to around forty. By the end of the year, after more attacks, the number would grow to 150. "A determined spirit exists among the Anti-Mormons," Thomas Sharp wrote, admitting that many gentiles were committed to driving the Mormons from the state, or at least would "die in the attempt." If Young was not already serious about relocating, his long-term plans were being made for him.[76]

Over a hundred teams of Mormon men and their horses were sent out to help relocate outlying saints to Nauvoo, bringing whatever goods and grain they could. The Mormons also alerted Jacob Backenstos, the county sheriff, to the mob violence and pled for protection. Backenstos, already unpopular with the non-Mormon population, promised to try to help. "My policy is to quell the mob peaceably if I can," he wrote, "and forcibly if we must." It was not an easy task. Anti-Mormon agitators accused Backenstos of shielding the Mormons from justice and forced him to flee, first from his Carthage home to Warsaw, and then from Warsaw to Nauvoo. During his perilous ride, he was cornered in the bottom of a ravine. Luckily for him, he stumbled upon two Mormons, including Orrin Porter Rockwell, the same man who had been charged with attempting to kill Missouri governor Lilburn Boggs. Rockwell told Backenstos that they had fifty-two loaded shots between them. Once the first three men chasing the sheriff crested the hill and raised their rifles, Backenstos gave Rockwell the approval to fire. At least one shot mortally hit a rider in the chest. Ironically, the dying man was Frank Worrell, the second lieutenant of the Carthage Greys, who had been in charge of the militia guarding the Smith brothers the previous June. The Mormons cried justice, while their opponents called for revenge.[77]

Though both Rockwell and Backenstos were later acquitted on the grounds of self-defense, the incident sent the Mormons' opponents into a frenzy. Worrell's death, announced Sharp, "will kindle a flame that cannot be quenched until every Mormon has left the vicinity." The next two weeks witnessed numerous deadly encounters and daring escapes. Backenstos requested the support of six hundred Mormons and two cannons as he set off to attack the Warsaw militias. Young counseled the saints that if the mobs moved on their homes and families, they were now authorized to "give them cold lead." The Mormons were passing the point of no return.[78]

While there was no climactic battle, there were several small skirmishes throughout the county, and these resulted in several fatalities. When news spread that two adversaries to the church, Phineas Wilcox and Andrew Daubenheyer, had gone missing, it was assumed they were victims of Mormon retaliation; Daubenheyer was last seen traveling to Carthage, and Wilcox disappeared while visiting Nauvoo. Eventually, Governor Ford concluded he had to step in. He convened the state's leading politicians, including Stephen A. Douglas, to find a solution to the crisis. He also assigned congressman John J. Harden to muster three hundred militiamen, bring an end to the fighting, and search for the missing persons. When the troops arrived in Nauvoo, they were told by locals that they were fools to search for Wilcox's body on land when there was a river nearby. His body was never found, but Daubenheyer's was later discovered in a shallow grave with a bullet hole in its head.[79]

The region was afire. Homes were burning, militias were forming, and political cover for the Mormons was growing thin. Zina Huntington wrote that when she looked around at her previously peaceful city, all she could see were men marching around with guns on their shoulders and rage in their eyes.[80]

Prompted by this violence, Brigham Young and other Mormon leaders finally made public their intentions to leave the state. They also entered into negotiations with officials from numerous counties in the region in the hope of forging a temporary peace. If the mobs left them alone, Young promised, the Mormons would leave Nauvoo by the following spring. Eventually, a convention was assembled in Carthage during the first days of October, with delegates from at least nine Illinois counties. They concluded the Mormons were at fault and had to leave, as no community could exist near the saints without being drawn into a collision with them. The governor's commission agreed that the crisis had become so dire that it would be impossible for the church to remain within the state. Governor Ford, though emphasizing that the state had no legal right to expel an entire community, urged the Mormons to follow the majority's opinion. Remaining in Illinois would mean living in a state of continual war.[81]

As part of the agreement the two sides struck, local and state officials promised the Mormons that they would not be harassed as long as they planned to depart the following spring, when the rivers thawed and the grass began to grow. John J. Hardin, still in command over the state troops, issued a proclamation urging anti-Mormon forces to stand down.[82]

But how could church leaders explain their momentous decision to their flock, let alone coordinate such a massive task? Convincing approximately twenty thousand people to pick up their lives and leave their country was no small thing. When the saints gathered for a general conference in October, Young and the Twelve emphasized the necessity of migrating west. They assured the audience that God's hand was behind their plan, as a new location would allow the church to grow and finally enjoy true liberty. While in New York on a mission, the apostle Orson Pratt attempted to put a positive spin on the move to those who lived on the eastern seaboard. It was an honor to be expelled from the wicked nation, he explained, as it was evidence that they were too righteous to live within such a corrupt society. America had become so depraved that complete separation was the only logical solution.[83]

The Twelve called for a halt to immigration to Nauvoo and arranged for saints in New York to charter a sea voyage around Cape Horn. Their ship would dock in California, and then they would rendezvous in the Great Basin region. The gathering would continue, but now beyond America's borders. Residents of Nauvoo were provided a list of necessary supplies for the trek and divided into companies of one hundred, each of which was presided over by a priesthood leader. While many Mormons hoped to sell their properties, they were aware of the difficulties they faced. "The most of the Saints are selling out although at a very low price," wrote Sally Randall. Not all were even that fortunate. "If we can't sell it we will leave it," wrote John S. Fullmer, even "if we have to walk off with a bundle on our backs." No matter the cost, Zion was moving west.[84]

Not everyone would go, however. Among those who were not planning to leave the city was Joseph Smith's widow, Emma. After the murder of her husband, Smith's relationship with the Quorum of the Twelve quickly soured. The final years of her marriage had been exceptionally contentious, and Brigham Young's political calculation and aggressive posturing suggested the same traits that had led Joseph into trouble. Given her leadership experience and role in organizing the Smith family estate, Emma chafed when Young asked her to sign over all her family's belongings with the understanding that the church would take care of her. Further, Young and the Twelve represented the most odious aspect of Emma Smith's Nauvoo experience: the expansion of plural marriage. To her, polygamy was where Joseph's vision failed. And now she was left to helplessly witness dozens more women enter the practice that brought her misery. She may have had an even more personal grievance: given that Young and Kimball had split Smith's other plural wives, it is possible they also approached Emma and offered to add her to their families. If such a proposal was made, regardless of whether it was done out of the men's sense of pastoral duty, it would have merely reminded the church's first lady of her secondary role within this new patriarchal kingdom.

In short, Brigham Young represented everything about Mormonism that Emma Smith hoped to escape. There were rumors that she openly questioned Young's claim to authority, and instead believed that William Marks, who held an ecclesiastical office that placed him over Nauvoo's congregations—and as someone who opposed polygamy—was next in line to succeed her husband. Some even wondered if Joseph

Photograph of Emma Smith, circa 1845. Emma and Joseph's final child, David Hyrum, was born in November 1844, only five months after Joseph's death. LIBRARY AND ARCHIVES, COMMUNITY OF CHRIST, INDEPENDENCE, MISSOURI.

and Emma's sons should be their father's successors. In Young's eyes, Emma Smith was evolving from a nuisance to a threat.[85]

If Young could not directly attack the widow of Mormonism's prophet, he could at least attack her institution, the Relief Society. As he saw it, internal dissension had led to Joseph's death, and he blamed Emma Smith's anti-polygamy crusade for stoking those fires. In early 1845, Young banned the Relief Society from holding official meetings, forcing them to gather informally and in private. "I say I will curse every man that lets his wife or daughters meet again," he proclaimed to a gathering of priesthood leaders in March. "What are relief societies for?" His answer was less than supportive: "To relieve us of our best men," just as "they relieved us of Joseph and Hyrum." Whereas Joseph Smith's vision for a divine kingdom involved a limited form of shared governance, Young's was even more explicitly patriarchal: "I don't want the advice or counsel of any woman—they would lead us down to hell." Young rarely minced words.[86]

Others shared Young's view. In December, speaking to those who were still part of the Quorum of the Anointed, Heber C. Kimball claimed that many of the men who had left the faith had done so due to their wives' influence. He warned that if such a pattern continued, women would no longer be admitted to these sacred gatherings. The position and authority of women within the Nauvoo experiment had always been precarious, but now, under Brigham Young, their second-class status was affirmed. Of course, Emma Smith refused to support this new direction, leading to her final alienation from the institution. Not that Young minded. When discussing the Mormon exodus with the Council of Fifty, he explained that he opposed allowing Emma to travel with them, as she was no better than the mobs trying to prevent their peaceful departure. "They [both] want to bind us down and make us pay tribute to them," he bellowed. To the satisfaction of both parties, Emma Smith stayed in Nauvoo, where she lived for most of the remainder of her life.[87]

Even as he was planning the Mormon trek west, Young wanted to cement his position of religious leadership. He had asked Illinois that the saints be allowed to stay through the spring of 1846 not only because a winter departure would likely be disastrous, but because it would also provide them a chance to finish the temple. In a very real way, Young staked his authority on its completion. The Twelve, he consistently argued, held the keys to priesthood governance, and the saints could not look to anyone else for leadership. Finally, in December 1845, the time came for the temple doors to open. Starting on December 15, thousands of believers filled the massive structure and performed sacred ordinances.

When it came to these rituals, Young mostly built upon the endowment, anointing, and sealing ceremonies Joseph Smith instituted in 1842, with a few alterations. For the participants, the rituals were the culmination of Nauvoo's theological project, as they were now pronounced clean and sealed as united families for the eternities. The experience also reaffirmed their commitment to their own, increasingly beleaguered community. "It was the most interesting scene of all my life," wrote one inductee. Young was satisfied with the enthusiasm, and he was dedicated to working in the temple nearly every day and night until their departure. For nearly two months, he and the Twelve basically lived in the temple, constantly performing the ordinances. After eight weeks, over five thousand Mormons had participated in these salvific rituals. Among them were Lewis Dana, who was permitted to marry a white woman, Mary Gont. Most Americans, including Mormons, opposed interracial unions, but Heber C. Kimball justified the sealing by claiming Dana "was civilized" due to having "been an Elder about four years."[88]

For Young, the rituals reaffirmed his role as the faith's chief priest. Not only did he preside over the ceremonies, but he used them to buttress his authority. As in Smith's rituals, participants were walked through different phases of mortality, including the creation, Garden of Eden, the present world, and finally the afterlife, and granted sacred tokens and keywords necessary for exaltation. But under Young's direction, inductees were now guided by men acting as Christ's ancient apostles—Peter, James, and John—a clear reference to apostolic authority within the kingdom. The final stage of the endowment was entrance into the "celestial kingdom," or the highest degree of glory, and the temple featured a celestial room that replicated heaven. Hanging on the walls of the majestic room were portraits of Brigham Young and his associate apostles. Everywhere saints looked in the temple, they were reminded of the Twelve's priesthood authority.[89]

Further, Young introduced a new ordinance, called the "adoption," that emphasized patriarchal dependence. The ceremony featured grown men and women being ritually adopted as "children" by priesthood leaders. The practice forged tangible linkages to presiding apostles at the very moment it seemed to the Mormons that the world was falling apart. One participant explained that "this order of Adoption will Link the chain of the Priesthood in such a way that it cannot be separated." Another saint wrote to Young pleading to be sealed to him, as without the priesthood connection he was merely "an Orphan wandering through a wicked world without a Father of promise." And if being sealed to Young was too great a request, then he would ask to be linked to another apostle, as long as they could be attached to someone

Photograph of Nauvoo Temple, circa 1847. After being under construction for five years, the temple's exterior was completed in late 1845. INTERNATIONAL SOCIETY DAUGHTERS OF UTAH PIONEERS, SALT LAKE CITY.

who held sufficient authority to assure eternal glory. Joseph Smith's salvific vision had always emphasized interdependence, but Brigham Young's reaffirmed hierarchical control. While the Mormon kingdom appeared tyrannical to outsiders, to the faithful it provided a much-desired stability. According to Young, an admittedly biased source, many Mormons wept when they were adopted into his family.[90]

These temple rituals also significantly expanded polygamy as part of the divine kingdom. Among those who received the rituals were dozens of women sealed as plural wives to the faith's leading men. In most instances, the man's first wife placed the hand of the new wife into the hand of her husband, and then stood as witness to the ceremony. The number of new inductees was staggering. On top of the fifteen wives Young had been sealed to over the past fifteen months, he was wed to eighteen more in December and January alone. Before leaving Nauvoo, he claimed nearly forty polygamous spouses. Heber C. Kimball was not far behind: he was sealed to thirty women, five of whom were already pregnant with his children. Their domestic kingdoms were quickly growing.

These family arrangements represented a new stage in Mormonism's evolving polygamous practice. Whereas previous circumstances— including Joseph Smith's reticence to be caught by his wife, the limited number of knowing participants, and the fear that rumors could spread—meant interactions between men and their plural wives were limited, the saints' final few months in Nauvoo brought much more transparency to the practice. Soon polygamy became an open secret, which simultaneously granted more stability to those involved as well as increasing the expectation for conjugal relations between spouses. While there were few documented cases of plural wives who became pregnant prior to Smith's death, that number quickly grew as the practice expanded and participants adapted to their new reality. Women were now expected to not only be sealed to Mormon men for eternity, but also to commence providing the numerous children promised to God's patriarchs.

Some women even offered themselves as plural wives. Percis Tippets, though already married, expressed a desire to be added to Young's growing family. "As my mind seems still to be placed upon you," she wrote, "I would ask a place in your kingdom." And Young and Kimball were far from the only patriarchs engaging in plural marriages. In total, around two hundred men and seven hundred women entered into such unions in Nauvoo during Young's reign. By the time they left Illinois, the Mormons were a broad and interconnected web of familial relations linked together in hopes of surviving modernity's storm.[91]

THROUGH THE WINTER, AS THE SAINTS' DEPARTURE from Illinois approached, the attacks on outlying Mormon communities continued, despite pleas from the governor. The springtime departure was therefore appearing increasingly unsettled. But more concerning to Nauvoo's leaders than the mobs was the federal government. On December 18, a grand jury indicted nearly a dozen Nauvoo residents, including Brigham Young, Willard Richards, John Taylor, Parley Pratt, and Orson Hyde, for counterfeiting. The charges stemmed from accusations that the saints were producing bogus money in both Illinois and Iowa, charges that followed a long stream of counterfeiting accusations in the Mormon city for the past two years and posed a serious threat to the church's plans.[92]

In the short term, church leaders did what they could to avoid arrest. When federal officials arrived at the Nauvoo temple on December 23, the saints orchestrated a ruse: they called Brigham Young's carriage to the door, where it picked up William Miller, a member of the Council of Fifty. Wearing a heavy coat and Young's cap, and surrounded by several women—including Orrin Porter Rockwell disguised in drag—Miller was a decoy. The hoax worked, as the officers arrested him and made it all the way to Carthage before realizing their mistake. But while "Bogus Brigham," as the dodge was later called, worked, the encounter spooked the saints. They worried that the federal government might not honor the state's promise of a peaceful exodus. Orson Hyde rushed a letter to Stephen A. Douglas, pleading for assurance that there would not be any more legal problems for Nauvoo.[93]

That assurance never came. Thomas Ford, weary of being attacked by both sides for failing to solve the Mormon problem, was anxious to finally rid himself of the Mormon nuisance. He began to spread rumors in early January 1846 that not only would the government continue to press the counterfeiting charges, but federal troops might stand in the way of the Mormon departure. He hoped the news would light a fire under church leaders. The plan worked well. Convinced that national and state leaders were conspiring against them, Young concluded on January 13 that the government planned to surround the saints and enable the mobs to finish off the church for good. They therefore had to speed their preparations. Young asked his deputies if a good number of the organized migration companies could be ready within a matter of hours. While that short a turnaround was deemed impossible, they decided to move up their departure date from April to February. The original agreement stipulated that the Mormons would not have to leave until the grass grew and the water flowed, but neither would be the case. Instead, the ground was still frozen solid and the river was pretty close.[94]

The final few weeks were bitter for many Mormons as they prepared to say farewell to their city and their country, but there were still a few sweet moments. On February 3, Young declared to a gathering of saints that they could no longer perform temple rituals, as it was time to close the grandiose structure and leave it behind. There would be future temples, he assured his audience. But after leaving the crowd for some time, he was surprised to find that many refused to disperse. They craved the temple's rituals, which they knew would buoy their faith for the difficult trip ahead. Young was moved, reversing his decision and performing the rituals for another twenty-four hours. He and other leaders endowed around three hundred persons in that short time.[95]

"Expulsion of the Mormons from Nauvoo." FOUND IN HENRY MAYHEW, *THE MORMONS, OR LATTER-DAY SAINTS* (AUBURN AND BUFFALO, NY: MILLER, ORTON & MULLIGAN, 1854), 214.

During the next week, on February 9, an overheated stovepipe caused a fire in the temple. Even though the structure avoided extensive damage, Young found the episode fitting. If it was the Lord's will for the temple to be burned rather than falling into gentile hands, he reasoned, "Amen to it." A trickle of wagons started crossing the daunting mile-wide Mississippi River on makeshift skiffs that week, the vanguard of what John Taylor dubbed "the great move of the Saints out of the United States." Young and other leaders departed on or around February 15, but remained just on the other side of the river as they attempted to orchestrate the remaining departures. Soon, thousands of saints were strung along the plains headed westward, migrating to a new promised land, though they did not know exactly where it would be. "My last act in that precious spot was to tidy the rooms, sweep up the floor, and set the broom in its accustomed place behind the door," remembered Bathsheba Smith. "I gently closed the door and faced an unknown future." At least she was not alone—while not every resident of the city followed Young, an estimated 15,000 Mormons left their belongings behind as they abandoned Nauvoo.[96]

A few months before the exodus, the Council of Fifty considered leaving America a parting gift: a written compilation of all the persecutions the Mormons had faced in the United States. Brigham Young called for a committee to gather "every mean, dastardly publication concerning us," and publish them for the world to see. They felt such an indictment would prove the lie in America's democratic tradition. But what title could they give such a compilation of villainy? They turned to bitter satire. Parley Pratt recommended "The beauties of American liberty"; David Fullmer volunteered "The land of the free, the home of the brave, the assylum for the opprest"; and William W. Phelps suggested "Hail Columbia happy land! Hail ye heroes see these bands." In the end, they could not decide which was the most appropriate, so they chose all of them. It was an ungainly solution, but a revealing expression of their disappointment in America's democratic promise. True liberty, the Mormons had concluded, could only be found beyond American democracy's borders.[97]

EPILOGUE

Legacies

Engraving of Nauvoo Temple ruins, 1853. Shortly after the Mormons left Nauvoo, much of the temple was destroyed by fire. The external shell was then devastated by a tornado several years later. FOUND IN FREDERICK PIERCY, *ROUTE FROM LIVERPOOL TO GREAT SALT LAKE VALLEY* (LIVERPOOL: FRANKLIN D. RICHARDS, 1855), 63.

Even before he arrived in Nauvoo, Thomas L. Kane, a young, rich, and handsome traveler, was impressed by its appearance. "I was descending the last hillside upon my journey," he explained in a public speech to a group of Philadelphia dignitaries, "when a landscape in delightful contrast broke upon my view." In front of him, across the Mississippi River, lay a beautiful city glittering in the sunrise. He could see tidy dwellings and lush gardens on the flats, and above, on a bluff, a noble marble edifice with a towering gold and white spire. The city appeared several miles wide, with farms littering the surrounding countryside. Kane noted "the unmistakable marks of industry, enterprise and educated wealth." It struck him as a scene of singular beauty.

Yet after procuring a skiff and crossing the river to see the city up close, he was met with silence. He didn't find a soul on the city's streets, and every building he entered was vacant. Kane wandered the empty streets, walked into abandoned homes, and explored the deserted shops. "The town lay as in a dream," he said, "under some deadening spell of loneliness, from which I almost feared to wake it." If he had visited only a year before, he would have encountered a bustling city of about twenty thousand inhabitants, one of the most populous urban settlements west of Cleveland. But in September 1846, all he found was a ghost town. Kane noted that the grass was not overgrown, nor all the footprints washed away. "Plainly it had not slept long," he concluded.[1]

His inspection continued, and he soon found the remnants of a large battle. Embers of a just-perished flame were all around him. He eventually encountered other people: men from the victorious side. Intoxicated militiamen were relaxing by the temple and sharing stories of their bravery. When Kane approached them, they leapt to their feet and demanded to know his business. Once assured he was not a Mormon, they offered to give him a tour of the majestic stone structure, which they admitted was not theirs. The men boasted that after several years of conflict with the "deluded persons" who had inhabited the city, they had finally evicted the last of the fanatics only a few days previous.

Kane listened to their rant before departing and making his way across the Mississippi into Iowa Territory. It was there that he found the battle's losers. Near the river, he stumbled upon a makeshift camp of over six hundred Mormons either too sick or too poor to move far-ther west. It was a dreadful scene. "They were there because they had no homes, nor hospital nor poor-house nor friends to offer them any," he recalled. Most of the Mormons had fled Nauvoo before the sum-mer, leaving behind only those who lacked the strength and provi-sions. Finally, they, too, were forced out, at gunpoint. They were now huddled on the west bank of the Mississippi as they waited for their church to send assistance. From across the river, Kane could still hear the ruffians drunkenly singing and shouting as they danced around the Mormon temple.[2]

FOLLOWING BRIGHAM YOUNG'S DEPARTURE from Nauvoo in mid-February, the Mormon exodus out of Illinois was a haphazard enter-prise. The rushed nature of their evacuation created complications. Only a few companies left with the first wave of migration, and several more departed over the following months. Compounding the prob-lems facing those who remained in Nauvoo was the arrival of mission-aries from a new Mormon schismatic faith based in Wisconsin. James J. Strang had only joined the faith in early 1844, a few months before Joseph Smith's death, but he turned out to be a bigger threat to Young and the Twelve than Sidney Rigdon ever was. Strang claimed to pos-sess a letter from Smith that designated him the prophet's successor, and he also spoke in detail about his experiences with angelic ordi-nations, buried plates, and translated scriptures—experiences that seemed reminiscent of Smith's own prophetic origin story.

Many in Nauvoo were convinced by the new prophet. William Marks, Nauvoo's stake president, joined the new church, officially titled Church of Jesus Christ of Latter Day Saints but colloquially known as the "Strangites," as did William Smith, the deceased prophet's only living brother. Rumors swirled that Emma and Lucy Mack Smith, Joseph's wife and mother, followed the charismatic leader. Strang also recruited a number of prominent figures who had held major positions in the church prior to Nauvoo, including David Whitmer and Martin Harris, two of the three witnesses of the Book of Mormon gold plates back in 1829. Even John C. Bennett, always seeking a new thrill, converted and took a high position in the church's leadership, though once again he would only last two years before being expelled. Especially for Mormons who were not fully supportive of Young's authority or unwilling to leave America for some unknown western future, Strang's appeal was readily apparent.[3]

When Wilford Woodruff, who had been overseeing the church's missionary work in Britain for the last eighteen months, returned to Nauvoo on April 14, 1846, he found those who remained struggling to catch up with the rest of the church who had already fled "in the wilderness." Two days later, he learned that Illinois's governor was planning to remove the troops guarding the city, prompting fear among the remaining Mormons of further mob violence. Woodruff and Orson Hyde, the other apostle assigned to help gather the last saints, led the last sizable group out of Nauvoo a month later, but only after overseeing a public celebration that officially dedicated the temple, just before they abandoned it.[4]

There were still a few hundred Mormons left in Nauvoo. Though these people were either too poor or too infirm to start the trek, Nauvoo's neighbors rejected all of their claims about their low condition. Starting in July, mobs once again attacked the community, and continued even after the state militia tried to intercede. Emma Smith relocated her family to a nearby town until the fighting subsided. Eventually, after a week-long siege in September, which gentile locals called "The Battle of Nauvoo," the last saints were evicted. Non-Mormon neighbors refused to allow any Mormons to stay behind. Now that the county had rid itself of all the Mormons, wrote Thomas Sharp, it was time "to obliterate, as far as possible, all the effects of their reign of terror." He recommended renaming any town or street that was associated with the faith. He and others wished to forget that Nauvoo ever existed. The county then returned to its quiet way of living, seemingly oblivious to the fact that their entire democratic system had nearly failed.[5]

The dissenters who had published the *Nauvoo Expositor*, the event that led to Smith's imprisonment and then death, also tried to move on from the Nauvoo episode. Francis Higbee and Robert Thompson remained in Hancock County for a few more years before relocating to the East Coast. William Law moved to northern Illinois, and later Wisconsin, where he eventually became known as a successful physician and surgeon. Chauncey Higbee remained in Illinois and would be elected to the state senate. Each of them sought stability after their turbulent years in Nauvoo. And while a number of Joseph Smith's former followers migrated between new schismatic Mormon creeds—including Strang's—over the years, these dissenters mostly stayed away. They had had enough of Mormonism.[6]

Thomas Kane visited Nauvoo only days after the final "battle." Though he presented himself in his account as an ignorant observer, he in fact knew the town was abandoned before he arrived. A member of a prominent Philadelphia family with strong political connections, Kane had taken pity on the saints as he followed their story in the national news. He rushed to meet Brigham Young when the new Mormon prophet was camped along the Missouri River in eastern Iowa, and Kane helped broker a deal between the Mormon church and the federal government. America needed men to fight in the Mexican-American War, just under way, and the Mormons were in dire need of provisions. Despite their disdain for the United States, and the fact that they had set out from Nauvoo in the hope of leaving the nation forever, Young agreed to muster a Mormon battalion of five hundred men to be sent south. The agreement was made out of desperation, and out of a lingering commitment to the country in which most Mormons were raised. To symbolize its ambivalent loyalty, the battalion marched to Mexico waving a homemade American flag with only thirteen stars— their devotion was to America's original ideals, not its current government. It was after making these arrangements that Kane went to Nauvoo to see the deserted City of God for himself. He hoped to write a book about the disenfranchised church as a way to raise sympathy for the community.[7]

For his part, Young eventually reached the Great Salt Lake Valley, just west of the Rocky Mountains, in the summer of 1847. Originally, the Mormons had wanted to move to the region because it was outside America's control, but the settlement of the Mexican-American War, and the land transfers involved, meant they were once again within the jurisdiction of the United States. Church authorities immediately petitioned for statehood—the State of Deseret—but government officials proved no more willing to work with Young than they had been with Smith, so they created the Utah Territory, a nod to the indigenous populations that preceded the Mormons in the area but were now being pushed out.

The next four decades witnessed continuing conflict between the Utah saints and Washington, at one point nearly resulting in war when President James Buchanan dispatched federal troops in 1857 to quell what he believed was a Mormon rebellion. Americans still worried that the Mormons, who pledged their allegiance to church leaders rather than the federal government, could never conform to democratic rule. Even Stephen A. Douglas, who had championed the saints' cause in Illinois, now refused to support Utah's attempts at self-sovereignty. In the meantime, Young oversaw one of the largest religious colonization efforts in North American history, as Mormon settlements spread throughout the Rocky Mountain region, south to Mexico, north to Canada, and west to California. It was not until 1896, after the church ceased practicing polygamy, gave up its theocratic rhetoric, and adopted the nation's two-party political system, that Utah was finally admitted to the Union as the forty-fifth state.[8]

Other aspects of Smith's project were more easily discarded, however. Soon after leaving Nauvoo, Young jettisoned early Mormonism's belief in an interracial priesthood. Though as late as 1847 he insisted that ordination had nothing to do with genealogy, because from "one blood has God made all flesh," he quickly reversed course. Later that same year, he received word of a black male convert marrying a white female member in Boston, and his disgust for mixed-race relationships overwhelmed his commitment to Smith's more inclusive racial vision. By 1852 he had instituted a policy of white supremacy: "Any man having one drop of the seed of Cane in him Cannot hold the priesthood," he bellowed, "& if no other Prophet ever spake it Before I will say it now in the name of Jesus Christ." Following his direction as territorial governor, the Utah legislature passed a series of laws that allowed the Mormons their own brand of coerced labor that, while they believed it was kinder than Southern slavery, still saw black men, women, and children enslaved. At the same time, their arrival and expansion in the region led to the removal and subjugation of the same Native tribes they had previously imagined as colleagues in their imperial project.[9]

These were especially difficult changes for Mormons such as Elijah Able and Jane Manning—now Jane Manning James, after she married Isaac James, another black Mormon—who had lived in Nauvoo. Though he had already been ordained an elder, Able was no longer recognized as a priesthood holder in the official church record; and while Manning had been offered some form of sealing by Joseph and Emma Smith, she was now denied any temple ordinances in Utah. Eventually, after she agitated for it, she was allowed to be sealed to Smith—but only as a servant, and the ritual was performed vicariously as she waited outside the temple walls. Meanwhile, the church's most famous Native convert, Lewis Dana, lost faith in Young and eventually joined a different Mormon breakaway sect. Mormonism's treatment of racial minorities may have been unexceptional at the time, but it was still troubling, especially in its movement from inclusiveness to racial exclusion.[10]

Another of Joseph Smith's legacies did survive, however. Once outside of Illinois, and thus beyond the reach of the state's laws, polygamy became much more open and pervasive. Brigham Young, Heber C. Kimball, and other leading men did not attempt to hide their new wives, and soon decided to take the practice public. Young assigned apostle Orson Pratt to announce it officially in 1852, and they soon disseminated the news to the world. The world, unsurprisingly, reacted with scorn and derision. The federal government immediately set itself to eradicating the practice, leading to a decades-long battle over Mormon sexuality. The very presence of polygamy, to most Americans, was a threat to American civilization.[11]

Mormon women in Utah had to learn to cope with the new family arrangements, as the practice soon became all-encompassing. Several of those women who were married to church leaders, especially as the latter were sealed to a growing number of wives, decided they could not accept the new dispensation. Mary Ann Pratt, who had married the apostle Parley Pratt in 1837, divorced him in 1853, and Marinda Hyde, who had married the apostle Orson Hyde in 1834, divorced him in 1870. Meanwhile, many of the women who chose to enter polygamous unions had second thoughts. Five women who were sealed to Brigham Young in the Nauvoo temple later asked for divorces, as did three women who were sealed to Wilford Woodruff during the trek west. Ironically, Utah, known for its patriarchal form of marriage, soon boasted some of the most liberal divorce laws in the nation, as the mechanism became common for couples that struggled to make polygamy work. These separations did little to diminish the Mormon leaders' expanding patriarchal empires: by his death in 1877, Young had fifty-five wives and fifty-nine children.[12]

While there was certainly discontent, the vast majority of women who entered polygamous unions remained within their new families. Some even offered a public defense of the practice. Belinda Marden Pratt, who was sealed to Parley Pratt as a plural wife in Nauvoo, wrote the first published apologia for polygamy authored by a woman in America. Titled *Defense of Polygamy, by a Lady of Utah*, the 1854 pamphlet argued that polygamy was biblically sanctioned and divinely inspired, and she assured readers that the institution brought stability, both on earth and in heaven. The reality was much more complicated. Some women insisted that they found support in their sister-wives—some took advantage of their shared marital duties to move away and get an education or enter the workforce—while others suffered immensely. Decades later, Utah surprised the nation by joining the suffragist movement, as the same women who defended polygamy also agitated for women's rights; the territory granted women's suffrage in 1870, and Susan B. Anthony and Elizabeth Cady Stanton visited the next year to praise the Mormon activists for their efforts. Yet a majority of America remained disgusted by what they heard was taking place in Utah households, and an increasing number of prosecutions, often resulting in adverse judicial decisions, as well as political pressure forced the Mormon church to publicly denounce the practice in 1890.[13]

Among those who were shocked and disgusted by the revelations of Mormon polygamy after they became public in 1852 were Joseph Smith's own sons, who were still living with Emma in Nauvoo. Emma had since remarried, and she refused to either force the Mormon faith on her children or explain to them the troubles that nearly sunk her first marriage. After years of anguish, her method for dealing with the most odious aspect of Smith's legacy was denial. Few could blame her. Yet the Smith family could not remain outside the fray for long. A number of men and women who had been part of the Mormon faith in Nauvoo but refused to acknowledge Brigham Young's leadership, and who had since dispersed among the surrounding communities, were anxious to restore the church back to its simplest form. In 1860, after several years of persistent agitation, they succeeded in drafting Joseph Smith III, the son of Mormonism's first prophet, as the new leader of yet another Mormon tradition. The denomination was later called the Reorganized Church of Jesus Christ of Latter Day Saints, and among its founding principles was a firm denial that Joseph Smith had ever practiced polygamy. While established in Nauvoo, where its members were not troubled by neighbors because the new church did not carry on the controversial actions of young Joseph's father, its headquarters soon relocated to Missouri. Once again, Nauvoo was left behind.[14]

TODAY, NAUVOO IS HOME TO ONLY TWO THOUSAND residents, a fraction of the number who lived there during its Mormon heyday. However, it continues to serve as a sacred tourist destination for denominations linked to Joseph Smith. While the town remains mostly quiet between September and May, a sleepy Midwestern community with few stores and even fewer restaurants, during the summer it is swarmed by thousands of believers from different Mormon faiths seeking out the city's history and tapping into its spiritual heritage. Both the Church of Jesus Christ of Latter-day Saints, still headquartered in Salt Lake City and now boasting over sixteen million members worldwide, and the Community of Christ, the renamed Reorganized Church and now based in Independence, Missouri, have built visitor centers, maintained historic homes, and reconstructed dozens of period buildings from the 1840s. The Latter-day Saint church even rebuilt the massive temple on the bluff in 2002. There are scripted pageants, games for children, and historic tours guided by earnest missionaries, both young and old. Some have dubbed Nauvoo the "Mormon Williamsburg."[15]

Like Colonial Williamsburg, Nauvoo today offers only a partial view of the city's true history. Its beautiful brick homes distract from the reality that, in the 1840s, Nauvoo predominantly consisted of dirty wooden shacks. Its self-presentation as a pilgrimage destination, and as a necessary intermediate step on the way to Utah, belies the fact that the Mormons under Smith had wanted to build their kingdom on the Mississippi. Further, historic tours put on by faithful missionaries from the Latter-day Saint church rarely cover the radical political, social, and polygamous experiments that were at the heart of Joseph Smith's Nauvoo vision.

That vision had as much to do with democracy as anything else, and this is why Nauvoo and its failure matter. The question the Mormons posed was not just about the boundaries of religious liberty; it concerned the limits of American democracy. Today, however divided and cacophonous our political and cultural battles may be, few believe that the only solution is to abandon the American experiment altogether. But the Mormons did just that, decades before Southern secession.

Democracy was envisioned to manage different interests and grant individual freedoms. With the Mormons, the process broke down. After facing repeated opposition, they determined that the only way to achieve stability and assure their rights was to question traditional American principles and, when that failed to bring redress, flagrantly challenge the political and legal system. In response, both their state and federal governments proved unsympathetic to the saints' pleas, and their gentile neighbors proved exacting in their revenge. Yet the saints were far from the first, or the last, group of dissenters to call into question traditional values in a desperate quest to realize freedom, however misbegotten, within a society driven by majority control. Even if their solutions only brought more problems, their struggles high-light real questions concerning democratic rule. If we are to account for the full history of American democracy, we must give voice not only to its victors, but also to its discontents.

ACKNOWLEDGMENTS

Joseph Smith believed that an individual could only be saved when part of a community; the same could be said about someone trying to write a book. The genesis of this project came when, as an undergraduate student, I had the privilege to participate in a Brigham Young University program in Nauvoo for four months. In part because of the program's teachers and fellow students, I quickly fell in love with the city and its history. I decided then and there that I wanted to write a book on Nauvoo's rise and fall, and that desire led directly to becoming a historian. To all my fellow Nauvooians, I salute you.

Three individuals performed the herculean work of reading this manuscript's entire first draft: Christopher Jones, my best friend and favorite critic, was as supportive as he was encouraging; Jenny Reeder, expert on nineteenth-century Mormon women, had a clear eye for issues related to audience, gender, and relevance; and Alex Smith, who knows more about Nauvoo than nearly anyone else currently alive, was always as insightful with his analysis as he was sharp with his wit. This book would have been far worse without the insight of these, my three most reliable readers.

A host of others read either entire chapters or sections, always providing useful feedback. Steve Evans, Matt Grow, David Grua, Lindsay Hansen-Park, Robin Jensen, Elizabeth Kuehn, Michael MacKay, Andrea Radke-Moss, Brent Rogers, Cristina Rosetti, Jonathan Stapley,

and Joseph Stuart: thank you. Matthew Bowman, one of the most pro-
lific and brilliant historians of American religion, and Jeffrey Mahas,
quickly becoming one of the foremost experts on Nauvoo, provided
particularly helpful critiques. Spencer McBride and Jordan Watkins,
two of my closest colleagues whose focus overlaps with mine, were
similarly obliging. I'm especially appreciative of Amy Thiriot for walking me through the presence of slavery in Nauvoo. And finally, Paul
Reeve, one of the best mentors in the field, and Quincy Newell, my col-
laborator in editing the *Mormon Studies Review*, helped me understand
Nauvoo's racial dimensions.

A scholarly army—no less intimidating than the Nauvoo Legion—
helped structure my academic world, either through personal conversation, conference comments, or indirect mentoring. Gary Bergera,
Joanna Brooks, Barbara Jones Brown, Richard Bushman, Frank Cogli-
ano, Rachel Cope, Kathleen Flake, Sally Gordon, Melissa Inouye, Lau-
rie Maffly-Kipp, Patrick Mason, Max Mueller, Ardis Parshall, Sarah
Pearsall, Steve Taysom, John Turner, and Laurel Ulrich: whether
you know it or not, you have shaped my historical mind. A special
thanks to my digital families—By Common Consent, the Junto, Juve-
nile Instructor, and all the #Twitterstorians—for always providing
camaraderie. On several trips to Nauvoo, Lachlan Mackay, always an
ambassador to scholars of all stripes, allowed me to stay in some of the
Community of Christ's treasured historic properties.

A number of institutions in Utah were indispensable for my project.
Any history of Nauvoo cannot be coherently written without the mon-
umental scholarship performed by the Joseph Smith Papers Project,
housed at the LDS Church History Department in Salt Lake City. The
many editors and researchers associated with that project are pillars of
the field and generous collaborators; all future work on early Mormonism will be built on their shoulders. The LDS Church History Library,
especially Anne Berryhill, Jennifer Barkdull, and Elise Reynolds, were
tremendously helpful in finding, acquiring, and digitizing sources.
Spencer Fluhman, my first and best mentor, provided a generous fellowship at BYU's Neal A. Maxwell Institute for Religious Scholarship

at a critical moment in the project's development. None of these individuals or organizations, of course, are to blame for this book's errors.

I have presented papers based on this project at the University of Missouri, Lamar University, College of Charleston, and Utah Valley University, annual conferences for the Mormon History Association, John Whitmer Historical Association, Society for United States Intellectual History, Society for Historians of the Early American Republic, and Consortium for the Revolutionary Era, as well as brownbags with Brigham Young University and Sam Houston State University. I thank everyone at all these venues, especially the designated respondents, for thoughtful questions, critiques, and suggestions. And besides the LDS Church History Library, the staffs at the Abraham Lincoln Presidential Library, Brigham Young University's Harold B. Lee Library, the Community of Christ's Library and Archives, the International Society Daughters of Utah Pioneers, the Library of Congress, the University of Chicago Library, the University of Utah's J. Willard Marriot Library, Western Illinois University's Leslie F. Malpass Library, and Yale University's Beinecke Rare Book and Manuscript Library provided assistance during my research trips.

Sam Houston State University has proven to be a wonderful academic home as I wrote this book. Sincere thanks to all the faculty for being hospitable, particularly to Pinar Emiralioglu for serving as a wonderful department chair, Brian Jordan for being the ideal colleague, and my many students for teaching me numerous lessons. Outside of Texas, I was twice able to participate in "Second Book" workshops that were put together by Emily Conroy-Krutz and Jessica Lepler. At the first, Amy Greenberg offered crucial advice concerning book proposals; at the second, Rosemarie Zagarri, Seth Cotlar, and David Head, as well as Emily and Jessica, provided feedback on chapter 3. If only all scholars could have such supportive networks.

This book would have never been possible were it not for several individuals taking a chance on an unproven author. My literary agent, Giles Anderson, helped me get the project off the ground and into a good home. At Liveright, the legendary Bob Weil not only saw promise in the proposal, but provided an exhaustive reading of the manuscript's first draft, pushing me on some misplaced assumptions and teaching me how to write for a general audience. Dan Gerstle then devoted countless hours to helping smooth my prose and finesse my arguments; in some instances, he came to comprehend the book's thesis much sooner than I did. The rest of the team at Norton, especially Gina Iaquinta, proved to always be responsive, thorough, and efficient—everything an author could want from a press.

My family has always been the most important foundation in my life. It was from my parents, Melanie and Richard, that I first gained a love of learning, and they continue to serve as examples in a myriad of ways. My brothers—Spencer, Jared, and Abe—are some of my best friends, and I think the world of them. My grandmother, Arlene, set an example of writing from my earliest years. My in-laws—Neil, Thelma, and Margaret—have been nothing but supportive. But, of course, it is those closest to me who deserve the most thanks: Sara, Curtis, and, especially, Catherine, you make life worth living. To you three, I owe everything.

NOTES

ABBREVIATIONS

AIC   George D. Smith, ed., *An Intimate Chronicle: The Journals of William Clayton* (Salt Lake City: Signature Books, 1995).

ALPL   Abraham Lincoln Presidential Library, Springfield, IL.

ATDR   *Alton* (IL) *Telegraph and Democratic Review*, 1836–1850.

BYJ   Brigham Young Journals, CHL.

BYOF   Brigham Young Office Files, CHL.

BYUS   *Brigham Young University Studies*. Quarterly, 1959–.

BYUSC   L. Tom Perry Special Collections, Harold B. Lee Library, Brigham Young University, Provo, UT.

C50   Matthew J. Grow, Ronald K. Esplin, Mark Ashurst-McGee, Gerrit J. Dirkmaat, and Jeffrey D. Mahas, eds., *Council of Fifty, Minutes, March 1844–January 1846*, vol. 1 of the Administrative Records series of *The Joseph Smith Papers*, edited by Ronald K. Esplin, Matthew J. Grow, and Matthew C. Godfrey (Salt Lake City: Church Historian's Press, 2016).

CHL   LDS Church History Library, Salt Lake City, UT.

COC   Library and Archives, Community of Christ, Independence, MO.

D6   Mark Ashurst-McGee, David W. Grua, and Elizabeth A. Kuhen, eds., *Documents, Volume 6: February 1838–August 1839*, vol. 6 of the Documents series of *The Joseph Smith Papers Project*, edited by Ronald K. Esplin, Matthew J. Grow, Matthew C. Godfrey, and R. Eric Smith (Salt Lake City: Church Historian's Press, 2017).

D7   Matthew C. Godfrey, Spencer W. McBride, Alex D. Smith, and Christopher James Blythe, eds., *Documents, Volume 7: September 1839–January 1841*, vol. 7 of the Documents series of *The Joseph Smith Papers Project*, edited by Ronald K. Esplin, Matthew J. Grow, Matthew C. Godfrey, and R. Eric Smith (Salt Lake City: Church Historian's Press, 2018).

ERSJ   Eliza R. Snow Journals, CHL.

GCM   General Church Minutes, CHL.

GLN   Glen Leonard, *Nauvoo: A Place of Peace, a People of Promise* (Salt Lake City: Deseret Book, 2002).

HFoF   Laurel Thatcher Ulrich, *A House Full of Females: Plural Marriage and Women's Rights in Early Mormonism, 1835–1870* (New York: Knopf, 2017).

J1   Dean C. Jessee, Mark Ashurst-McGee, and Richard L. Jensen, eds., *Journals, Volume 1: 1832–1839*, vol. 1 of the Journals series of *The Joseph Smith Papers*, edited by Dean C. Jessee, Ronald K. Esplin, and Richard Lyman Bushman (Salt Lake City: Church Historian's Press, 2008).

J2   Andrew H. Hedges, Alex D. Smith, and Richard Lloyd Anderson, eds., *Journals, Volume 2: December 1841–April 1843*, vol. 2 of the Journals series of *The Joseph Smith Papers*, edited by Dean C. Jessee, Ronald K. Esplin, and Richard Lyman Bushman (Salt Lake City: Church Historian's Press, 2011).

J3   Andrew H. Hedges, Alex D. Smith, and Brent M. Rogers, eds., *Journals, Volume 3: May 1843–June 1844*, vol. 3 of the Journals series of *The Joseph Smith Papers*, edited by Ronald K. Esplin and Matthew J. Grow (Salt Lake City: Church Historian's Press, 2015).

JMH   *Journal of Mormon History.* Quarterly, 1974–.

JS   Joseph Smith.

JSC   Joseph Smith Collection, CHL.

JSLB   Joseph Smith Letterbook, CHL.

JSJ   Joseph Smith Journals, in J1, J2, and J3.

JSOP   Joseph Smith Office Papers, CHL.

JSP   Joseph Smith Papers Project, https://www.josephsmithpapers.org.

JWHAJ   *John Whitmer Historical Association Journal.* Biannual, 1981–.

KFL   Pat Geisler, ed., Kimball Family Letters, Heber C. Kimball Family Association, typescript, CHL.

KoM   Robert Bruce Flanders, *Nauvoo: Kingdom on the Mississippi* (Urbana: University of Illinois Press, 1965).

LoC   Library of Congress, Washington, DC.

MHC-C1   Manuscript History of the Church, vol. C-1, covering November 2, 1838, to July 31, 1842, CHL, found on JSP.

MHC-D1   Manuscript History of the Church, vol. D-1, covering August 1, 1842, to July 1, 1843, CHL, found on JSP.

MHC-E1   Manuscript History of the Church, vol. E-1, covering July 1, 1843, to April 30, 1844, CHL, found on JSP.

NCCDM	Nauvoo City Council Draft Minutes, in John S. Dinger, ed., *The Nauvoo City and High Council Minutes* (Salt Lake City: Signature Books, 2011).
NCCM	Nauvoo City Council Minutes, found on JSP.
NHCM	Nauvoo High Council Minutes, in John S. Dinger, ed., *The Nauvoo City and High Council Minutes* (Salt Lake City: Signature Books, 2011).
NMCMB	Nauvoo Municipal Court Docket Book, CHL.
NN	*Nauvoo* (IL) *Neighbor*, 1842–1846.
NRSMB	Nauvoo Relief Society Minute Book, in Jill Mulvay Derr, Carol Cornwall Madsen, Kate Holbrook, and Matthew J. Grow, eds., *The First Fifty Years of Relief Society: Key Documents in Latter-day Saint Women's History* (Salt Lake City: Church Historian's Press, 2016).
PPPC	Parley P. Pratt Collection, CHL.
QW	*Quincy* (IL) *Whig*, 1838–1856.
R4	Robin Scott Jensen and Brian M. Hauglid, ed., *Revelations and Translations, Volume 4: Book of Abraham and Related Manuscripts*, vol. 4 of the Revelations and Translations series of *The Joseph Smith Papers Project*, edited by Ronald K. Esplin, Matthew J. Grow, Matthew C. Godfrey, and R. Eric Smith (Salt Lake City: Church Historian's Press, 2018).
RSR	Richard Lyman Bushman, *Joseph Smith: Rough Stone Rolling* (New York: Knopf, 2005).
SJ	*Sangamo Journal* (Springfield, IL), 1831–1853.
T&S	*Times and Seasons* (Nauvoo, IL), 1841–1846.
UofU	J. Willard Marriott Library Special Collections, University of Utah, Salt Lake City, UT.
WCJ	William Clayton Journals, CHL. The journals are currently restricted. References are either from AIC, C50, HFoF, J3, or JSP.
WLJ	William Law Journal, in Lyndon Cook, ed., *William Law* (Salt Lake City: Grandin Book, 1994).
WRCC	William Robertson Coe Collection of Western Americana, YBL.
WRJ	Willard Richards Journals, CHL.
WRP	Willard Richards Papers, CHL.
WS	*Warsaw* (IL) *Signal*, 1841–1845.
WWC	Wilford Woodruff Collection, CHL.
WWJ	Wilford Woodruff Journals, CHL, online collection, https://history.lds.org.
YBL	Beinecke Rare Book & Manuscript Library, Yale University, New Haven, CT.
ZDHJ	Zina Diantha Huntington Jacobs Journals, CHL

PROLOGUE

1   Benjamin Franklin, quoted in James Madison, *Notes of Debates in The Federal Convention of 1787* (New York: W.W. Norton, 1987), 53.

2   The rained-out Sunday meeting is mentioned in JSJ, April 14, 1844, in J3:230. The weather is reported in William Mosley to Kingsley Mosley, February 18, 1844, CHL. Jacob Scott to Mary Warnock, April 5, 1844, CHL.

3   C50 Minutes, April 18, 1844, in C50:109–10, 114. WCJ, April 18, 1844, in AIC:131.

4   See C50.

5   This book will continue to frequently use "Mormon," "Mormon church," and "Mormonism"; however, both for the sake of simplicity as well as to remain faithful to the language of the Nauvoo period, I also frequently refer to members of the faith as "saints," and those who were not part of the church as "gentiles," as those, too, were terms used during the era covered in this study, and they reflect the religious framework in which the faithful understood themselves. Further, the spelling of the church's official name often vacillated during the early period, sometimes as "Latter Day Saints." For consistency, I will use the "Latter-day Saint" spelling.

6   The standard treatment of Nauvoo has been KoM, published in 1965. For an exhaustive social, if devotional, history of Nauvoo directed to faithful Mormons, see GLN. A readable and engaging history of Smith's death, and the trial of those charged with his murder, is found in Alex Beam, *American Crucifixion: The Murder of Joseph Smith and the Fate of the Mormon Church* (Chicago: PublicAffairs, 2014). The definitive biography of Joseph Smith is RSR, though it understates the centrality of polygamy to Smith's other Nauvoo duties. For scholarly arguments that Mormonism diverged from its surrounding culture, see Marvin S. Hill, *Quest for Refuge: The Mormon Flight from American Pluralism* (Salt Lake City: Signature Books, 1989), and Kenneth H. Winn, *Exiles in a Land of Liberty: Mormons in America, 1830–1846* (Chapel Hill: University of North Carolina Press, 1989).

7   The best treatment on Mormon polygamy is HFoF. See also Lawrence Foster, *Religion and Sexuality: The Shakers, the Mormons, and the Oneida Community* (Urbana: University of Illinois Press, 1984).

8   See HFoF, 386–87; Rachel Cope et al., eds., *Mormon Women's History: Beyond Biography* (Madison, NJ: Fairleigh Dickinson University Press, 2017); Ann Braude, "Women's History *Is* American Religious History," in *Retelling U.S. Religious History*, ed. Thomas A. Tweed (Berkeley: University of California Press, 1997), 87–107.

9   *St. Louis* (MO) *Weekly Gazette*, May 18, 1844. Josiah Quincy, *Figures of the Past from Leaves of Old Journals* (Boston: Roberts Brothers, 1883), 380–81. Charles Francis Adams Diary, May 15, 1844, Massachusetts Historical Society, Boston. W. Aitken, *A Journey Up the Mississippi River, From Its Mouth to Nauvoo, the City of the Latter Day Saints* (Ashton-Under-Lyne: W. B. Micklethwaite, 1845), 37. For general descriptions of Smith's physical appearance, including his clothing accessories, see Henry Caswall, *The City of the Mormons, or Three Days at Nauvoo, in 1842* (London: J. G. F & J. Rivington, 1843), 35; W. M. Busey to T. R. Webber, January 2, 1843, YBL; Wandle Mace, Journal, 37, CHL.

10 Elizur Wolcott to Samuel Wolcott, October 17, 1842, YBL. Robert A. Gilmore to John Richey, July 5, 1844, CHL. The minutes for the C50 meeting on April 18

do not specify where they took place. They frequently met in the Masonic Hall, finished only a week previous, but that building was occupied on this day. Joseph Smith's red-brick store is the most likely location, given the frequency with which it was used for events like this, though it is also possible they met in the home of Henry Miller.

11 *Pittsburgh* (PA) *Gazette*, September 15, 1843.
12 Aitken, *A Journey Up the Mississippi River*, 37.
13 Joseph Smith to John C. Calhoun, January 2, 1844, in MHC-E1, 1847.
14 Alexis de Tocqueville, *Democracy in America*, trans. and ed. Harvey C. Mansfield and Delba Winthrop (1835; Chicago: University of Chicago Press, 2000), 236–37.
15 *Lee County Democrat* (Fort Madison, IA), April 16, 1842.

CHAPTER 1: SOIL

1 JS to the Church and Edward Partridge, March 20, 1839, in D6:363.
2 Andrew Jenson, *Latter-day Saint Biographical Encyclopedia*, vol. 2 (Salt Lake City: A. Jenson History Co., 1914), 372.
3 Sarah M. Kimball, quoted in Jill Mulvay Derr, *Sarah M. Kimball* (Salt Lake City: Utah State Historical Society, 1976). Sarah M. Kimball, "Our Sixth Sense, or the Sense of Spiritual Understanding," *Woman's Exponent* (Salt Lake City, UT), April 15, 1895. For background on Sarah and Hiram, see Jill Mulvay Derr, *Sarah M. Kimball* (Salt Lake City: Utah State Historical Society, 1976).
4 *Woman Suffrage Leaflet* (Salt Lake City), January 1892.
5 *New York Herald*, June 17, 1842.
6 Daniel H. Rumfield, report, January 13, 1839, CHL. SJ, January 17, 1839. Heber C. Kimball to Joseph Fielding, March 11, 1839, CHL. Eliza R. Snow to Isaac Streator, February 22, 1839, photocopy, CHL.
7 "Far West Committee Minutes, January–April 1839," January 26, 1839, CHL. The "covenant" and its signatures follow the January 29 entry in the "Far West Committee Minutes." The frozen river is mentioned in Edward Partridge to JS, March 5, 1839, in D6:330.
8 Mary Fielding Smith to Joseph Fielding, June 1839, CHL. For the suffering of Mormon women during the Missouri crisis, see Andrea Radke-Moss, "Silent Memories of Missouri: Mormon Women and Sexual Assault in Group Memory and Identity," in *Beyond Biography: Sources in Context for Mormon Women's History*, ed. Rachel Cope, Amy Easton-Flake, Keith A. Erekson, Lisa Olsen Tait (Madison, NJ: Fairleigh Dickinson University Press, 2017): 49–82.
9 QW, February 23, 1839.
10 QW, March 2, March 16, March 23, April 27, June 8, 1839. Quincy Democratic Association, quoted in *Quincy* (IL) *Argus*, March 16, 1839.
11 "Far West Committee Minutes," February 7, 1839, CHL. Albert P. Rockwood to Family, January 1839, WRCC.
12 MHC-C1, 888. Isaac Galland to D. W. Rogers, February 26, 1839, JSLB 2:1–3. *Quincy Argus*, April 20, 1839. Edward Partridge to Joseph Smith, March 5, 1839, in D6:329.
13 See RSR, 382; Gordon A. Madsen, "Joseph Smith and the Missouri Court of Inquiry: Austin A. King's Quest for Hostages," BYUS 43, no. 4 (2004): 93–136.

14 T&S, November 1839.

15 JS to the Church and Edward Partridge, March 22, 1839, in D6:391–392. Minutes, April 24, GCM. WWJ, May 4, 1839, 331. Minutes, May 4–5, May 6, 1839, GCM. WWJ, May 15, 18, and 20, 1839.

16 JSJ, May 10, 1839, in J1:338. For background on the land and its purchase, see KoM, 28–38; GLN, 41–61.

17 ATDR, November 14, 1840. MHC-C1, 954. T&S, January 15, 1841. The names Commerce and Nauvoo coexisted for alternate purposes and spaces for several years. See GLN, 59.

18 JS, discourse, circa July 1839, in Willard Richards Pocket Companion, 69–70, CHL. See E. Brooks Holifield, *Theology in America: Christian Thought from the Age of the Puritans to the Civil War* (New Haven: Yale University Press, 2003), 300–301.

19 See GLN, 61. On land speculation, see KoM, 115–53.

20 Mary Fielding Smith to Joseph Fielding, June, 1839, CHL.

21 Thomas Jefferson to John Holmes, April 22, 1820, LoC. For the Missouri Crisis in general, see Robert Pierce Forbes, *The Missouri Compromise and Its Aftermath: Slavery and the Meaning of America* (Chapel Hill: University of North Carolina Press, 2007).

22 For the Book of Mormon and its connection to early Mormon belief concerning indigenous populations, see Mark Ashurst-McGee, "Zion Rising: Joseph Smith's Early Social and Political Thought" (PhD Dissertation: Arizona State University, 2008), 108–55; Terryl L. Givens, *By the Hand of Mormon: The American Scripture That Launched a New World Religion* (New York: Oxford University Press, 2002); Jared Hickman, "The Book of Mormon as Amerindian Apocalypse," *American Literature* 86, no. 3 (March 2016): 429–61; Max Mueller, *Race and the Making of the Mormon People* (Chapel Hill: University of North Carolina Press, 2017), 31–59.

23 For the story of early Mormonism in Jackson County, see Kenneth H. Winn, *Exiles in a Land of Liberty: Mormons in America, 1830–1846* (Chapel Hill: University of North Carolina Press, 1989), 85–105; Ashurst-McGee, "Zion Rising," 156–389; Matthew Bowman, *The Mormon People: The Making of a Mormon People* (New York: Random House, 2012), 32–62.

24 For segregation as the solution to racial problems in early America, see Nicholas Guyatt, *Bind Us Apart: How Enlightened Americans Invented Racial Segregation* (New York: Basic Books, 2016). For the stripping of Mormon whiteness and the relatedness between the creation of Caldwell County and Native reservations, see W. Paul Reeve, *Religion of a Different Color: Race and the Mormon Struggle for Whiteness* (New York: Oxford University Press, 2015), 64–67.

25 JS, motto, in JSJ, March 1838, in J1:237–38.

26 Memorial to Congress, 1839, in Clark V. Johnson, eds., *Mormon Redress Petitions: Documents of the 1833–1838 Missouri Conflict* (Provo, UT: BYU Religious Studies Center, 1992), 108. For an overview of the Mormon-Missouri War, see Stephen C. LeSueur, *The 1838 Mormon War in Missouri* (Columbia: University of Missouri Press, 1987); Alexander L. Baugh, *A Call to Arms: The 1838 Mormon Defense of Northern Missouri*, Dissertations in Latter-day Saint History (Provo, UT: Joseph Fielding Smith Institute for Latter-day Saint History and BYU Studies, 2000); Leland H. Gentry and Todd M. Compton, *Fire and Sword: A History of Latter-day Saints in Northern Missouri, 1836–39* (Salt Lake City: Kofford Books, 2010), 169–394.

27 A copy of the transcript is found in Sampson Avard, witness testimony, November 12, 1838, Mormon War Papers, 1837–1841, Missouri State Archives. For the organization of the Danites, see Leland H. Gentry, "The Danite Band of 1838," BYUS 14, no. 4 (1974): 421–50. Stephen C. LeSueur, "The Danites Reconsidered: Were They Vigilantes or Just the Mormons' Version of the Elks Club?" JWHAJ 14 (1994): 35–51. For the uses of the Declaration of Independence's words and ideals in extralegal actions, see Christian G. Fritz, *American Sovereigns: The People and America's Constitutional Tradition Before the Civil War* (Cambridge: Cambridge University Press, 2007), 277–78.

28 Avard, witness testimony.

29 Sidney Rigdon, *Oration Delivered by Mr. S. Rigdon, on the 4th of July, 1838* (Far West: Journal office, 1838), 12. Lilburn Boggs, Executive Order #44, Mormon War Papers.

30 David Lewis, petition to Congress, in Johnson, *Mormon Redress Petitions*, 276. For the racialized tones of extermination, see Reeve, *Religion of a Different Color*, 69–72. For the Hawn's Mill Massacre (previously, based on dated scholarship, known as "Haun's Mill"), see Thomas M. Spencer, "'Was This Really Missouri Civilization?': The Haun's Mill Massacre in Missouri and Mormon History," in Thomas M. Spencer, ed., *The Missouri Mormon Experience* (Columbia: University of Missouri Press, 2010), 100–118; Alexander L. Baugh, *Tragedy and Truth: What Happened at Hawn's Mill* (Salt Lake City: Covenant Communications, 2014).

31 Christopher Waldrep, *The Many Faces of Judge Lynch: Extralegal Violence and Punishment in America* (New York: Palgrave Macmillan, 2004), 27–48; Irene Quenzler Brown and Richard D. Brown, *The Hanging of Ephraim Wheeler: A Story of Rape, Incest, and Justice in Early America* (Cambridge: Harvard University Press, 2003). For the racial dimensions of these forms of justice, see Sally E. Hadden, *Slave Patrols: Law and Violence in Virginia and the Carolinas* (Cambridge: Harvard University Press, 2001).

32 For the significance of the Missouri tribulations to later Mormon thought, see David W. Grua, "Memoirs of the Persecuted: Persecution, Memory, and the West as a Mormon Refuge" (Brigham Young University: Master's Thesis, 2008).

33 Background for Illinois's political culture comes from James Simeone, *Democracy and Slavery in Frontier Illinois: The Bottomland Republic* (DeKalb: Northern Illinois University Press, 2000); Gerald Leonard, *The Invention of Party Politics: Federalism, Popular Sovereignty, and Constitutional Development in Jacksonian Illinois* (Chapel Hill: University of North Carolina Press, 2002); Richard Lawrence Miller, *Lincoln and His World: Prairie Politician, 1834–1842* (Mechanicsburg, PA: Stockpile Books, 2008) Sidney Blumenthal, *A Self-Made Man: The Political Life of Abraham Lincoln, Vol. 1, 1809–1849* (New York: Simon & Schuster, 2016). For the economic context, see Gabor S. Boritt, *Lincoln and the Economics of the American Dream* (Urbana: University of Illinois Press, 1994).

34 Andrew Jenson, "Lyman Wight," *Historical Record* 5 (December 1886): 108.

35 Lyman Wight to Thomas Benton, March 30, 1839, in QW, May 11, 1839.

36 Robert B. Thompson to First Presidency, May 13, 1839, in D6:462–464. WWJ, May 12, 1839, 333. Thompson and the apostles might have been particularly perturbed that Wight published his letters in a newspaper that had been particularly harsh on them. See, for instance, QW, November 10, December 8, 1838; Though

their tone shifted after the Mormons temporarily settled in Quincy, the *Whig* still republished many attacks on the faith. In April, they accused the Mormons of paying off their rival paper, the *Quincy Argus*, and in May they published letters that attacked Mormonism's origins. QW, April 27, May 18, 1839.

37 First Presidency to the editors of QW, May 17, 1839, in D6:466–67. Joseph Smith to Lyman Wight, May 27, 1839, in D6:484–85. QW, May 18, 1839. See also First Presidency to Robert B. Thompson, May 25, 1839, in D6:478–479. The First Presidency's statement appeared in QW, May 25, 1839; *Quincy Argus*, June 1, 1839. Statements of bi-partisan support are found in QW, May 11, 1839; *Quincy Argus*, May 11, 1839.

38 S. K. Lathrop, *The Nature and Extent of Religious Liberty* (Boston: I. R. Butts, 1838), 3. For the formation of Christian politics based on individual liberty, see Nathan O. Hatch, *The Democratization of American Christianity* (New Haven: Yale University Press, 1989); Philip Hamburger, *Separation of Church and State* (Cambridge: Harvard University Press, 2002), esp. 193–251. For the role of ministers in taking advantage of a democratized culture, see Jonathan D. Sassi, *A Republic of Righteousness: The Public Christianity of the Post-Revolutionary New England Clergy* (New York: Oxford University Press, 2001); Amanda Porterfield, *Conceived in Doubt: Religion and Politics in the New American Nation* (Chicago: University of Chicago Press, 2012); Spencer W. McBride, *Pulpit and Nation: Clergymen and the Politics of Revolutionary America* (Charlottesville: University of Virginia Press, 2017). For the birth of a new religious establishment, see David Sehat, *The Myth of American Religious Freedom* (New York: Oxford University Press, 2011).

39 Samuel Seabury, *The Supremacy and Obligation of Conscience: Considered with Reference to the Opposite Errors of Romanism and Protestantism* (New York: Billin and Brother, 1860), 21. Philip Hamburger argues that it is in response to the Catholic threat that "Protestants would eventually elevate separation of church and state as an American ideal." Hamburger, *Separation of Church and State*, 202.

40 J. B. Turner, *Mormonism in All Ages, or the Rise, Progress and Cause of Mormonism* (New York: Platt and Peters, 1842), 8.

41 Udney Hay Jacob to Martin Van Buren, March 19, 1840, ALPL. QW, October 17, 1840.

42 T&S, April 1840.

43 Thompson to First Presidency, May 13, 1839, in D6:463.

44 JS et al. to Edward Partridge and the Church, March 22, 1839, D6:398–99.

45 *Daily National Intelligencer* (Washington, DC), September 26, 1839. Sidney Rigdon to Joseph Smith, April 10, April 1839, in D6:397.

46 JS, Sidney Rigdon, and Elias Higbee, "Memorial to Congress" (1839), in Johnson, *Mormon Redress Petitions*, 103, 108, 116, 117, 118.

47 Isaac Leany affidavit, May 6, 1839, in Johnson, *Mormon Redress Petitions*, 266–67. Nathan K. Knight affidavit, April 13, 1839, in Johnson, *Mormon Redress Petitions*, 260. Benjamin Crandell affidavit, May 11, 1839, in Johnson, *Mormon Redress Petitions*, 173. James R. Bingham affidavit, undated, in Johnson, *Mormon Redress Petitions*, 141. JS affidavit, June 4, 1839, in Johnson, *Mormon Redress Petitions*, 350.

48 Abraham Lincoln, "Address to the Young Men's Lyceum of Springfield, Illinois, January 27, 1838," in Lincoln, *Speeches and Writings, 1832–1858*, ed. Don E. Fehrenbacher (New York: Library of America, 1989), 28–36.

49 Tocqueville, *Democracy in America*, 239–42. See James T. Kloppenberg, *Toward Democracy: The Struggle for Self-Rule in European and American Thought* (New York: Oxford University Press, 2016), 633–36.

50 Lemira Calkins affidavit, undated, in Johnson, *Mormon Redress Petitions*, 153. Lydia English affidavit, May 10, 1839, in Johnson, *Mormon Redress Petitions*, 197. Nancy Cary affidavit, undated, in Johnson, *Mormon Redress Petitions*, 157. Sophia Higbee affidavit, May 6, 1839, in Johnson, *Mormon Redress Petitions*, 235. Catherine McBride affidavit, May 18, 1839, in Johnson, *Mormon Redress Petitions*, 282. Almira Covey to Harriett Mack Whittemore, January 19, 1840, in Harriett Mack Whittemore Correspondence, CHL.

51 Background for Emma Smith comes from Linda King Newell and Valeen Tippetts Avery, *Mormon Enigma: Emma Hale Smith* (New York: Knopf, 1984).

52 Leonora Taylor to John Taylor, September 9, 1839, CHL. Phebe Woodruff to Wilford Woodruff, September 19, 1839, CHL. For domestic life in early Nauvoo, see HFoF, 30–56.

53 Background for Rigdon comes from Richard S. Van Wagoner, *Sidney Rigdon: A Portrait of Religious Excess* (Salt Lake City: Signature Books, 1994).

54 James Adams, Letter of Introduction, November 9, 1839, in D7:55. JS and Elias Higbee to Hyrum Smith and High Council, December 5, 1839, in D7:70. John Reynolds, *My Own Times; Embracing Also the History of My Life* (Belleville, IL: B. H. Perryman 1855), 575. See also JS to Seymour Brunson, December 7, 1839, in D7:77–81.

55 JS and Higbee to Smith, December 5, 1839, in D7:69.

56 Ibid., in D7:69–71.

57 Elias Higbee to JS, February 20, 1840, in D7:181. Elias Higbee to JS, February 26, 1840, in D7:199. The Senate of the United States of America, Report, March 4, 1840, in *Public Documents Printed by Order of the Senate of the United States*, vol. 5 (1840). For a summary of this trip and the political issues involved, see Spencer W. McBride, "When Joseph Smith Met Martin Van Buren: Mormonism and the Politics of Religious Liberty in Nineteenth-Century America," *Church History* 85, no. 1 (March 2016): 150–58. For the Jacksonians and the Democratic Party, see Sean Wilentz, *The Rise of American Democracy: Jefferson to Lincoln* (New York: Norton, 2005), 312–440; David Walker Howe, *What Hath God Wrought: The Transformation of America, 1815–1848* (New York: Oxford University Press, 2007), 411–45.

58 JS to Elias Higbee, March 7, 1840, in D7:218. JS and Higbee to Smith, December 5, 1839, in D7:72. Hyrum Smith to JS, January 2, 1840, in D7:97.

59 JS and Higbee to Smith and High Council, December 5, 1840. JS, discourse, April 7, 1840, in D7:341. *Peoria (IA) Register and North-Western Gazetteer*, April 17, 1840.

60 JS to Robert Foster, March 11, 1840, in D7:228. R. F. Haynes to F. G. Williams, November 4, 1840, CHL. Phebe Woodruff to Wilford Woodruff, March 8, 1840, WWC. *Ohio Democrat and Dover Advertiser* (Canal Dover, OH), May 15, 1840.

CHAPTER 2: SEEDS

1 Elisha Atwood to Lorren S. Atwood, July 19, 1841, CHL.

2 T&S, April 1, 1841. Elisha Atwood to Lorren S. Atwood, July 19, 1841, CHL. David Jenkins to Leonard Pickel, September 28, 1841, in Leonard Pickel Papers, 1841–

1844, CHL. The estimate of 3,000 Nauvoo residents comes from T&S, January 15, 1841.

3   T&S, April 15, 1841. The report of attendance—both for those watching and those in the Legion—was recorded in *Western World* (Warsaw, IL), April 7, 1841.

4   T&S, January 15, 1841. T&S, April 15, 1841.

5   WS, May 19, 1841. T&S, June 1, 1841. WS, June 2, 1841.

6   Ralph Waldo Emerson, quoted in Oliver Wendell Holmes, *Ralph Waldo Emerson* (Boston: Houghton, Mifflin, 1884), 164.

7   See Adam Jortner, *The Gods of Prophetstown: The Battle of Tippecanoe and the Holy War for the American Frontier* (New York: Oxford University Press, 2012).

8   Revelation, November 1, 1831 [D&C 1:1], JSP. Revelation, July 20, 1831 [D&C 57:3], JSP. JS, Plat of the City of Zion, circa June 1833, text and drawing by Frederick G. Williams, JSP. For these plats and their significance, see Benjamin E. Park, "To Fill Up the World: Joseph Smith as Urban Planner," *Mormon Historical Studies* 14, no. 1 (Spring 2013): 1–27; Richard Bushman, "Making Space for the Mormons," in Richard Bushman, *Believing History: Latter-day Saint Essays*, ed. Reid L. Neilson and Jed W. Woodworth (New York: Columbia University Press, 2004): 173–98. The best treatment of Joseph Smith's early Zion project is Mark Ashurst-McGee, "Zion Rising: Joseph Smith's Early Social and Political Thought" (PhD Dissertation: Arizona State University, 2008).

9   James Adams to JS, January 4, 1840, in D7:107. John B. Weber to JS, January 6, 1840, in D7:108. *North American and Daily Advertiser* [Philadelphia, PA], May 30, 1840. The estimate for conference attendance comes from the *Salt River Journal* (Bowling Green, MO), May 16, 1840. Heber C. Kimball et al. to JS, May 25, 1840, in D7:288. Heber C. Kimball to JS, July 9, 1840, in T&S, April 1, 1845. JS, discourse, July 19, 1840, in D7:336–37, 342.

10   John C. Bennett to JS, July 25, 1840, in D7:349. John C. Bennett to JS, July 27, 1840, in D7:352. John C. Bennett to JS, July 30, 1840, in D7: 370. John C. Bennett to JS, August 15, 1840, in D7:375. JS to John C. Bennett, August 8, 1840, in D7:371–73. Bennett wrote his August 15 letter before he received the one dated August 8 from Smith. For background on Bennett, see Andrew F. Smith, *The Saintly Scoundrel: The Life and Times of Dr. John Cook Bennett* (Urbana: University of Illinois Press, 1997).

11   T&S, October 1840. Phebe Woodruff to Wilford Woodruff, October 6–19, 1840, WWC. Vilate Kimball to Heber C. Kimball, October 11, 1840, KFL.

12   Act to Incorporate the City of Nauvoo, December 16, 1840, in D7:472–88. T&S, January 15, 1841. Robert Flanders aptly noted that "the charter itself seemed harmless; what the Mormons accomplished under its provisions did not." KoM, 98. The other five cities whose charters served as models were Alton, Chicago, Galena, Springfield, and Quincy.

13   Ford, *History of Illinois*, 263–65. T&S, January 1, 1841. See D7:373.

14   City Oaths, February 3, 1841, JSP. Nauvoo Legion Minutes, February 4, 1841, JSP. Nauvoo Legion Minutes, February 20, 1841, JSP. T&S, February 15, 1841. See GLN, 108–9.

15   John S. Fullmer to James Rucker, March 7, 1841, CHL. T&S, July 1, 1841.

16   The size of the Legion is mentioned in T&S, January 1, 1842. The number of supplies comes from ATDR, July 23, 1842.

17   JS, discourse, September 29, 1839, in D7:14–16. JS, discourse, July 30, in D7:368.

18 1 Corinthians 15:29 (King James Version). Vilate Kimball to Heber C. Kimball, September 6, 1840, KFL. For context to the ritual, see Ryan G. Tobler, " 'Saviors on Mount Zion': Mormon Sacramentalism, Mortality, and the Baptism for the Dead," JMH 39, no. 4 (Fall 2013): 182–238.

19 Vilate Kimball to Heber C. Kimball, October 11, 1840, KFL. John Smith, journal, October 2–10, CHL. Phebe Woodruff to Wilford Woodruff, October 6–19, 1840, WWC. T&S, October 1840. T&S, December 15, 1840.

20 T&S, November 15, 1841. Phebe Woodruff to Wilford Woodruff, October 6–19, 1840, WWC. For Smith's purchase of the plot of land for the temple, see GLN, 235.

21 JS, discourse, July 19, 1840, in D7:344.

22 T&S, January 15, 1841. JS, revelation, January 19, 1841, in D7:517–18.

23 JS, discourse, March 28, 1841, JSP. JS, discourse, January 5, 1841, in D7:494–95. JS, Instruction on the Priesthood, October 5, 1840, in D7:434–35.

24 JS, discourse, March 21, 1841, JSP.

25 T&S, April 15, 1841.

26 Franklin D. Richards, journal, January 22, 1869, CHL. Joseph Noble, affidavit, 1869, Joseph F. Smith Affidavit Book, CHL. For Beman, sometimes spelled "Beamon" or "Beaman," see Todd M. Compton, In Sacred Loneliness: The Plural Wives of Joseph Smith (Salt Lake City: Signature Books, 1997), 55–70.

27 RSR, 437–40. For a general overview of documents related to Smith's polygamous relationships, see Brian C. Hales, Joseph Smith's Polygamy, 3 vols. (Draper, UT: Kofford Books, 2013). Many historians argued that Smith was married to Fanny Alger around 1836, and some argue for a sealing to Lucinda Pendleton around 1838. There is some evidence that Smith might have entered plural marriage in 1840. However, due to the chronological developments of Smith's cosmology in the fall of 1840, and the evolution of temple theology in early 1841, the most compelling evidence places Louisa Beman as the first plural wife in April of that year. For arguments for these earlier dates, see Don Bradley, "Mormon Polygamy before Nauvoo? The Relationship of Joseph Smith and Fanny Alger," in Newell G. Bringhurst and Craig L. Foster, eds., The Persistence of Polygamy: Joseph Smith and the Origins of Mormon Polygamy (Independence, MO: John Whitmer Books, 2010): 14–58; Compton, In Sacred Loneliness, 43–54; Gary James Bergera, "Memory as Evidence: Dating Joseph Smith's Plural Marriages to Louisa Beamon, Zina Jacobs, and Presendia Buell," JMH 41, no. 4: 95–131.

28 See Rosemarie Zagarri, Revolutionary Backlash: Women and Politics in the Early American Republic (Philadelphia: University of Pennsylvania Press, 2007); Marilyn J. Westerkamp, Women in Early American Religion, 1600–1850: The Puritan and Evangelical Traditions (New York: Routledge, 2005), 73–182; Catherine A. Brekus, Strangers and Pilgrims: Female Preaching in America, 1740–1845 (Chapel Hill: University of North Carolina Press, 1998).

29 For Matthias, see Paul E. Johnson and Sean Wilentz, Kingdom of Matthias: A Story and Sex and Salvation in 19th-Century America, 2nd ed. (New York: Oxford University Press, 2012). Richard Bushman wrote that, "like Abraham of old, Joseph [Smith] yearned for familial plentitude. He did not lust for women so much as he lusted for kin." RSR, 440.

30 Zina D. H. Young, Biographical Sketch #1, in Zina Card Brown Family Collection, CHL.

31 Ibid.

32 Zina D. H. Young, quoted in Hales, *Joseph Smith's Polygamy*, 1:254.

33 Deuteronomy 25:5 (King James Version). BYJ, January 6, 1842, CHL. Compton, *In Sacred Loneliness*, 153. George D. Smith, *Nauvoo Polygamy: "but we called it celestial marriage"* (Salt Lake City: Signature Books, 2008), 86–125. Hales, *Joseph Smith's Polygamy*, 1:253–76.

34 See Gary James Bergera, "Identifying the Earliest Mormon Polygamists, 1841–44," *Dialogue* 38, no. 3 (Fall 2005): 17.

35 John Sweat to Samuel Akers, April 16, 1843, CHL. See GLN, 92–97.

36 NCCM, February 8, February 22, March 29, 1841.

37 T&S, October 1840. NCCM, March 1, 1841. Parley P. Pratt, *Late Persecution of the Church of Jesus Christ of Latter-day Saints* (New York: J. W. Harrison, 1840), 59. For the racialization of Nauvoo during this period, see W. Paul Reeve, *Religion of a Different Color: Race and the Mormon Struggle for Whiteness* (New York: Oxford University Press, 2015), 22–24.

38 WWJ, July 30, 1840. Bond to Elijah Able, December 8, 1839, in D7:81–85. WWJ, November 9, 1840. Though Woodruff's journal does not identify the Native American convert as Dana, the connection seems likely.

39 Joseph Smith, *The Book of Mormon: An Account Written by the Hand of Mormon, Upon Plates Taken from the Plates of Nephi* (Palmyra, NY: E. B. Grandin, 1830), 102.

40 Scholarship on early Mormon race relations is voluminous. The best overview is Reeve, *Religion of a Different Color*, 52–74, 106–39. For Mormonism's early universalistic theologies of race, see Max Perry Mueller, *Race and the Making of the Mormon People* (Chapel Hill: University of North Carolina Press, 2017), 31–59.

41 Joseph Smith, Old Testament Revision, circa 1830–1831, 16, JSP.

42 JS to Vilate Kimball, March 2, 1841, JSP. T&S, April 15, 1841. T&S, July 1, 1842. The "young woman" may have been Catherine Fuller, who the following year accused Bennett of unwanted advances. NCCM, May 25, 1842.

43 T&S, July 1, 1842. T&S, August 15, 1842. *The Wasp* (Nauvoo, IL), July 27, 1842. Smith, *Saintly Scoundrel*, 78–80.

44 Heber C. Kimball to Parley Pratt, July 15, 1841, PPPC.

45 T&S, September 1, October 15, 1841.

46 WWJ, December 19, 1841. BYJ, January 6, 1842. See John Taylor, "Sermon in Honor of the Martyrdom," June 27, 1854, CHL.

47 NHCM, January 18, 1842, 400–401.

48 T&S, February 15, 1842.

49 JS to Robert D. Thompson, March 11, 1840, in D7:227–28.

50 For background to Douglas, see Martin H. Quite, *Stephen A. Douglas and Antebellum Democracy* (New York: Cambridge University Press, 2012).

51 *Illinois State Register* (Springfield, IL), November 13, 1840.

52 Stephen A. Douglas to John C. Bennett, May 3, 1841, in T&S, May 4, 1841. JSJ, May 7, 1842, in J2:55.

53 Requisition for JS, September 1, 1840, State of Missouri v. JS for Treason [Warren Co. Cir. Ct. 1841], JS Extradition Records, ALPL. T&S, September 1840. T&S, June 15, 1841. See RSR, 425–27.

54 WS, May 19, 1841. George R. Gayler, "A Social, Economic, and Political Study of the Mormons in Western Illinois" (PhD dissertation: University of Indiana, 1955),

161–62. KoM, 221–22. For Browning's speech, see MHC-C1, 1205–6. For Mormon voting patterns, see KoM, 220–21; George W. Gayler, "The Mormons in Illinois Politics: 1839–1844," *Journal of the Illinois State Historical Society* 49 (1956): 50–51; GLN, 289–95.

55 T&S, January 1, 1842. (Emphasis in original.)

56 QW, January 22, 1842. *Peoria Register and Northwestern Gazetteer,* January 21, 1842.

57 NN, August 2, 1843. WWJ, July 4, 1843.

58 John Harper to JS, July 13, 1842, JSP. Harper to JS, July 14, 1842, JSP.

59 William Wright to JS, July 24, 1842, JSP. ATDR, July 23, 1842. SJ, June 10, 1842.

60 Illinois, Hancock County, Nauvoo Precinct Election returns, August 1, 1842, CHL.

61 *Niles National Register* (Washington, DC), August 6, 1842. John J. Hardin to John Stuart, December 28, 1842, CHL. See KoM, 220–21.

62 Thomas Ford, "Message of the Governor of Illinois in Relation to the Disturbances in Hancock County, December 21, 1844," *Reports Made to the Senate and House of Representatives of the State of Illinois, 1844* (Springfield, 1844), 71. JSJ, August 13, 1843, in J3:79.

CHAPTER 3: ROOTS

1 *The Weekly Herald* (New York), January 15, 1842.

2 Tocqueville, *Democracy in America,* 483. Ralph Waldo Emerson, quoted in Lawrence Buell, *Emerson* (Cambridge: Harvard University Press, 2004), 228.

3 JSJ, January 6, 1842, in J2:25–26.

4 JSJ, December 22, 1841, and January 1, 1845, in J2:17, 21. Joseph Smith to Edward Hunter, January 5, 1842, JSP. See Robert T. Bray, *Archaeological Investigations at the Joseph Smith Red Brick Store, Nauvoo, Illinois* (Columbia: University of Missouri Press, 1973); Roger D. Launius and F. Mark McKiernan, *Joseph Smith, Jr.'s, Red Brick Store* (Macomb: Western Illinois University, 1985).

5 SJ, February 9, 1842. The same day Joseph Smith wrote about the opening of his store, he was sealed to his deceased brother's wife, Agnes Moulton Coolbrith, in his office upstairs. BYJ, January 6, 1842. Mary Rollins Lightner also later recalled that she was taught plural marriage in the red-brick store in January 1842. Mary Elizabeth Rollins Lightner, "Mary Elizabeth Rollins" photocopy of holograph, Susa Young Gates Papers, CHL.

6 MHC-B1, 596. The literature on the origins of the Book of Abraham is voluminous. See RSR, 285–93; Brian M. Hauglid, *A Textual History of the Book of Abraham: Manuscripts and Editions* (Provo, UT: Neal A. Maxwell Institute for Religious Scholarship, 2010); Robert K. Ritner, *The Joseph Smith Egyptian Papyri: A Complete Edition* (Salt Lake City: Signature Books, 2013); R4.

7 JS, Editorial Draft, circa March 1, 1842, JSP. WWJ, February 19, 1842. JS to Edward Hunter, March 7, 1842, JSP. JSJ, March 8 and 9, in J2:42. Jacob Scott to Mary Warnock, March 24, 1842, CHL.

8 T&S, March 15, 1842, in R4:319. I argue that all the text published in this issue of T&S was of recent production. Everything preceding it—what is now canonized in the LDS faith as Abraham 1–2:18—was transcribed in Kirtland. There are three Ohio-era manuscripts that contain Book of Abraham text, and none of them

go further than that verse. Further, the portion published in the March 15 issue marks a shift in tone and focus from the earlier portion, suggesting that the material published in the March 1 issue was from 1835, and the material published two weeks later was produced in early March 1842.

9   T&S, March 15, 1842, in R4:317–19. JS, discourse, in WWJ, April 1, 1842. The "stars in the sky" phrase frequently appears in Genesis, including 15:5, 22:17, and 26:4 (King James Version). See Samuel Brown, "The Early Mormon Chain of Belonging," *Dialogue: A Journal of Mormon Thought* 44, no. 1 (Spring 2011): 1–52.

10 For Smith's reliance on other sources, see Benjamin E. Park, "Reasonings Sufficient: Joseph Smith, Thomas Dick, and the Context(s) of Early Mormonism," JMH 38, no. 3 (Summer 2012): 210–24.

11 For astronomy and American political discourse, see Eran Shalev, "'A Republic Amidst the Stars': Political Astronomy and the Intellectual Origins of the Stars and Stripes," *Journal of the Early Republic* 31, no. 1 (Spring 2011): 39–74.

12 T&S, October 3, 1841. JS, discourse, in WWJ, March 20, 1842. (Though the T&S issue was dated March 15, Wilford Woodruff's journal noted that it didn't come off the press until March 19. WWJ, March 19 and 20, 1842.) JSJ, March 20, 1842, in J2:46.

13 T&S, April 1, 1842.

14 T&S, April 1, 1842.

15 *Lee County Democrat* (Fort Madison, IA), April 16, 1842. JSJ, March 11, in J2:43. Minutes of the Nauvoo Legion, March 12, 1842, in "Nauvoo Legion: Minutes and Ordinances of the Organization," Nauvoo Legion Records, JSP.

16 JS, revelation, July 8, 1838, JSP. JS to Edward Partridge and the Church, March 22, 1839, JSP. The march is detailed in WWJ, March 15, 1842. GLN, 313–18.

17 Michael W. Homer, *Joseph's Temples: The Dynamic Relationship Between Freemasonry and Mormonism* (Salt Lake City: University of Utah Press, 2014), 138–50. For Masonry as a central fraternal order in early American society, see Steven C. Bullock, *Revolutionary Brotherhood: Freemasonry and the Transformation of the American Social Order, 1730–1840* (Chapel Hill: University of North Carolina Press, 1996); David G. Hackett, *That Religion in Which All Men Agree: Freemasonry in American Culture* (Berkeley: University of California Press, 2014), 55–110.

18 Masonic Lodge, Minutes, March 15–16, 1842, in Records of the Nauvoo Lodge, JSP. Homer, *Joseph's Temples*, 150–51.

19 Thomas Smith Webb, quoted in Homer, *Joseph's Temples*, 202. T&S, March 15, 1842. JS, discourse, in WWJ, March 20, 1842.

20 JSJ, May 1, 1842, in J2:53.

21 Smith's earliest vision account is found in JS, history, circa summer 1832, JSP.

22 Willard Richards, draft notes, May 4, 1842, quoted in J2:54, fn. 198. See Homer, *Joseph's Temples*, 204–7.

23 Willard Richards to Levi Richards, March, 1842, Richards Family Letters, CHL. Heber C. Kimball to Parley P. Pratt, June 17, 1842, PPPC. See Samuel Morris Brown, *In Heaven as It is On Earth: Joseph Smith and the Early Mormon Conquest of Death* (New York: Oxford University Press, 2012), 183–88.

24 Oliver Olney, diary, June 4, 1842, YBL. Joseph Fielding diary, in Andrew Ehat, ed., "'They Might Have Known That He Was Not a Fallen Prophet': The Nauvoo Journal of Joseph Fielding," BYUS 19, no. 2 (1979): 7.

25 JSJ, May 7, 1842, in J2:53–54. WWJ, May 7, 1842. Heber C. Kimball to Parley P. Pratt, June 17, 1842, PPPC.

26 *Millennial Star* (Liverpool, UK), September 1842.

27 Sarah M. Kimball, "Autobiography" (1883), quoted in Jill Mulvay Derr, Janath Russell Cannon, and Maureen Ursenbach Beecher, *Women of Covenant: The Story of the Relief Society* (Salt Lake City: Deseret Book, 1992), 26. Jill Mulvay Derr, Carol Cornwall Madsen, Kate Holbrook, and Matthew J. Grow, eds., *The First Fifty Years of Relief Society: Key Documents in Latter-day Saint Women's History* (Salt Lake City: Church Historian's Press, 2016), 3–16. Ann Firor Scott called these female societies "miniature democratic laboratories" in her essay "On Seeing and Not Seeing: A Case of Historical Invisibility," *Journal of American History* 71 (June 1948): 7–21, quoted in Derr, Cannon, and Ursenbach, *Women of Covenant*, 26.

28 NRSMB, March 17, 1842, 6–8, 11–12.

29 See Lori D. Ginzberg, *Women and the Work of Benevolence: Morality, Politics, and Class in the 19th-Century United States* (New Haven: Yale University Press, 1990); Ginzberg, *Women in Antebellum Reform* (New York: Wiley-Blackwell, 2000).

30 NRSMB, April 28, 1842, 48. NRSMB, March 17, 1842, 7. NRSMB, May 17, 1842, 48. T&S, April 1, 1842.

31 NRSMB, March 24, March 31, April 14, 1842, 17–18, 23, 26. A few months later, Eliza R. Snow published a poem that outlined the society's obligations which included, besides philanthropic endeavors, "to put the tattler's coinage, scandal, down, / And make corruption feel its with'ring frown." T&S, July 1, 1842.

32 NRSMB, March 31, 1842, 22. JSJ, April 28, 1842, JSP J2, 52. Eliza R. Snow, "Female Relief Society," quoted in Derr, Madsen, Holbrook, and Grow, *The First Fifty Years of Relief Society*, 271.

33 See Jonathan Stapley, "Mormon Women and Authority," in Kate Holbrook and Matthew Bowman, eds., *Women and Mormonism: Historical and Contemporary Perspectives* (Salt Lake City: University of Utah Press, 2016), 101–120.

34 NRSMB, March 31, 1842, 22.

35 NRSMB, March 31, 1842, 22, 24, 87.

36 NRSMB, March 24, June 9, 1842, 17–18, 61.

37 Due to the scarcity of records from the period, it is difficult to identify both plural unions and their sealing dates, which make it difficult, if not impossible, to decipher overall trends. Evidence for Lucinda Pendleton, for example, is sparse, and there are conflicting dates for Presendia Huntington.

38 Andrew Jenson, "Plural Marriage," *Historical Record* 6 (July 1887): 232.

39 SJ, August 19, 1842. JSJ, May 12, 13, 1842, in J2:55–56. See Richard S. Van Wagoner, *Sidney Rigdon: A Portrait of Religious Excess* (Salt Lake City: Signature Books, 1994), 294–302. The authenticity of Smith's letter to Nancy Rigdon is questioned in Gerrit Dirkmaat, "Search for 'Happiness': Joseph Smith's Alleged Authorship of the 1842 Letter to Nancy Rigdon," JMH 42, no. 3 (July 2016): 94–119. While a salacious narrative of the event was published in a letter from John C. Bennett after he left the church (SJ, July 8, 1842), but the most detailed overview of the Nancy Rigdon proposal comes from an affidavit from her brother, John Wickliffe Rigdon, dated July 28, 1905, CHL. The issues with these sources have caused some historians to doubt the reality of this proposal. It is possible that, when Smith and Rigdon reconciled on May 13, Smith denied the proposal, or at least only gave a part of the story, because

there would be another breach between the two six weeks later. This later conflict perhaps coincided with Nancy Rigdon agreeing to turn over the letter to Bennett, as well as Sidney learning more details concerning the episode. Regardless, the arguments found in the letter match Smith's teachings from the period.

40 NCCM, May 14, 1842. See Gary James Bergera, "'Illicit Intercourse,' Plural Marriage, and the Nauvoo Stake High Council, 1840–1844," JWHAJ 23 (2003): 59–90.

41 Martha Brotherton, affidavit, July 13, 1842, published in SJ, July 22, 1842. T&S, April 15, 1842. See John G. Turner, *Brigham Young: Pioneer Prophet* (Cambridge: Harvard University Press, 2012), 91–94. The problems with Brotherton's account draw primarily from the fact that they were filtered through John C. Bennett, who by that time was on a crusade against the church and exaggerated other reports. Further, the allegation that it was men, rather than women, who introduced the practice to Brotherton is also discordant with other accounts.

42 JSJ, April 10, 29, 1842, in J2:50, 53. In the latter entry, Smith's secretary scribbled the initials "J.C.B." in the margins to identify Bennett as the root of the conspiracy.

43 For an overview of the Bennett scandal, see Andrew Smith, *The Saintly Scoundrel: The Life and Times of Dr. John Cook Bennett* (Urbana: University of Illinois Press, 1997), 89–98.

44 Abraham Jonas to George Miller, May 4, 1842, in Records of the Nauvoo Lodge, JSP. Masonic Lodge, Minutes, May 7, 1842, in Records of the Nauvoo Lodge, JSP. "Notice," May 11, 1842, JSP. The precise details of these events are impossible to recreate given the secrecy with which they dealt with at the time and the partisanship that framed later accounts. Smith and other Mormons flooded the press with their side of the story in later months—most notably in a letter from Joseph Smith, dated June 23, and published in T&S, July 1, 1842—but these were aimed to shield the church against Bennett's increasingly radical accusations.

45 JSJ, May 19, 1842, in J2:58. NCCM, May 19, 1842, JSP. John Cook Bennett affidavit, May 17, 1842, in T&S, August 1, 1842. It is possible that Hiram Kimball did not know about Smith's proposal to his wife, though the tension between the two men seems to suggest some form of conflict.

46 JSJ, May 19, 1842, in J2:58. *The Wasp* (Nauvoo, IL), May 21, 1842.

47 NRSMB, May 19, 1842, 48.

48 Catherine Warren statement, May 25, 1842, in NN, May 29, 1844. Matilda Nyman statement, May 24, 1842, in NN, May 29, 1844. NHCM, May 21, 24, 25, 26, 27, 28, 1842, 414–19.

49 JSJ, May 26, 1842, in J2:63. NRSMB, May 26, 1842, 51–53.

50 NRSMB, June 9, 1842, 62. WWJ, May 27, 1842.

51 Oliver Olney, diary, June 18, 1842, YBL.

52 WWJ, June 18, 1842. T&S, July 1, July 15, and August 1, 1842. Smith, *Saintly Scoundrel*, 99–101.

53 William Phelps to Parley Pratt, June 16, 1842, PPPC.

54 ERSJ, June 29, 1842. Snow later affirmed that she was sealed to Smith on this day in an affidavit recorded twenty-seven years later. Eliza R. Snow Smith, Affidavit, June 7, 1869, in Affidavits about Celestial Marriage, CHL. For Johnson and McBride, see Hales, *Joseph Smith's Polygamy*, 1:497–98.

55 For the matriarchal power associated with these polygamous sealings, see Kathleen Flake, "The Emotional and Priestly Logic of Plural Marriage," Leonard J.

Arrington Mormon History Lecture, Series No. 15 (Logan, UT: Utah State University Press, 2010).

56 Eliza R. Snow, "The Slaughter on Shoal Creek, Caldwell County, Missouri," 1839, in Jill Mulvay Derr and Karen Lynn Davidson, eds., *Eliza R. Snow: The Complete Poetry* (Provo, UT: Brigham Young University Press, 2009), 105. Eliza R. Snow, "Missouri," December 9, 1843, in Derr and Davidson, *The Complete Poetry*, 278. The source detailing Snow's Missouri experience is late, yet evidence seems to confirm the possibility of its veracity. The culture of shame and silence made it so that few women during the nineteenth century recorded their own accounts of rape, and the male accounts—including those written by Mormon men—erased the names of survivors. Information concerning these assaults were mostly passed down through oral traditions in intimate settings. Radke-Moss discusses the source, its problems, and the broader significance of sexual violence in the Missouri War in "Silent Memories of Missouri: Mormon Women and Men and Sexual Assault in Group Memory and Religious Identity," in Rachel Cope, Amy Easton-Flake, Keith A. Erekson, and Lisa Olson Tait, eds., *Mormon Women's History: Beyond Biography* (Madison, NJ: Fairleigh Dickinson University Press, 2017), 49–82.

57 ERSJ, June 29, 1842, CHL. See also Snow, "The Bride's Avowal," August 13, 1842, in Derr and Davidson, *The Complete Poetry*, 210.

58 ERSJ, September 23, 1842.

59 Henry Kearns to Leonard Pickel, December 7, 1842, in Leonard Pickel Papers, CHL. Wilford Woodruff to Parley Pratt, Jun 18, 1842, PPPC. (Emphasis in original.)

CHAPTER 4: TRUNK

1 JSJ, June 30, 1843, in J3:45.

2 W. M. Busey to T. R. Webber, January 2, 1843, YBL.

3 "The Spirit of God," in Emma Smith, comp., *A Collection of Sacred Hymns for the Church of Latter Day Saints* (Kirtland, OH: F. G. Williams & Co., 1835), 120. JSJ, January 1, 1843, in J2:208.

4 JSJ, August 17, 1842, in J2:96.

5 JS to the Church and Edward Partridge, March 20, 1839, JSP. WWJ, May 15, 1842.

6 QW, May 21, May 22, 1842. *The Wasp* (Nauvoo, IL), May 28, 1842. JSJ, June 26–27, in J2:68, 70.

7 JS to Thomas Carlin, June 24, JSP. Thomas Carlin to JS, June 30, 1842, JSP. JS to James Arlington Bennet, June 30, 1842, JSP. Bennett's first accusations concerning Smith and Boggs appeared in *St Louis* (MO) *Bulletin*, July 14, 1842; SJ, July 15, 1842.

8 Draft of Petition, July 22, 1842, in WRP.

9 WWJ, June 18, 1842. Aldrich & Chittenden to JS, July 28, 1842, JSP. ERSJ, July 29, 1842. Thomas Carlin to JS, July 27, 1842, JSP. For the relief society petition, see HFoF, 74–75.

10 Lilburn Boggs, Affidavit, Jackson Co., MO, July 20, 1842, ALPL. State of Missouri, Requisition of Thomas Reynolds, July 22, 1842, ALPL.

11 Thomas Carlin, writ, August 2, 1842, ALPL.

12 NCCM, August 8, 1842.

13 JSJ, August 8, 1842, in J2:81. Thomas Carlin to Emma Smith, September 7, 1842, JSP.

14 Much of my work on Nauvoo and habeas corpus is reliant on Alex D. Smith, "Untouchable: Joseph Smith's Use of the Law as Catalyst for Assassination," *Journal of the Illinois State Historical Society* 112, no. 1 (Spring 2019): 8–42. See also John S. Dinger, "Joseph Smith and the Development of Habeas Corpus in Nauvoo, 1841–44," JMH 36, no. 3 (Summer 2010): 135–71; Jeffrey N. Walker, "Habeas Corpus in Early Nineteenth-Century Mormonism: Joseph Smith's Legal Bulwark for Personal Freedom," BYUS 52, no. 1 (2013): 4–97. For the broader context of habeas corpus, see Paul D. Halliday, *Habeas Corpus: From England to Empire* (Cambridge: Harvard University Press, 2010).

15 NCCM, November 14, 1842.

16 NCCM, August 8, 1842. T&S, August 15, 1842.

17 Willard Richards to James Arlington Bennett, November 20, 1842, WRP.

18 JSJ, August 12, 1842, in J2:85.

19 JSJ, August 10, 13, 1842, in J2:83, 86. JS to Wilson Law, August 15, 1842, JSP. Wilson Law to JS, August 15, 1842, JSP. JSJ, August 29, 1842, in J2:124. ERSJ, August 28, 1842.

20 Emma Smith to Thomas Carlin, August 16, 1842, JSP. Thomas Carlin to Emma Smith, August 24, 1842, JSP. Emma Smith to Thomas Carlin, August 27, 1842, JSP. Thomas Carlin to Emma Smith, September 7, 1842, JSP.

21 ERSJ, September 4, 1842. Justin Butterfield to Sidney Rigdon, October 20, 1842, Rigdon Collection, CHL. James Arlington Bennett to Joseph Smith, August 16, 1842, in COC. Willard Richards to James Arlington Bennett, November 20, 1842, draft, in WRP. The Mormons began counseling with Douglas in October, as mentioned in JSJ, October 5, 1842, in J2:161.

22 JSJ, December 17, 27, 29, 31, 1842, in J2:179, 195–97, 205.

23 *Proceedings of the Illinois State Bar Association* (Springfield, IL: The Association, 1877), 104.

24 JSJ, January 2, 1843, in J2:209. JSJ, January 6, 1843. On the whole trial, see Andrew H. Hedges and Alex D. Smith, "Joseph Smith, John C. Bennett, and the Extradition Attempt," in *Joseph Smith, the Prophet and Seer*, ed. Richard Neitzel Holzapfel and Kent P. Jackson (Provo, UT: Religious Studies Center, 2010), 437–66; Morris A. Thurston, "The Boggs Shooting and Attempted Extradition: Joseph Smith's Most Famous Case," BYUS 48:1 (2009): 4–56.

25 JSJ, January 7, 1843, in J2:236–240. JSJ, January 18, 1843, in J2:245–46. Eliza R. Snow, "Jubilee Song," in *Poems, Religious, Historical, and Political*, vol. 1 (Liverpool: F. D. Richards, 1856), 130–32. JSJ, January 5, 1842, in J2:233–34.

26 SJ, July 15, 1842. For Bennett's distance from Smith, see Hales, *Joseph Smith's Polygamy*, 1:549–54. For Bennett's unreliable narrative, see HFoF, 78–82.

27 Orson Pratt to Sarah Pratt, July 14, 1842, CHL.

28 JSJ, July 15, 1842, in J2:77–78. Brigham Young to Parley Pratt, July 17, 1842, PPPC. T&S, August 1, 1842. WWJ, August 20, 1842.

29 See Compton, *In Sacred Loneliness*, 342–63.

30 Elizabeth Ann Whitney, "A Leaf from an Autobiography," *Woman's Exponent* (Salt Lake City, UT), December 15, 1878, 146. John Wickliffe Rigdon to Arthur Willing, quoted in Hales, *Joseph Smith's Polygamy*, 1:504. (The letter refers to a conversation with Elizabeth Whitney in 1863.) The concern about Horace is documented in Helen Mar Kimball Whitney, "Scenes in Nauvoo after the Martyrdom of the Prophet and Patriarch," in Jeni Broberg Holzapfel and Richard Neitzel Holzapfel,

eds., *A Woman's View: Helen Mar Whitney's Reminiscences of Early Church History* (Provo, UT: Religious Studies Center, 1997), 146.

31 JS, revelation, July 27, 1842, Revelations Collection, CHL. For the meaning and context of this revelatory text, see Kathleen Flake, "The Development of Early Latter-day Saint Marriage Rites, 1831–1853," JMH 41, no. 1 (January 2015): 77–103. For the definition of the priesthood, a structure that ordered heaven, see Stapley, *Power of Godliness*, 34–56.

32 JS, revelation, July 27, 1842. Helen Mar Whitney, in Jeni Broberg Holzapfel and Richard Neitzel Holzapfel, eds., *A Woman's View: Helen Mar Whitney's Reminiscences of Early Church History* (Provo, UT: Religious Studies Center, 1997), 196–97, 482. See J. Spencer Fluhman, "'A Subject That Can Bear Investigation': Anguish, Faith, and Joseph Smith's Youngest Plural Wife," *Mormon Historical Studies* 11, no. 1 (Spring 2010): 41–51.

33 JS to Emma Smith, August 16, 1842, JSP. Joseph Smith to the Whitneys, August 18, 1842, JSP.

34 Deed to Sarah Ann Whitney, September 6, 1842, JSP. Deed to Helen Mar Whitney, June 7, 1843, JSP.

35 NRSMB, August 31, 1842, 81. T&S, October 1, 1842. SJ, October 14, 1842.

36 Udney Hay Jacob, *An Extract from a Manuscript Entitled The Peacemaker, or the Doctrines of the Millennium* (Nauvoo, IL: J. Smith, [1842]), 1. See Kenneth W. Godfrey, "A New Look at the Alleged Little Known Discourse by Joseph Smith," BYUS 9 (1968): 5–6; Lawrence Foster, "A Little-Known Defense of Polygamy from the Mormon Press in 1842," *Dialogue* 9, no. 4 (1974): 21–24; HFoF, 102–6.

37 For Robert Matthias, see Paul E. Johnson and Sean Wilentz, *The Kingdom of Matthias: A Story of Sex and Salvation in 19th-Century America*, 2nd ed. (New York: Oxford University Press, 2010).

38 T&S, December 1, 1842. On the issue of divorce, Ulrich claims that "as many as 20 percent of women who became plural wives before Joseph Smith's death had at some point been married to other men" (HFoF, 105). At least one Nauvoo resident assumed that Smith was the ghostwriter of the pamphlet. See Oliver Olney, journal, January 1, 1843, YBL. John D. Lee later claimed it was "a feeler among the people, to pave the way for celestial marriage." *Mormonism Unveiled; or The Life and Confessions of the Late Mormon Bishop John D. Lee* (St. Louis, MO: Bryan, Brand, 1878), 146. However, according to a letter Jacob sent Smith the following year, they had still not met. Udney Hay Jacob to JS, January 6, 1844, JSP.

39 JSJ, January 4, 1843, in J2:220. The role of the fugitive slave law in prompting America's legal code is detailed in David Brion Davis, *The Problem of Slavery in the Age of Emancipation* (New York: Knopf, 2014), 244–50; Manisha Sinha, *The Slave's Cause: A History of Abolition* (New Haven, CT: Yale University Press, 2016), 421–60; Martha S. Jones, *Birthright Citizens: A History of Race and Rights in Antebellum America* (New York: Cambridge University Press, 2018). Pope, one of the architects of Illinois statehood, was an outspoken critic of Missouri's slave practice, as seen in his extended comments during Smith's hearing.

40 JSJ, January 2, 1843, in J2:212. For the politics of slavery during the decade, see Matthew Mason, *Slavery and Politics in the Early American Republic* (Chapel Hill: University of North Carolina Press, 2006), 213–38; Sinha, *The Slave's Cause*, 228–65.

41 JSJ, January 2, 1843, in J2:212. T&S, March 15, 1842. See Max Mueller, in *Race and the Making of the Mormon People* (Chapel Hill: University of North Carolina Press, 2017).

42 WRJ, December 30, 1842, CHL.

43 Information on slavery in Nauvoo comes from Amy Tanner Thiriot's book manuscript, "Slaves in Zion: African American Servitude in Utah Territory."

44 Jane Manning James, autobiography, circa 1902, transcribed by Elizabeth Roundy, CHL. A notice in one of the city's newspapers requesting help to find Manning's luggage places her arrival in Nauvoo prior to December 1843. NN, November 6, 1843. For Manning's narrative, see Quincy Newell, "The Autobiography and Interview of Jane Elizabeth Manning James," *Journal of Africana Religions* 1, no. 2 (2013): 251–91. For Manning's life in general, see Quincy Newell, *Your Sister in the Gospel: The Life of Jane Manning James, a Nineteenth-Century Black Mormon* (New York: Oxford University Press, 2019).

45 James, autobiography. Hyrum Smith, Patriarchal Blessing of Jane Manning, March 6, 1844, reproduced in Newell, *Your Sister in the Gospel*, 140. Mueller, in *Race and the Making of the Mormon People*, 135–37, argues that Manning might have received a marital sealing to Joseph Smith. Such a possibility is quite remote, however, given that she arrived during a period Smith was not taking many plural wives. Further, it is unlikely that Emma Smith would have proposed a marriage given her staunch views on the topic. And finally, Joseph Smith was quite adamant in his disapproval of interracial marriages.

46 Mormon attempts to reach out to indigenous tribes during this period are outlined in Ronald W. Walker, "Seeking the 'Remnant': The Native American During the Joseph Smith Period," JMH 19, no. 1 (Spring 1993): 1–33. W. Paul Reeve outlines the tensions between Mormonism's racial relations and America's racial boundaries in *Religion of a Different Color: Race and the Mormon Struggle for Whiteness* (New York: Oxford University Press, 2015). For the rise and fall of American Protestant hope in Native missions, see John Demos, *The Heathen School: A Story of Hope and Betrayal in the Age of the Early Republic* (New York: Knopf, 2014).

47 John C. Bennett, *The History of the Saints; or, an Exposé of Joe Smith and Mormonism* (Boston: Leland and Whiting, 1842), 193. (Emphasis in original.)

48 Henry King to John Chambers, July 14, 1843, JSP. Helen Mar Whitney, "Scenes and Incidents in Nauvoo," in *Women's Exponent* (Salt Lake City, UT), October 1, 1882. JSJ, April 18, 1843, in J3:363. WCJ, April 18, 1843, quoted in J3:363. Letter from Potawatomi Indians, circa August 1843, JSP. For fears of Mormon/Indian alliances, see Reeve, *Religion of a Different Color*, 64–74. That Smith's secretary referred to the tribal leaders as a "delegation"—and another attendee referred to them as three "Indian Chiefs"—revealed the diplomatic nature in which they viewed the conference.

49 King to Chambers, July 14, 1843. (Emphasis in original.)

50 JS to Potawatomi Indians, August 28, 1843, JSP.

51 JSJ, November 4, 1842, in J2:166. John Bernhisel to JS, October 1, 1842, JSP. John C. Bennett to Sidney Rigdon and Orson Pratt, January 10, 1843, Rigdon Collection, CHL. JSJ, January 18 and 20, 1843, in J2:245–46, 248. WWJ, January 20, 1843. Sarah was also baptized with Orson that day, but left the church decades later. For her later accusations, see Hales, *Joseph Smith's Polygamy*, 1:589–93.

52 Emily Dow Young, "Incidents in the Life of a Mormon Girl," 185, CHL. Lucy
    Walker Kimball, statement, n.d., typescript, CHL. Eliza Maria Partridge, "Life and
    Journal of Eliza Maria Partridge (Smith)," 1877, UofU, 7.

53 JS, blessing to Sarah Ann Whitney, March 23, 1843, JSP.

54 JS, blessing to Joseph Kingsbury, in Joseph Kingsbury, diary, March 23, 1843, JSP.
    Joseph C. Kingsbury, "History of Joseph C. Kingsbury," photocopy of manuscript,
    in Ronald and Ilene Kingsbury Collection, UofU. Marriage Certificate for Joseph
    Kingsbury and Sarah Ann Whitney, April 29, 1843, JSP. Whitney and Kingsbury
    received their blessings on the same day, March 23, which likely implies the agree-
    ment struck between families. For the connection between polygamy and deceased
    spouses, see Samuel Morris Brown, *In Heaven as It Is on Earth: Joseph Smith and the
    Early Mormon Conquest of Death* (New York: Oxford University Press, 2012), 236–46.

55 Levi Richards, diary, May 14, 1843, CHL. WCJ, May 23, 1843, in AIC, 105.

56 WCJ, May 16, 1843, JSP. JS, discourse, May 21, 1843, JSP. WCJ, May 26, 1843, in
    AIC, 106. Brigham Young later explained his side of Hyrum's conversion, likely
    embellishing his own role, in 1866. See Andrew F. Ehat, "Joseph Smith's Introduc-
    tion of temple Ordinances and the 1844 Mormon Succession Question" (Brigham
    Young University: Master's Thesis, 1981), 56–59.

57 JSJ, May 29, 1843, in J3:25–26. Lyndon W. Cook, *Nauvoo Marriages, Proxy Sealings,
    1843–1846* (Provo, UT: Grandin Books, 2004), 5.

58 See Linda King Newell and Valeen Tippetts Avery, *Mormon Enigma: Emma Hale
    Smith*, 2nd ed. (Urbana: University of Illinois Press, 1994), 130–56; RSR, 493–
    494. The Partridge sisters later recalled that their second sealing to Smith took
    place on May 11, but this is unlikely, given that Emma was in St. Louis on that day.
    Willard Richards's diary places the sealing on May 23, which fits the other events
    that were taking place that week. WRJ, May 23, 1843, CHL.

59 Emily Dow Partridge, "Diary and Reminiscences, 1874–1899," 2, BYUSC.

60 WCJ, May 23, 1843, in AIC, 105–6. ERSJ, July 20, 1843. WCJ, August 16, 1843, in
    AIC, 117. WCJ, June 23, 1843, in AIC, 108. Though Eliza does not specify Emma as
    the woman who confronted her on July 20, Laurel Ulrich notes how internal clues
    make it very likely that it was the prophet's wife who visited her that day. HFoF, 93.
    It is noteworthy that Snow served as secretary for the Relief Society for the last time
    in 1843 just before this episode, and was replaced by Phoebe Wheeler just afterward.

61 WCJ, July 12, 1843, in AIC, 110. JS, Revelation, July 12, 1843, JSP.

62 JS, Revelation, July 12, 1843, JSP.

63 WCJ, July 12, 1843, in AIC, 110. William Clayton, affidavit, February 16, 1874, CHL.

64 WCJ, July 13, 1843, in AIC, 110. Deed to Emma Smith and others, July 12, 1843, JSP.

65 Vilate Kimball to Heber C. Kimball, June 27, 1843, KFL.

66 *The Wasp* (Nauvoo, IL), January 23, 1843.

67 Sylvester Emmons to JS, January 29, 1843, JSP. Perhaps as a consolation, Emmons
    was elected to the City Council. Election results are in *The Wasp*, February 8, 1843.

68 *Journal of the Senate of the Thirteenth General Assembly of the State of Illinois, at
    Their Regular Session . . .* (Springfield, IL: William Walters, 1842), 33. JSJ, Decem-
    ber 13, 1842, in J2:173. Willard Richards to James Arlington Bennett, December
    22, 1842, draft, WRP. JSJ, December 28, 1842, in J2:196. James Adams to JS,
    March 14, 1843, JSP. JS to James Arlington Bennett, March 17, 1843, JSP. JSJ, April
    2, 1843, in J2:324.

69 Davis County Circuit Court Records, vol. A, 372. Indictment, June 1843, State of
    Missouri v. Joseph Smith for Treason, Western Americana Collection, YBL. Warrant for Joseph Smith, June 17, 1843, JSC.
70 ERSJ, June 20, 1843. WCJ, June 21, 1843, in J3:39, fn.153.
71 ERSJ, June 25, June 30, 1843. JSJ, June 30, 1843, in J3:42. Writ of Habeas Corpus, Nauvoo Municipal Court to Joseph H. Reynolds, June 30, 1843, Nauvoo City
    Records, CHL. Other details of the episode come from Thomas Ford to Thomas
    Reynolds, August 14, 1843, in T&S August 15, 1843; JSJ, June 25, 1843, in J3:40. The
    saints defended bringing JS to Nauvoo by claiming it was the "nearest tribunal"
    within the fifth judicial circuit authorized to hear writs of habeas corpus. However, Knox, Warren, and Henderson Counties were all closer to Dixon and were
    similarly authorized.
72 JSJ, June 30, 1843, in J3:43. WWJ, June 30, 1843. WCJ, June 30, 1843, JSP.
73 JSJ, June 30, 1843, in J3:44. WWJ, June 30, 1843. T&S, August 1, 1843. *Illinois
    State Register*, reprinted in NN, July 19, 1843. For this whole episode, see Andrew
    H. Hedges, "Extradition, the Mormons, and the Election of 1843," *Journal of the
    Illinois State Historical Society* 109, no. 2 (Summer 2016): 127–47.
74 Thomas Ford to Joseph H. Reynolds, July 6, 1843, JSOP. Thomas Ford to Mason
    Brayman, July 3, 1843, Illinois Governor's Correspondence, Military Affairs, 1843,
    Illinois State Archives, Springfield, IL. Mason Brayman to JS, July 29, 1843, CoC.
    George J. Adams to Peter Hess, July 7, 1843, CHL.
75 WWJ, July 4, 1843.
76 JSJ, July 16, 23, and August 6, 1843, in J3:61–62, 65, 72–73. WCJ, July 16, 1843, in
    AIC: 110.
77 Ford, *History of Illinois*, 318. JSJ, August 7, 1843, in J3:74.
78 *Chicago Democrat*, August 23, 1843. "Political Ruse" from William Mulder and A.
    Russell Mortensen, eds., *Among the Mormons: Historic Accounts by Contemporary
    Observers* (New York: Knopf, 1958), 127. Andrew Moore to Levi B. Moore, October
    15, 1843, YBL. JSJ, August 6, 1843, in J3:73. For the electoral votes, see NN, August
    16, 1843; KoM, 238–39. There was even a rumor that Governor Ford had "delayed
    making a decision" of extraditing Smith to Missouri "until after the election, so
    as by intimidation to compel the Mormons to vote the democratic ticket." T&S,
    August 15, 1843.
79 Andrew Moore to Levi B. Moore, October 15, 1843, YBL. Ford, *History of Illinois*,
    318.

CHAPTER 5: BRANCHES

1 WLJ, January 8, 1844, 47.
2 William Law to Isaac Russell, November 10, 1837, and William Law to Isaac Russell, November 29, 1840, in Lyndon W. Cook, "'Brother Joseph is Truly a Wonderful Man, he is All We Could Wish a Prophet to Be': Pre-1844 Letters of William
   Law," BYUS 20, no. 2 (Spring 1980): 4–6. T&S, August 1, 1842. For background
   on Law, see Lyndon W. Cook, "William Law, Nauvoo Dissenter," BYUS 22, no. 1
   (1982): 47–72.
3 WLJ, January 1, 1844, 37.
4 John Frierson to Hon. F. H. Elmore, October 12, 1843, in NN, June 5, 1844. Back-

ground for Frierson is found in QW, May 22, 1844; *History of Western Iowa: Its Set-
tlement and Growth, A Comprehensive Compilation of Progressive Events concerning
the Counties, Cities, Towns and Villages—Biographical Sketches of the Pioneers and
Business Men, with an Authentic History of the State of Iowa* (Sioux City, IA: Western
Publishing Company, 1882), 52; Benjamin F. Shambaugh, ed., *Executive Journal of
Iowa, 1838–1841* (Iowa City: State Historical Society of Iowa, 1906), 77–78; Charles
Ray Aurner, *Leading Events in Johnson County, Iowa History*, 2 vols. (Cedar Rapids,
IA: Western Historical Press, 1912), 1:123–24.

5 Joseph L. Heywood to JS, October 23, 1843, JSC. JS to Joseph L. Heywood, November 2, 1843, Phillips Library, Peabody Essex Museum, Salem, MA.

6 Descriptions of the city come from Thomas Cooper to Joseph D. Murray, March 2,
1843, CHL; W. Aitken, *A Journey Up the Mississippi River, From Its Mouth to Nauvoo,
the City of the Latter Day Saints* (Ashton-Under-Lyne: W. B. Micklethwaite, 1845),
36. Description of JS comes from Albert and Swan Taggart to Samuel and Henry
Taggart, September 1843, in Albert Taggart Correspondence, 1842–1848, CHL.
Wilford Woodruff noted that "it was late & we had not time during the evening so
we dispersed." WWJ, November 25, 1843.

7 Jacob Scott to Mary Warnock, April 5, 1844, CHL. For background on the Mansion House, see E. Cecil McGavin, *Nauvoo the Beautiful* (Salt Lake City: Bookcraft,
1946), 45–54.

8 "Memorial to the United States Senate and House of Representatives," November
28, 1853, JSOP. JSJ, November 26 and 28, 1843, in J3:134–35.

9 Alexis de Tocqueville, *Democracy in America*, trans. and ed. by Harvey C. Mansfield
and Delba Winthrop (1835; Chicago: University of Chicago Press, 2000), 236–37. For
a general overview of these political developments, see RSR, 512–17. See also Brian
Balogh, *A Government Out of Sight: The Mystery of National Authority in Nineteenth-
Century America* (Cambridge: Cambridge University Press, 2009), 112–276.

10 James Madison to Thomas Jefferson, October 15, 1788, in *The Papers of James Madison, Congressional Series*, ed. William T. Hutchinson et al., 17 vols. (Charlottesville: University of Virginia Press, 1962–1991), 11:285–86. T&S, July 15, 1842.

11 T&S, July 16, 1842.

12 For background on these petitions, see Brent M. Rogers, "To the 'Honest and Patriotic Sons of Liberty': Mormon Appeals for Redress and Social Justice, 1843–1844,"
JMH 39, no. 1 (Winter 2013): 36–67.

13 NCCM, December 8, 1843, 188.

14 NCCM, December 16, 1843, 190–191. C50, April 18, 1844, in JSP C50:121–26.

15 "An Ordinance for the Protection of the People Styled the Church of Jesus Christ
of Latter Day Saints residing on the Western Borders of the State of Illinois," in
MHC-E1, 1812, 1814–5, 1821–2. JSJ, December 16, 1843, in J3:145. The saints probably expected a letter of support from the local government, as the manuscript history, into which they copied the memorial, included a drafted preamble from "the
Inhabitants of Hancock County," followed by blank space. The original petition is
found in "Hyrum Smith et al., Memorial to U.S. Senate and House of Representatives, December 21, 1843," Record Group 46, Records of the U.S. Senate, National
Archives, Washington, DC.

16 NHCM, August 12, 1843. For Joseph Smith's list of wives, see Hales, *Joseph Smith's
Polygamy*, 2:263–314; Smith, *Nauvoo Polygamy*, table 3.1.

17 David Fuller, Affidavit, June 15, 1869, in Joseph F. Smith Affidavit Book, CHL. Franklin D. Richards, notebook, August 12, 1843, CHL. Most of the details for this meeting
can only be gleaned through later affidavits. Besides David Fuller's, see also Thomas
Grover, Affidavit, July 6, 1869, Joseph F. Smith Affidavit Book, CHL. For the broader
Nauvoo context, see Gary James Bergera, " 'Illicit Intercourse,' Plural Marriage, and
the Nauvoo Stake High Council, 1840–1844," JWHAJ 23 (2003): 84–85.

18 NHCM, August 12, 1843, 467.

19 Charlotte Haven to "My Dear friends at home," transcribed in "A Girl's Letters
from Nauvoo," *Overland Monthly* 16 (December 1890): 635–36. NHCM, September
1, 1843. For Cowles's opposition to polygamy, see the late reminiscence in Ebenezer
Robinson, "Items of Personal History," *The Return* 3 (February 1891): 29.

20 NHCM, September 7, 1843. T&S, September 15 and October 14, 1843.

21 NHCM, November 25, 1843. WWJ, November 25, 1843. Sagers's later adoption of
plural marriage is stated in Nathan Tanner, Affidavit, August 28, 1869, in Joseph
F. Smith Affidavit Book, CHL. See Bergera, "Illicit Intercourse," 88–89.

22 WWJ, January 21, 1844.

23 Jacob Scott to Mary Warnock, January 5, 1844, CHL. Augusta Cobb is quoted in
Catherine Lewis, *Narrative of Some of the Proceedings of the Mormons; Giving an
Account of Their Iniquities* (Lynn, MA, 1848), 5. See Hales, *Joseph Smith's Polygamy*,
2:144–51. For the number who entered plural marriage during this period, see Gary
James Bergera, "Identifying the Earliest Mormon Polygamists, 1841–1844"; George
Smith, *Nauvoo Polygamy*, appendix B; Hales, *Joseph Smith's Polygamy*, 2:163–65.

24 Lewis, *Narrative*, 5. (Emphasis in original.) For the dynastic nature of these sealings,
see Todd Compton, "A Trajectory of Plurality: An Overview of Joseph Smith's Thirty-
Three Plural Wives," *Dialogue: A Journal of Mormon Thought* 29, no. 2 (Summer
1996): 1–38; J. Spencer Fluhman, " 'A Subject that can Bear Investigation': Anguish,
Faith, and Joseph Smith's Plural Wife," *Mormon Historical Studies* 11, no. 1 (Spring
2010): 41–51. For polygamy providing an avenue of marital choice, see Laurel
Thatcher Ulrich, "Runaway Wives, 1830–1860," JMH 42, no. 2 (April 2016): 1–26.

25 For social and sexual experimentation during the era, see Lawrence Foster, *Religion and Sexuality: The Shakers, the Mormons, and the Oneida Community* (Urbana:
University of Illinois Press, 1984).

26 JS, revelation, July 12, 1843, JSP. JSJ, September 28, 1843, in J3:104. CWJ, October
19, 1843, 122. For an example of female involvement in these ordinances, see Bath-
sheba W. Smith, testimony, in Devery S. Anderson and Gary James Bergera, eds.,
Joseph Smith's Quorum of the Anointed, 1842–1845: A Documentary History (Salt
Lake City: Signature Books, 2005), 45–46.

27 JS, revelation, July 12, 1843, JSP. (Emphasis added.) For the background to this quorum, see Anderson and Bergera, eds., *Joseph Smith's Quorum of the Anointed*, xiii–
xxxix. For the evolution of "priesthood" as an inter-gender construction during
this period, see Jonathan Stapley, "Women and Mormon Authority," in *Women
and Mormonism: Historical and Contemporary Perspectives*, ed. Kate Holbrook and
Matthew Bowman (Salt Lake City: University of Utah Press, 2016), 101–20.

28 Ebenezer Robinson to Jason W. Briggs, January 28, 1880, CHL. Laurel Ulrich
argues that "personal restraint, uncertainty about the meaning of sealing, fear of
exposure, and limited opportunity" were key factors in the low conception rate.
HFoF, 95–96.

29 Vilate Kimball to Heber C. Kimball, June 29, 1843, KFL.

30 The Clayton narrative and quotations comes from HFoF, 94–98.

31 "Letter from Gen. Bennett," October 28, 1843, in *Hawk Eye* (Burlington, IA), December 7, 1843. T&S, February 1, 1844. WS, February 7, April 25, 1844. Helen Mar Hayden to Flora Heydon Drake, April 7, 1844, Flora Heydon Drake Family Correspondence, 1842–1844, CHL. Gary James Bergera persuasively argues for Higbee's authorship of the Warsaw editorials in "Buckeye's Laments: Two Early Insider Exposés of Mormon Polygamy and Their Authorship," *Journal of the Illinois State Historical Society* 95, no. 4 (Winter 2002/2003): 350–90.

32 Details concerning Law's introduction to the practice can only be surmised through later interviews, supported by similar patterns during the period. See "Law Interview," March 30, 1887, and "1885 Affidavit of William Law," both in Cook, ed., *William Law.*

33 JSJ, October 5, October 9, and October 11, 1843, in J3:107, 109. WCJ, June 12, 1844, in AIC:132–33. Jane missed quorum meetings on September 28, October 1, and October 8.

34 JSJ, October 11, 1843 in J3:112. The journal entry mentions that "Ladies" were present, but does not specify who. WCJ, October 11, 1843, in AIC:121, notes that Smith had "gone to the Benbows to dine," and that he was gone so long he missed his evening appointments. Though no records from the period detail what was discussed at the dinner, it is likely that the discussion included a heated debate concerning polygamy, and especially the Lawrence sisters, because of two factors. First, William Law never fully participated in leadership or ecclesiastical activities after this point, which demonstrated a growing chasm between him and Smith. And second, when Law initiated a lawsuit against Smith for adultery the following spring, he singled out Maria Lawrence and provided October 12 as the start of the union. That date likely reflects not the day he believes Smith inaugurated the plural relationship, but rather the first date he could prove there was an unlawful relationship. It is possible that Law created written evidence the day after the dinner at Benbow farm, or perhaps that Maria Lawrence was present at the dinner itself. I appreciate Tom Kimball's help on understanding these events.

35 The broadside, originally printed in McDonough County, Illinois, was republished in the *Macomb* (IL) *Journal* decades later. It is transcribed in John Hallwas and Roger D. Launius, eds., *Cultures in Conflict: A Documentary History of the Mormon War in Illinois* (Logan: Utah State University Press, 1999), 192.

36 *Warsaw* (IL) *Message*, September 13, November 29, 1843.

37 WWJ, December 7, 1843. JS to Thomas Ford, December 6, 1843, JSOP. Thomas Ford to Joseph Smith, December 12, 1843, JSC. NCCM, December 8, 12, 1844.

38 WWJ, December 7, 1843. JS to Thomas Ford, December 6, 1843, JSOP. Thomas Ford to Joseph Smith, December 12, 1843, JSC. NCCM, December 8, 12, 21, 29, 1843. For the language of "foreign" and "kidnapping," see, for instance, NCCM, December 21, 1843. JS learned of the Averys' case in JSJ, December 5 and 6, 1843, in J3:139–40. See Brent M. Rogers, "'Armed men are coming from the state of Missouri': Federalism, Interstate Affairs, and Joseph Smith's Final Attempt to Secure Federal Intervention in Nauvoo," *Journal of the Illinois State Historical Society*, 109, no. 2 (Summer 2016): 148–79. The ordinance on searches and seizures would be amended three weeks later to better reflect state laws. NCCM, January 10, 1844.

39 NCCDM, December 19, 1843, 197. Smith reported that Rockwell warned Missouri "did not design to try me[,] but hang me, and that they had a man in our midst who would fix me out if they could not get me without." NCCDM, January 3, 1844, 201.

40 WLJ, January 2, 1844, 38.

41 NCCDM, January 3, 1844, 199, 202. WLJ, January 2, 1844, 38.

42 NCCDM, January 3 and 5, 1844, 203, 206, 207. Hyrum's metaphor comes from MHC-E1, 1855.

43 NCCDM, January 3 and 5, 1844, 203, 204, 207. WLJ, January 3, 1844, 41, 45. JSJ, January 3 and January 4, 1844, in J3:156–157.

44 JSJ, January 4, 1844, in J3:157.

45 WLJ, January 4, 1844, 42.

46 JSJ, November 2, 1843, in J3:124. *Niles National Register*, February 3, 1844.

47 John C. Calhoun to JS, December 2, 1843, in MHC-E1, 1845–1846. Henry Clay to Joseph Smith, November 15, 1843, quoted in RSR, 514.

48 JS to John C. Calhoun, January 2, 1844, in MHC-E1, 1846–1849. (Emphasis in original.) *Warsaw Message*, January 24, 1844. See also James B. Allen, "Joseph Smith vs. John C. Calhoun: The States' Rights Dilemma and Early Mormon History," in Reid L. Neilson and Terryl L. Givens, eds., *Joseph Smith, Jr.: Reappraisals After Two Centuries* (New York: Oxford University Press, 2008): 73–91.

49 JSJ, January 29, 1844, in J3:169. MHC-E1, 1869–1870. On February 6, Smith proposed a number of people to serve in administrative positions, including Willard Richards as Secretary of State and Orson Pratt as Secretary of the Treasury. "Proposed Plan for a Moot Organization and Congress," February 6, 1844, JSOP. Smith's skepticism concerning the Whig Party remained obvious at the meeting. "The Whigs are striving for a king under the garb of Democracy," he stated—a comment that becomes more ironic a few months later. JSJ, February 6, 1844, in J3:170. Richard Bushman, in "Joseph Smith's Presidential Ambitions," in Randall Balmer and Jana Riess, eds., *Mormonism and American Politics* (New York: Columbia University Press, 2015), posits Smith as a "protest candidate." See also Richard D. Poll, "Joseph Smith and the Presidency," *Dialogue: A Journal of Mormon Thought* 3 (Autumn 1868): 17–21; Spencer W. McBride, "The Council of Fifty and Joseph Smith's Presidential Ambitions," in Matthew Grow and Eric Smith, eds., *The Council of Fifty: What the Records Reveal about Mormon History* (Provo, UT: BYU Religious Studies Center, 2017), 21–30.

50 Henry Clay to James T. B. Stapp, November 16, 1843, in James Hopkins et al., ed., *The Papers of Henry Clay, 1797–1842*, 11 vols. (Lexington: University of Kentucky Press, 1959–1992), 9:891. *New York Herald*, republished in NN, March 20, 1844. For the election year, see Daniel Walker Howe, *What Hath God Wrought: The Transformation of America, 1815–1848* (New York: Oxford University Press, 2007), 680–82; John Bicknell, *America 1844: Religious Fervor, Westward Expansion and the Presidential Election That Transformed the Nation* (Chicago: Chicago Review Press, 2014).

51 NN, February 14, 1844. WWJ, February 8, 1844. William Hyde, autobiography, 18, CHL.

52 JS, *General Smith's Views of the Powers and Policy of the Government of the United States* (Nauvoo: John Taylor, 1844), 3.

53 JS, *General Smith's Views*, 6. (Emphasis in original.) *Illinois State Register* (Springfield, IL), March 15, 1844. For other claims that Smith's was a Whig campaign, see *National Intelligencer* (Washington, DC), March 19, 1844. *Erie Observer* [PA], March 23, 1844. *Democratic Free Press* (Detroit), May 30, 1844.

54 JS, *General Smith's Views*, 6–7. JSJ, February 24, 25, 1844, in J3:183.

55 JSJ, March 3, 1844, in J3:189. Willard Richards to James Arlington Bennet, March 4, 1844, in MHC-E1, 1902–1904. JSJ, March 7, 1844, in J3:196–97. They discuss Bennet's eligibility in JSJ, March 8, 1844, in J3:198. Wilford Woodruff offered the vice-presidency in a letter to Solomon Copeland, March 19, 1844, JSOP. For background on Bennet, see Lyndon W. Cook, "James Arlington Bennet and the Mormons," BYUS 19, no. 2 (Winter 1979): 247–49.

56 WS, March 13, 1844. *Wayne County Sentinel* (New York), March 20, 1844. The positive responses were featured in NN, March 20 and April 10, 1844. Joseph Smith's defense is found in NN, April 17, 1844.

57 JSJ, March 7, 1844, in J3:194, 196. WWJ, March 7, 1844.

CHAPTER 6: FRUIT

1 C50 Minutes, April 5, 1844, in C50:82.

2 *New-York Observer*, February 3, 1844. *Salem Gazette*, reprinted in *Auburn Journal and Advertiser* (Auburn, NY), November 29, 1843.

3 Ralph Harding to Dwight Harding, August 22, 1844, Ralph Harding Correspondence, 1844–1846, CHL.

4 NRSMB, March 17, 1842, 36.

5 Examination of John Scott, City of Nauvoo v. Bostwick, February 26, 1844, Nauvoo, IL, Records, 1841–1845, CHL. JSJ, February 26, March 7, 1844, in J3:183–84, 191–93. The attendance is reported in WWJ, March 7, 1844. The physical description of the grove is found in W. Aitken, *A Journey Up the Mississippi River, From Its Mouth to Nauvoo, the City of the Latter Day Saints* (Ashton-Under-Lyne: W. B. Micklethwaite, 1845), 37.

6 Joseph Smith's journal recorded that Phelps was "writing on O F Bostwick for women." While it is possible that Phelps was writing on behalf of Joseph, a more likely reading, based on the contents of the statement as well as Emma's later use, is that Emma requested it on behalf of the Relief Society. JSJ, February 28, 1844, in J3:184. For the document's reception at the public meeting, see JSJ, March 7, 1844, in J3:194. It was published as "Virtue Will Triumph," NN, March 20, 1844. See discussion of the document in NRSMB, 151–53. For Phelps as Smith's ghostwriter, see Samuel Brown, "The Translator and the Ghostwriter: Joseph Smith and W. W. Phelps," JMH 34, no. 1 (Winter 2008): 26–62.

7 Emma Smith's edition of the "Voice of Freedom," with her edits and emendations, is found in NRSMB, 154–56. It is possible that Emma was only one of several speakers, but she certainly would have had control of the meeting. See Jill Mulvay Derr, Janath Russell Cannon, and Maureen Ursenbach Beecher, *Women of Covenant: The Story of the Relief Society* (Salt Lake City: Deseret Book, 1992), 61.

8 NRSMB, March 16, 1844, 130. (Emphasis in original.)

9 JS, discourse, May 26, 1844, JSP.

10 WS, March 20, 1844. (Emphasis in original.) T&S, March 15, 1844.

11 NHCM, April 13, 1844, 490–91. "The Trial of Harrison Sager defendant and his wife Lucinda Sagers," Nauvoo Stake High Council Court Papers, CHL.

12 T&S, July 15, 1842. WWJ, March 7, 1844. NCCM, March 18, 1844, 231.

13 Kathleen Flake, "Ordering Antinomy: An Analysis of Early Mormonism's Priestly Offices, Councils and Kinship," *Religion and American Culture* 26, no. 2 (Summer 2016): 139–83.

14 C50 Minutes, March 10, 1844, in C50:39. JSJ, March 10, 1844, in J3:201. WCJ, March 11, 1844, in AIC:126.

15 C50 Minutes, March 11, 14, 1844, in C50:40–44, 48.

16 Ibid.

17 C50 Minutes, March 19, 1844, in C50:52–54. WWJ, March 24, 1844. For the use of Daniel 2's prophecy in early America, see Eran Shalev, *American Zion: The Old Testament as a Political Text from the Revolution to the Civil War* (New York: Oxford University Press, 2013), 61. For Mormon uses of the prophecy, see David J. Whittaker, "The Book of Daniel in Early Mormon Thought," in *By Study and Also by Faith: Essays in Honor of Hugh Nibley*, ed. John M. Lundquist and Stephen D. Ricks (Salt Lake City: Deseret Book, 1990): 155–99.

18 Robert L. Tsai, "John Brown's Constitution," *Boston College Law Review* 51, no. 4 (2010): 151–207. "Constitution of the Confederate States; March 11, 1861," The Avalon Project, Yale Law School, http://avalon.law.yale.edu/19th_century/csa_csa.asp (accessed September 2016).

19 C50, April 5, 1844, in C50:81–84. See Benjamin E. Park, "Joseph Smith's Kingdom of God: The Council of Fifty and the Mormon Challenge to American Democratic Politics," *Church History: Studies in Christianity and Culture* 87, no. 4 (December 2018): 1029–55.

20 C50, April 11, 1844, in C50:88, 90, 92, 95–96. (Emphasis added.)

21 Ibid., 97, 100–101, 105–6. For Smith's conception of "theodemocracy," see Patrick Q. Mason, "God and the People: Theodemocracy in Nineteenth-Century Mormonism," *Journal of Church and State* 53, no. 3 (Summer 2011): 349–75.

22 C50, April 18, 1844, in C50:110–14.

23 Ibid. C50, April 25, 1844, in C50:137. This echoed Smith's instructions to the Female Relief Society two years earlier—he instructed their leadership to "serve as a constitution" and that "all their decisions be considered law"—but this time it was to a political body of men. NRSMB, March 17, 1842, 31.

24 Ibid., 121–26, 128. (Emphasis in original.) For previous uses of the term "proper source," see C50:128, fn. 38. For the political and cultural implications of these debates over revelation and knowledge, see David F. Holland, *Sacred Borders: Continuing Revelation and Canonical Restraint in Early America* (New York: Oxford University Press, 2011).

25 Ibid., 127–29.

26 WCJ, April 18, 1844, in AIC:131. C50 Minutes, May 10, 1845, in C50:454.

27 Quorum of the Twelve Apostles, minutes, April 24, 1843, CHL, quoted in C50:17, fn. 2. JSJ, October 27, 29, 1843, in J3:120, 122. The petition is detailed in C50 Minutes, March 26, 1844, in C50:67.

28 *United States Magazine, and Democratic Review* (Washington, DC), July/August 1845. For the origins of annexation, see Joel Silbey, *The Storm over Texas: The*

Annexation Controversy and the Road to Civil War (New York: W. W. Norton, 2005); David Walker Howe, *What Hath God Wrought: The Transformation of America, 1815–1848* (New York: Oxford University Press, 2007), 677–82. For the imperial designs of westward expansion, see Amy Greenberg, *Manifest Manhood and the Antebellum American Empire* (New York: Cambridge University Press, 2005); Walter Nugent, *Habits of Empire: A History of American Expansion* (New York: Knopf, 2008); Steven Hahn, *A Nation Without Borders: The United States and Its World in an Age of Civil Wars, 1830–1910* (New York: Viking, 2016), 114–52.

29 Joseph Smith, *General Smith's Views of the Powers and Policy of the Government of the United States* (Nauvoo: John Taylor, 1844), 6–9. JSJ, March 7, 1844, in J3:197–98. WWJ, March 7, 1844. JS encounters Clay's arguments in JSJ, February 29, 1844, in J3: 185. For Mormonism's interest in Texas during this period, see Michael Scott Van Wagenen, *The Texas Republic and the Mormon Kingdom of God* (College Station: Texas A&M University Press, 2002), 23–37.

30 Lyman Wight et. al to Joseph Smith, February 15, 1844, JSC.

31 JSJ, March 10, 1844, in J3:200–201.

32 For American fears concerning the British interfering in the Texas territory, see Sam W. Haynes, *Unfinished Revolution: The Early American Republic in a British World* (Charlottesville: University of Virginia Press, 2010), 230–50; Matthew Karp, *This Vast Southern Empire: Slaveholders at the Helm of American Foreign Policy* (Cambridge: Harvard University Press, 2016), 70–102.

33 JSJ, March 7, 1844, in J3:197. C50, March 19, 1844, in C50:53. Memorial to US Senate and House of Representatives, 26 March 1844, Record Group 46, Records of the US Senate, National Archives, Washington, DC; copy in JSC. They also wrote a similar petition directed to the president in case Congress refused to take action. JSJ, March 31, 1844, in J3:211.

34 Joseph Fielding Journal, May 3, 1844, in Andrew F. Ehat, ed., "'They Might Have Known That He Was Not a Fallen Prophet'—The Nauvoo Journal of Joseph Fielding," BYUS 19, no. 2 (Winter 1979): 8. Orson Hyde to Joseph Smith, April 30, 1844, JSP. John Walton to Joseph Smith, June 3, 1844, JSC. It is not known if Smith saw the letter from Walton before his death. For these early discussions with Houston, see Van Wagenen, *The Texas Republic and the Mormon Kingdom of God*, 38–51.

35 C50 Minutes, May 3, 1844, in C50:140–46. Brigham Young and Willard Richards to Reuben Hedlock, May 3, 1844, draft, BYOF. C50 Minutes, May 6, 1844, in C50:151, 155–57.

36 Hyrum Smith, Address, April 9, 1844, in GCM. C50 Minutes, April 25, 1844, in C50:133–35. For a general overview of this campaigning effort, see Derek Sainsbury, "The Cadre for the Kingdom: The Electioneer Missionaries of Joseph Smith's 1844 Presidential Campaign" (PhD dissertation: University of Utah, 2016).

37 David S. Hollister to JS, June 26, 1844, JSP. For the rise of party politics and national platforms, see Sean Wilentz, *The Rise of American Democracy: Jefferson to Lincoln* (New York: W. W. Norton, 2005), 482–520; Stan M. Haynes, *The First American Political Conventions: Transforming Presidential Nominations, 1832–1872* (Jefferson, NC: McFarland, 2012).

38 *The Prophet* (New York), June 2, 1844. William Hyde Autobiography, CHL. Lewis Ziegler to Joseph Smith, May 25, 1844, JSP. David S. Hollister to JS, June 26, 1844, JSP.

39 *The Prophet*, June 15, 1844.

40 C50 Minutes, March 21, 1844, in C50:60.

41 Orson Hyde to Sidney Rigdon et al., April 25, 1844, JSC. For the congressional debate over the petition, see *Congressional Globe*, 28th Congress [1844], 1st session, 64.

42 Hyde to Rigdon, April 25, 1844, JSC; Hyde to Rigdon, April 26, 1844, JSC.

43 Ibid.

44 Hyde to Rigdon, April 25, 1844, JSC; Hyde to Rigdon, April 26, 1844, JSC; Hyde to John E. Page, May 6, 1844, photocopy in CHL.

45 C50 Minutes, May 13, 1844, in C50:160–62. Willard Richard to Orson Hyde and Orson Pratt, May 13, 1844, in WRP. (Emphasis in original.)

46 Orson Hyde to "Dear Brethren," June 9, 1844, JSP; Hyde to "Dear Brethren," June 11, 1844, JSP. Willard Richards to Orson Hyde, May 25, 1844, WRP. C50 Minutes, May 31, in C50:171.

47 W. D. Abernethy to John Hardin, March 19, 1844, CHL.

CHAPTER 7: HARVEST

1 Thomas Sharp, "The Very Thing," undated editorial, in Cecil A. Snider, Newspaper Source Material Collection, 1838–1848, ALPL.

2 William W. Phelps, C50 minutes, March 4, 1845, in C50:285.

3 James Brattle to Charles Brattle, July 5, 1844, CHL.

4 James Robbins to Mother and Friends, June 16, 1844, CHL. WS, May 29, 1844. For background on Robbins, see *The History of Adams County, Illinois* (Chicago: Murray, Williamson & Phelps, 1879), 1873–74.

5 WS, May 29, 1844.

6 Wesley Williams to John Wesley Williams, June 26, 1844, in John E. Hallwas Cultures in Conflict Collection, Western Illinois University Special Collections.

7 WLJ, January 8, 1844, 46.

8 JSJ, January 7–8, 1844, in J3:158–59. WWJ, January 7, 1844. NHCM, May 22, 1842, 414. NCCM, January 5, 1844. Francis Higbee to JS, January 10, 1844, JSP. Joseph H. Jackson, *A Narrative of the Adventures and Experience of Joseph H. Jackson, in Nauvoo* (Warsaw, IL: self-pub., 1844).

9 RSR, 528–29. GLN, 357–59. Thomas Ford to the *Warsaw Signal*, January 29, 1844, in WS, February 14, 1844.

10 JSJ, March 7, 1844, in J3:195. WWJ, March 24, 1844. JSJ, March 25, 1844, in J3:207–8.

11 NN, April 17, 1844. WWJ, April 6–7, 1844. Joseph Fielding journal, April 7, 1844, in Andrew F. Ehat, ed., "They Might Have Known That He Was Not a Fallen Prophet': The Nauvoo Journal of Joseph Fielding," BYUS 19, no. 2 (Spring 1979): 8. WLJ, April 15, 1844, 49.

12 JSJ, March 6–8, 1844, in J3:245–46. NMCDB, March 6–8, 1844.

13 JSJ, April 25, 1844, in J3:235. NMCDB, May 16, 23, 1844. ATDR, June 15, 1844. WS, May 15, 1844. (Emphasis in original.) See Smith, "Untouchable."

14 People vs. Joseph Smith, May 24, 1844, indictments and arrest warrant, CHL. State of Illinois v. JS for Perjury, May 24, 1844, photocopy, CHL. JSJ, May 25, 1844, in J3:260–61. JS, discourse, May 26, 1844, JSP. JSJ, May 27, 1844, in J3:263–65.

15 JSJ, April 28, 1844, in J3:239. WWJ, May 6, 1844. WS, May 8, 15, 1844.

16 JS, discourse, May 12, 1844, JSP. JSJ, May 7, 1844, in J3:245.

17 *Nauvoo Expositor*, June 7, 1844.

18 JSJ, June 7, 1844, in J3:273.

19 *Nauvoo Expositor*, June 7, 1844.

20 NCCM, June 8, 1844. JSJ, June 8, 1844, in J3:274.

21 NCCM, June 10, 1844.

22 NCCM, June 10, 1844. NN, June 17, 1844. JSJ, June 10, 1844, in J3:277.

23 WCJ, June 11, 1844, in J3:227, fn. 1261. WS, June 11, 14, 1844.

24 Hancock Justice of the Peace, Warrant, Carthage, June 11, 1844, CHL. JSJ, June 12–13, 1844, in J3:279–81. JS, Petition for Writ of Habeas Corpus, June 12, 1844, State of Illinois v. JS on *Habeas Corpus*, JSC. NMCDB, June 13, 1844.

25 WCJ, June 12, 1844, in AIC:133. JS to Thomas Ford, June 14, 1844, JSC. WS, June 14, 1844. The number of attendees at the Carthage meeting is from JSJ, June 13, 1844, in J3:281.

26 JSJ, June 15–16, 1844, in J3:283, 286. NN, June 19, 1844. JS to Ford, June 16, 1844, JSC.

27 Isaac Morley et al. to Smith, June 16, 1844, JSC. JS to John Smith, June 17, 1844, JSC. Hyrum Smith to Brigham Young, June 16, 1844, JSC. See also William Clayton, "Daily Account of Joseph Smith's Activities," June 15, 1844, in J3:334; JS to Morley, June 16, 1844, JSC; John Smith to JS, June 16, 1844, JSC.

28 Clayton, "Daily Account of Joseph Smith's Activities," June 18, 1844, in J3:336. JS to John Tyler, June 20, 1844, draft, CHL.

29 JSJ, June 18, 1844, in J3:290–91. JS, Proclamation, June 18, 1844, JSC.

30 Ford to Smith, June 21, 1844, JSC. JS to Ford, June 22, 1844, JSC.

31 Ford to JS, June 22, 1844, JSC.

32 Ford to Smith, June 21, 1844, JSC. JS to Ford, June 22, 1844, JSC. Ford to JS, June 22, 1844, JSC. JS to Ford, June 22, 1844, JSC. Clayton, "Events of June 1844," in C50:198.

33 Clayton, "Event of June 1844," in C50:198. JS to Emma Smith, June 23, 1844, JSC. Clayton, "Events of June 1844," in C50:198–99. Vilate Kimball to Heber C. Kimball, June 24, 1844, KFL.

34 Ford to JS, June 24, 1844, JSC. WRJ, June 24, 1844, in J3:306. WCJ, June 24, 1844, in J3:306.

35 WRJ, June 25–27, 1844, in J3:307, 310, 311, 319, 322. Writ for JS, Hancock Co. IL, June 24, 1844, JSOP. Willard Richards, List of Witnesses in Carthage and Nauvoo, June 26, 1844, JSOP.

36 Thomas L. Barnes, undated letter to Miranda Haskett, transcripts in John E. Hallwas Cultures in Conflict Collection, Western Illinois University Special Collections. (Barnes was a Carthage resident who treated the bodies after the attack on the jail.)

37 Warsaw Committee of Safety, "To His Excellency Thomas Ford," broadside, YBL.

38 JS to Emma Smith, June 27, 1844, JSC. WRJ, June 27, 1844, in J3:326–27.

39 T&S, August 1, 1844. WRJ, June 27, 1844, in J3:327–29. NN, July 24, 1844. William M. Daniels, affidavit, July 4, 1844, JSOP. Samuel O. Williams to John A. Pricket, July 10, 1844, Chicago Historical Society, Chicago, IL. See William M. Daniels, *Correct Account of the Murder of Generals Joseph and Hyrum Smith* (Nauvoo: John Taylor, 1845).

40 NN, July 24, 1844.

41 ZDHJ, June 27, 1844.

42 Willard Richards and John Taylor to Nauvoo, June 27, 1844, WRP. SJ, July 11, 1844. GLN, 398–99.

43 Almira Mack Covey to Harriet Mack Hatch Whittemore, July 18, 1844, CHL.

44 ZDHJ, July 1, 1844. WCJ, June 28, 1844, in AIC:136. Vilate Kimball to Heber C. Kimball, June 30, 1844, KFL. ZDHJ, June 29, 1844.

45 Richard Van Wagoner and Steven C. Walker, "The Joseph/Hyrum Funeral Sermons," BYUS 23, no. 1 (Winter 1983): 15. T&S, July 1, 1844. ZDHJ, July 4, 1844.

46 T&S, July 1, 1844. *The Doctrine and Covenants of the Church of Jesus Christ of Latter Day Saints; Carefully Selected from the Revelations of God* (Nauvoo: John Taylor, 1844): 111:3.

47 WS, June 29, 1844. James Brattle to Charles Brattle, July 5, 1844, CHL. William Law to Isaac Hill, July 20, 1844, CHL.

48 ATDR, July 20, 1844. Vilate Kimball to Heber C. Kimball, June 30, 1844, KFL. Thomas Ford to M. R. Deming, June 30, 1844, WRP. See also Ford to W. W. Phelps, July 22, 1844, in WRP. GLN, 403–4. The bodies were removed once more and buried near Joseph and Emma's first home later that year.

49 WCJ, July 6, 1844, in AIC:137. NCCM, July 1, 2, 1844.

50 WCJ, July 6, 1844, in AIC:137. WWJ, July 8, 13, 18, 1844.

51 WWJ, August 7, 1844. *New York Herald*, July 8, 1844. For rumors, see James Blakesley to Jacob Scott, August 16, 1844, CHL.

52 William Huntington journal, August 4, 1844, UofU. WWJ, August 7, 1844.

53 WWJ, July 18, 1844. See John G. Turner, *Brigham Young: Pioneer Prophet* (Cambridge: Harvard University Press, 2012), 111–15.

54 BYJ, August 8, 1844. WWJ, August 8, 1844. T&S, September 15, 1844.

55 WCJ, August 8, 1844, in C50:207. WWJ, August 8, 1844.

56 Henry and Catherine Brooke to Pickel, November 15, 1844, Leonard Pickel Papers, CHL. Zilpha Cilley Williams to Samuel Cilley, Nauvoo, July 13, 1845, Zilpha Baker Cilley Williams Letters, CHL.

57 BYJ, August 11, 1844. WRJ, August 12, 1844.

58 T&S, September 15, October 15, 1844. William Huntington journal, November 22, 1844, UofU.

59 BYJ, September 19, 1845. See Turner, *Pioneer Prophet*, 132–40.

60 WS, August 7, 1844. T&S, August 15, 1844. GLN, 465.

61 Josiah Lamborn to Brigham Young, January 28, 1845, BYOF. Jacob Backenstos to Brigham Young, January 25, 1845, BYOF. NN, January 29, 1845. GLN, 464–67.

62 Nauvoo High Priest Quorum, minutes, February 2, 1845, CHL. For background to Dana, see Ronald Walker, "Seeking the 'Remnant': The Native American During the Joseph Smith Period," JMH 19, no. 1 (Spring 1993): 23; Jeffrey David Mahas, "'The Lamanites will be our Friends': Mormon Eschatology and the Perception of American Indians in the Council of Fifty," *Religion & American Culture* (forthcoming).

63 William Richards to George Miller, January 14, 1845, BYOF. (Emphasis in original.) NN, February 5, 1845. WS, February 10, 1845. Notably, Richards's proposal would have stripped the Mormon reservation of habeas corpus.

64 T&S, July 15, 1845. See Reeve, *Religion of a Different Color.*

65 Orson Spencer, drafted petition, in C50:242–44.

66 WCJ, February 26, 1845, C50:257.

67 C50 minutes, March 21, 1844, C50:58. Sally Randall to "Dear Parents and Brothers and Sisters," January 15, 1845, in Kenneth W. Godfrey, Audrey M. Godfrey, and Jill Mulvay Derr, eds., *Women's Voices: An Untold History of the Latter-day Saints, 1830–1900* (Salt Lake City: Deseret Book, 1982), 143. My analysis on the Council of Fifty's attempt at a Mormon–Indian alliance is drawn from Mahas, "The Lamanites will be our Friends."

68 GCM, March 16, 1845.

69 BYJ, January 24, 1845. For the dam's construction, see GLN, 492–95.

70 WCJ, August 24, 1845, in HFoF, 125. Brigham Young to Wilford Woodruff, June 27, 1845, BYOF. Brigham Young to Parley Pratt, May 4, 1845, BYOF.

71 C50 minutes, March 1, 1845, in C50:258–60. GCM, March 16, 1845.

72 Dwight Webster to Wilford Woodruff, May 4, 1845, WWC. NN, April 23, May 7, 1845. See Jeffrey David Mahas, "'I Intend to Get Up a Whistling School': The Nauvoo Whistling and Whittling Movement, American Vigilante Tradition, and Mormon Theocratic Thought," JMH 43, no. 4 (October 2017): 37–67.

73 WCJ, May 6, 1845, in C50:440–41. Brigham Young to Parley Pratt, May 26, 1845, BYOF.

74 Huntington, journal, May 26, 1845, UofU. GLN, 417. C50 minutes, March 18, 1845, in C50:336. Dallin H. Oaks and Marvin S. Hill, *Carthage Conspiracy: The Trial of the Accused Assassins of Joseph Smith* (Urbana: University of Illinois Press, 1975). Alex Beam, *American Crucifixion: The Murder of Joseph Smith and the Fate of the Mormon Church* (New York: PublicAffairs, 2014).

75 Orson Spencer, quoted in GLN, 517. Brigham Young to Wilford Woodruff, August 21, 1845, BYOF. Parley Pratt to Isaac Russell, September 6, 1845, PPPC. C50 Minutes, September 9, 1845, in C50:472. See also Council of Twelve to Addison Pratt, August 28, 1845, CHL.

76 Solomon Hancock and Alanson Ripley to Brigham Young, September 11, 1845, BYOF. NN, extra, September 12, 1845. WS, September 17, December 19, 1845.

77 Brigham Young to Jacob Backenstos, September 13, 1845, BYOF. Backenstos to Young, September 13, 1845, BYOF. WCJ, September 17, 1845, in AIC:183. See GLN, 523–29.

78 WS, September 17, 1845. Backenstos to Young, September 18, 1845, BYOF. Young to the Saints in Ramus, September 16, 1845, BYOF.

79 QW, October 1, 1845. WS, October 22, 1845. Hosea Stout, journal, quoted in Hallwas and Launius, *Cultures in Conflict,* 279. Ford, *History of Illinois,* 409. GLN, 533–34.

80 ZDHJ, September 18, 1845.

81 Carthage Committee, resolutions, "Manuscript History of the Anti-Mormon Disturbances in Illinois," circa 1845, Thomas C. Sharp and Allied Anti-Mormon Papers, YBL. John Hardin, William Warren, Stephen A. Douglas, and James McDougall to the First President & High Council of the Church of Latter Day Saints, October 3, 1845, in C50:489.

82 NN, October 29, 1845. ATDR, May 2, 1846. John J. Hardin et al. to The Anti Mormon Citizens of Hancock and the Surrounding Counties, October 6, 1845, Hardin Family Papers, Chicago History Museum, Chicago, IL.

83 T&S, November 1, December 1, 1845. NN, October 29, 1845.

84 Sally Randall to family, July 1, 1846, CHL. John S. Fullmer to John Fullmer, November 18, 1845, CHL. GLN, 542–586.

85 For Emma Smith's relationship to Brigham Young following her husband's death, see Linda King Newell and Valeen Tippetts Avery, *Mormon Enigma: Emma Hale Smith*, 2nd ed. (Urbana: University of Illinois Press, 1994), 199–209.

86 Brigham Young, sermon, March 9, 1845, High Priests Quorum Record, CHL.

87 WCJ, December 23, 1845, in AIC:223. C50 minutes, September 30, 1845, in C50:482.

88 Norton Jacob, journal, December 12, 1845, in Ronald Barney, ed., *The Mormon Vanguard Brigade of 1847: Norton Jacob's Record* (Logan: Utah State University Press, 2005), 60. BYJ, January 12, 1846. Heber C. Kimball, journal, October 14, 1845, UofU.

89 For the inclusion of apostolic leaders in the endowment, see WCJ, December 13, 1845, in AIC:210. For the portraits in the temple, see Jill C. Major, "Artworks in the Celestial Room of the First Nauvoo Temple," BYUS 41, no. 2 (Spring 2002): 47–69.

90 George Laub, journal, February 5, 1846, CHL. George Dyke to Brigham Young, August 17, 1846, BYOF. BYJ, January 25, 1846. For the practice of adoption, see Jonathan A. Stapley, "Adoptive Sealing Ritual in Mormonism," JMH 37, no. 3 (Summer 2011): 53–117.

91 Percis Tippets to Brigham Young, December 27, 1845, BYP. See Turner, *Pioneer Prophet*, 134–135. HFoF, 132. George D. Smith, *Nauvoo Polygamy: "but we called it celestial marriage"* (Salt Lake City: Signature Books, 2008), 573–656.

92 See Kathleen Kimball Melonakos, "Counterfeiting in Early Mormonism: The Historical Record," JWHAJ 37, no. 2 (Fall/Winter 2017): 83–98; GLN, 564–65.

93 Turner, *Pioneer Prophet*, 126–28. Orson Hyde to Stephen A. Douglas, December 31, 1845, in the Stephen A. Douglas Papers, University of Chicago Special Collections, Chicago, IL.

94 Ford, *History of Illinois*, 290–303. C50 minutes, January 13, 1845, in C50:522.

95 BYJ, February 3, 1846.

96 BYJ, February 9, 1846. T&S, February 1, 1846. GLN, 569–86.

97 C50 minutes, October 4, 1845, in C50:495–96.

EPILOGUE: LEGACIES

1 Thomas L. Kane, *The Mormons: A Discourse Delivered Before the Historical Society of Pennsylvania* (Philadelphia: King and Baird, 1850), 3–4.

2 Kane, *The Mormons*, 6, 10.

3 See Vickie Cleverley Speek, *God Has Made Us a Kingdom: James Strang and the Midwest Mormons* (Salt Lake City: Signature Books, 2006); Robin Scott Jensen, "Mormons Seeking Mormonism: Strangite Success and the Conceptualization of Mormon Ideology, 1844–50," in Newell G. Bringhurst and John C. Hamer, eds., *Scattering of the Saints: Schism Within Mormonism* (Independence, MO: John Whit-

mer Books, 2007): 115–40; Robin Scott Jensen and Benjamin E. Park, "Debating Succession, March 1846: John E. Page, Orson Hyde, and the Trajectories of Joseph Smith's Legacy," JMH 39, no. 1 (Winter 2013): 181–205.

4 WWJ, April 14, 16, 30; May 1, 3, 16, 1846. Though the temple had been in use since the previous December, lingering construction issues had delayed the dedication.

5 WS, January 16, 1847. GLN, 587–621.

6 Lyndon W. Cook, "William Law, Nauvoo Dissenter," BYUS 22, no. 1 (Spring 1982): 71.

7 See Matthew J. Grow, *"Liberty to the Downtrodden": Thomas L. Kane, Romantic Reformer* (New Haven: Yale University Press, 2009), 47–92. There are two possible flags the battalion carried on their march. One that is known to have been possessed by the battalion is discussed in Michael de Groote, "Secrets of the Patriarch's Bear Flag," *Deseret News*, January 7, 2010. The LDS Church History Library also houses another thirteen-star flag (LDS 93–134), but it is unknown whether it accompanied the march. I appreciate Mark Staker for helping me trace down these flags.

8 See Brent M. Rogers, *Unpopular Sovereignty: Mormons and the Federal Management of Early Territorial Utah* (Lincoln: University of Nebraska Press, 2017); Edward Leo Lyman, *Political Deliverance: The Mormon Quest for Utah Statehood* (Urbana: University of Illinois Press, 1986).

9 GCM, March 26, 1847. Brigham Young, "Address to the Territorial Utah Government," February 5, 1852, CHL. See W. Paul Reeve, Christopher B. Rich, Jr., and LaJean Purcell Carruth, *"Enough to Cause the Angels in Heaven to Blush": Race, Servitude, and Priesthood among the Mormons* (Salt Lake City: University of Utah Press, forthcoming).

10 See Reeve, *Religion of a Different Color*, 106–214; Mueller, *Race and the Making of the Mormon People*, 153–180; Newell, *Your Sister in the Gospel*, 114–16.

11 Polygamy was publicly announced in *Deseret News Extra* (Salt Lake City, UT), September 14, 1852. For the resulting conflict, see Sarah Barringer Gordon, *The Mormon Question: Polygamy and Constitutional Conflict in Nineteenth-Century America* (Chapel Hill: University of North Carolina Press, 2002).

12 Terryl L. Givens and Matthew J. Grow, *Parley P. Pratt: The Apostle Paul of Mormonism* (New York: Oxford University Press, 2011), 317–19. Jeffrey Johnson, "Defining 'Wife': The Brigham Young Households," *Dialogue: A Journal of Mormon Thought* 20, no. 3 (Summer 1987): 62–63. Eugene E. Campbell and Bruce L. Campbell, "Divorce Among Mormon Polygamists: Extent and Explanations," *Utah Historical Quarterly* 46 (Winter 1978): 4–23. According to Laurel Ulrich, "divorce was perhaps the safety valve that made polygamy work." HFoF, 280.

13 Belinda Marden Pratt, *Defense of Polygamy, by a Lady of Utah* (Salt Lake City: n.p., 1854). HFoF, 361–388.

14 For the beginnings of the Reorganized Church, see Roger D. Launius, *Joseph Smith III: Pragmatic Prophet* (Urbana: University of Illinois Press, 1988), 77–114.

15 For the restoration of historic Nauvoo, see Scott C. Esplin, *Return to the City of Joseph: Modern Mormonism's Contest for the Soul of Nauvoo* (Urbana: University of Illinois Press, 2018).

INDEX

Page references in *italics* indicate figures. Page references followed by *n* indicate notes.